CRIMINOLOGY IN AFRICA

Editor
Tibamanya mwene Mushanga

Fountain Publishers

This book was first published by United Nations Interregional Crime and Justice Research Institute, via Guilia 52,00186 Rome, Italy

Fountain Publishers
Plot 55 Nkrumah Road
Kampala, Uganda
Email: fountain@starcom.co.ug
Website: www.fountainpublishers.co.ug

ISBN 9970 02 403 5

Table of Contents

PREFACE TO THE SECOND EDITION

It is most fitting that the second issue of Criminology in Africa, first published in Rome in 1992 should be republished in Africa. Crime, like political instability, poverty, hunger, AIDS and dependence continues to be a serious problem in nearly all countries of Africa and especially in fast growing cities such as Kampala, Nairobi, Johannesburg, Kinshasa, Lagos and Abidjan. From very scanty information collected from newspapers, it is evident that crime, especially violent crime, corruption and drug trafficking are experiencing rapid increase but without empirical research, it is not easy to identify some of the contributing factors to this trend. But from what we are able to observe as armchair participant observers of social change in Africa, some of the increase in criminology is a result of:

1. Rapid breakdown of normative socio-cultural and economic order due to the modernisation process.
2. The impact of external forces, facilitated by quick means of communication.
3. Lack of democratic procedures and practices on the part of African leaders.
4. The widening gap between the rich and the poor.
5. Lack of serious commitment to fight and control corruption.
6. Rapid population increase and the extraordinary population growth of cities and towns.

Crimes of violence have become widespread in those countries that are experiencing political upheaval such as the Sudan, Rwanda, Burundi, Uganda, Angola, Sierra Leone. Violence as Professor Smit of South Africa indicated in this book, is used as a weapon by the dispossessed for the amelioration of their conditions.

In several African states, violence is used by the state for its political ends. For example, the governments in Rwanda and Burundi, as well as that in the Sudan, have been using violence over them. Opposition groups in Uganda, in Sierra Leone, and in the Democratic Republic of Congo have been using violence to effect their desired political change. Economic violence is equally increasing as armed robberies are becoming a real problem in many countries, sometimes carried out by members of the armed forces not a problem a decade or so ago is now a transnational crime in which some people are becoming professionals. The countries most affected are Mali, Nigeria, South Africa, Zimbabwe and Kenya. This kind of crime will require a concerted effort to control it on the part of police and politicians in affected countries.

Corruption is the most fast-spreading and most devastating and crippling of all crimes in Africa south of the Sahara. Professor Adeyemi's article focuses on Nigeria, but what he had to say about his country applies to other countries as well. No country is free from corruption. In Uganda, it has been reported that the police and the judiciary are the worst offenders, but on closer look one finds that practically every department of the public service is affected, almost without exception.

In Uganda, men who were a mere decade ago almost barefooted are now seen around in four-wheel-drive Japanese vehicles.

Corruption in law enforcement organs of state presents a special problem for the citizens in that the latter are denied the right of lawful redress.

One other evil of corruption is that it retards national development as large sums of money needed for construction, for the purchase of medical drugs or scholastic material for textbooks are diverted to personal use by political leaders and their relatives. Many countries in Africa are crippled by their leaders through corruption; Congo under President Mobutu and Nigeria under a succession of corrupt leaders are recent examples.

It is, in fact suspected that it is because of widespread corruption among African leaders that corruption, like inefficiency and nepotism is never seriously tabled for general discussion at the annual meetings of the Organisation of African Unity (OAU).

It would also appear that for the same reason, African governments have not been enthusiastic about making use of the facilities of the United Nations Crime Prevention Institute (UNAFRI) in Kampala in their fight against crime in general.

The publication of Criminology in Africa, in Uganda will, one hopes, help to stimulate some interest, at least in academic circles, in more research into more pressing crime problems of corruption during trafficking, violence, new slavery, and other transnational crimes.

Tibamanya Mwene Mushanga
Kagango Sheema
Bushenyi - Uganda
July 2003

PREFACE

Both crime and criminal activities and the organised official approach to counteracting these phenomena are of major concern in the world today.

The international nature of crime and criminal activities requires corresponding action both in terms of national, as well as international co-operation and research activities represent an important contribution to the analysis, policy formulation and evaluation. In view of this, it is important to appreciate the potential of criminological thinking and research for the development of appropriate social and criminal policy, not only within national boundaries, but at the regional and interregional levels.

Within the context of criminology in developing world, account must be taken of the relationship between development and crime. All those involved in criminal justice and socio-economic development are increasingly concerned with the crime-generating influences of development, and for crime prevention/controlling industries and costs, themselves influencing allocation of limited developmental resources and energies. New developmental and criminal justice strategies are needed as well as further development of criminology united with, rather than divorced from, issued of social structure and social change.

In many countries crime rates have grown to such an extent and have reached such proportions that they indicate the presence of a serious threat to sustainable development. The costs of crime in terms of the formulation and implementation of prevention and control policies and the processing of offenders through the criminal justice system place a very heavy strain on fragile economies, while the alarming growth in the phenomenon of juvenile and young adult crime denies nations the manpower necessary to achieve economic and developmental goals.

To further explore these phenomena, the United Nations Interregional Crime and Justice Research Institute (UNICRI), produced and published in 1990 the first volume of a series on crime in developing countries entitled "Criminologia en America Latina" - (Criminology in Latin America).

As a sequence to this volume on Africa, we plan to commence work on a third volume entitled *Criminology in Asia*.

Criminology in Africa has been produced with contributions from leading African authors who have focussed on the various problems facing Africa today regarding crime and criminal justice, and they have, at the same time, put forward their ideas and suggestions for coming to terms with these massive problems.

The task we set ourselves was not an easy one since much of the information our contributors provided was difficult for them to obtain at

i

times. It is a well-known fact that Africa lacks both criminal justice data as well as research-based information, and as the authors pointed out, the existing data was often unreliable. This is why I feel that the results will prove to be of tremendous interest to criminologists and policy-makers/administrators alike.

I would like to express my appreciation to the following Associate Research Officers: Maria Luisa Fornara for her work during the initial stages, and Angela Patrignani, for preparing this volume for publication.

Finally, I think we have managed to present to some extent some of the difficulties that exist in Africa South of the Sahara and this has been facilitated in great part by the invaluable contribution and assistance made by Ambassador Mushanga who graciously agreed to be the Editor of this volume and made this endeavour possible.

Rome, November 1992 *Ugo Leone*
Director

INTRODUCTION

In its 1988 Work Programme, the United Nations Social Defence Research Institute (UNSDRI), as it was then called, noted that:

> "There is little comprehensive systematically collected knowledge and information on the history, main trends and state of the art of criminological theory and research in the developing countries and on the relationships between such theory and research, on the one hand, and criminal justice policy and practice in the developing world, on the other". That "as in many other fields, information flow in the criminological-theory-research field is presently limited to flows within the developed world to developing countries. It is well recognised that there should be a more complete global glow of information and knowledge especially in terms of a reciprocal flow from developing to developed countries and a "South-South" flow within the developing world."

The Institute set out to tackle these objectives by collecting criminological information with respect to the types of crimes, and all relevant information related to them as regards their trends and extent, who the victims and perpetrators were, and the social and official reactions to these acts of criminality.

The task the Institute set itself was not an easy one. Collecting criminological information from any African country is a formidable task that must not be underrated. Lack of accurate, reliable and comparable crime statistics is a universal characteristic of all the countries in Africa South of the Sahara.[1]

This scarcity of criminal statistics is compounded by developmental factors that have become the hallmark of Africa's backwardness among which is included, inadequate or insufficient training of law enforcement officials whose duty it is to collect, compile, tabulate and publish criminal statistics. Then there is political instability and economic chaos, together with illiteracy, lack of communication, and in many cases, the breakdown of

---

1   Mushanga T. 1988. *Crime and Deviance: An Introduction to Criminology*. Nairobi. Kenya Literature Bureau, p.79.

law and order, bordering on the state of nature where the Rule of Law has remained an illusion.

Looking at the socio-economic conditions now prevailing in Africa South of the Sahara, a recent commentator has succinctly lamented that:

> "Africa has a genius for extremes, for the beginning and the end. It seems simultaneously connected to some memory of Eden to some foretaste of apocalypse. Nowhere is day more vivid nor night darker. Nowhere are forests more luxuriant. Nowhere is there a continent more miserable. Africa - Sub-Sahara, at least, - has begun to look like an immense illustration of chaos theory. Much of the continent has turned into a battle ground of contending dooms: AIDS and over population, poverty, starvation, illiteracy, corruption, social breakdown, vanishing resources, overcrowded cities, drought, war and the homelessness of war's refugees. Africa has become the basket case of the planet, the "Third World of the Third World", a vast continent in free fall, a sort of neo-colonial breakdown."[2]

The political and economic situation in most African states, makes it impossible for any government to be organised in such a way that it can gather criminal data. Consider the fighting that has been going on in Chad; in Angola between the MPLA and UNITA; in Mozambique between the RENAMO and the FRELIMO; in Uganda between the northern Nilotics and the southern Bantu; in northern Nigeria between Moslems and Christians; in The Sudan between northern Arabs and south Africans; in Somalia between rival clans after the overthrow of President Siad Barre; in Liberia between contending factions; also between opposed groups in Sierra Leone; in Ethiopia between the Oromos, the Eritreans and others; in Rwanda between the minority Tutsi and the majority Bahutu; in Kenya between the Kalenjin and their neighbouring Luyia, Kikuyu and Luo; in Burundi between the ruling elites and the Bahutu people and in South Africa between blacks and blacks on the one hand and blacks and whites on the other hand, making the future of that country difficult to predict with any degree of accuracy, and this goes for almost all the nations in Africa South of the Sahara.

Criminology, as an intellectual discipline for academic serious study, is in its infancy; very little attention has been paid to this subject; in many countries, courses in criminology and criminal law are given in universities,

---

2   Morrow L. 1992. *Africa: The Scramble for Existence*. In: Time Magazine. Vol. 140, No. 10, September 7, p.26.

mostly in departments of sociology for the former and in the faculties of law for the latter. It is only in the Republic of South Africa that fully-staffed departments of criminology can be found offering courses at undergraduate and graduate levels.

Research in the field of criminology has been erratic to say the least. Individual scholars have emerged here and there on the continent but, with the lack of serious academic supervision, encouragement and support, not much has come out of their attempts at research and publication. This lack of official support has led to the scarcity of literature in this field apart from newspaper reports of crimes in general.

In Africa, perhaps more so than in other parts of the world, crime is on the increase, as can be testified by police records where these happen to be available. Crimes against property as a category by themselves have increased enormously, in many countries, since independence in the 1960s.[3] Violent crimes committed by armed soldiers in the countries that have experienced political upheavals mixed with military conflicts have also increased, as we have noted above. In many countries, political violence has been on such a wide scale that the number of victims runs into millions as was in the case in Uganda.

There are crimes that appear to increase as a result of abrupt social change; that is, as society changes from pre-literate hunting-gathering and rudimentary agriculture status to semi-sedentary, semi-literate and semi-urbanised and to developing status, new situations are created that give rise, not only to the increase in crime, but also to entirely new crimes. For example, the forging of bank cheques and even bank robbery itself, may be viewed as new crimes of development, as is currency counterfeiting and drug trafficking. The development process stimulates the desire for wealth and also makes more products available for stealing such as motor vehicles, bicycles, video cameras, watches, television sets and a host of other goods that are in great demand for the masses, most of whom are either under-employed or not employed at all, but who, nevertheless, have a great desire for the goods that have good prices, and for which modern life demands, but which the economy cannot provide.

Other crimes that are parasitic, *vis-a-vis* the development process, include prostitution. Prostitution, in the western culture, is term the "oldest profession"; but it is a relatively newcomer on the African criminological landscape, at least in the sense of being a career. Prostitution has now

---

3 Clinard M.B., Abbott D.H. 1973. *Crime in Developing Countries: A Comparative Perspective.* New York. John Wiley and Sons., chapter 2.

become a major social problem in most African cities and especially so in the advent of the AIDS pandemic.

Drug addiction and drug trafficking, as Professor Tolani Asuni has shown, is spreading in major cities that have direct route connections with other major cities outside of Africa. And in this connection, it is important to note that the involvement in drug trafficking, and even drug use and addictions, may be closely related to the intensity of development activity taking place within a given country. So that where you find more economic activity in the development sector, you also find more drug trafficking and also drug addiction.

Illegal trade, contraband and smuggling are some of the offshoots of criminal nature that accompany development and modernisation. Smuggling and illegal trade across international borders increases, especially with the breakdown of law and order in one or two neighbouring countries. This, too, applies to currency exchange. There are people who have made fortunes at the borders of Uganda, Kenya and Rwanda through the illegal exchanges of currency, taking advantage of the laxity of law enforcement or due to the breakdown of the Rule of Law in the country.[4]

Rapid means of communication by fast cars and telephones, also facilitate the commission of certain types of crime, especially those of an international nature, like, again, drug trafficking and the smuggling of currency notes.

There are many other indicators to show that there has been an increase in the volume of crime in Africa. One of such indicators is the mushrooming of private security agencies, commonly known as "Securico" in many countries. These are privately recruited and maintained personnel that are detailed to keep security around some important persons, homes, businesses and banks. In many countries, these "Securico" guards may be armed with firearms, while others may be armed with clubs, spears or bows and arrows.

These private guards are very often recruited and in some cases, preferred to the local police for the protection of homes and property.

Another indication of the increase of crime is the merging of Neighbourhood Watch Groups or vigilantes. These are usually young male adults who are organised to patrol their villages at night in order to keep out thieves and other delinquents from disturbing the peace in the villages. In some countries, they have been known to reduce cattle theft and the theft of food crops from the gardens at night. In one African country, these young

---

4   Newman D.J., Anderson P.R. 1989. *Introduction to Criminal Justice*. (4th ed.). New York. Random House, Inc., p.40.

men have been given one or two months of para-military training and some have been armed to do their jobs more efficiently.

To me, this volume on *Criminology in Africa*, is an eye-opener for the leaders of Africa. It is a beckon to the leaders to begin to take the study of criminology more seriously, to give more support and encouragement to the scholars, researchers and law enforcement personnel to collect, compile and analyse criminological data, in a more systematic manner, in order to be of use to the policy makers in the field of criminal justice and in order to protect human lives and property, and to also promote the respect of human rights and the Rule of Law.

The countries of Europe and North America are constantly stepping up and up-grading their institutes of crime control and law enforcement in the way of training and data gathering, compilation, analysis and publications. Africa must emulate this practice if it has to avoid being engulfed in criminal syndicates that now characterise some countries around the world. Crime is human behaviour and it can be reduced and controlled by human action. Legislation is an important tool in the fight against crime, but it must be based on facts and not on fiction, the rates and trends of crime and the characteristics of the offenders, victims and situations in which crimes take place, must be identified in order to give adequate guidance to law makers to formulate effective criminal policies and preventive programmes.

As far as I am aware, it is only recently that African leaders through the Organization of African Unity (OAU), have shown more interest in the problem of crime in Africa. This matter has generally been left to individual countries to deal with their crime problems, but all indications show that there is an urgent need for a combined effort in the field of criminological data collection; in crime prevention programmes, in the training of law enforcement personnel, in the academic training of criminological researchers and in the publication of research findings, in order to share information throughout the entire sub-continent.

More and more serious crimes are being committed across international borders and that makes it imperative that national leaders co-ordinate their efforts in the fight against crime. There are now massive movements of large populations of people from one country to another, taking with them their criminal habits. And as more countries open their borders for international communication and trade, so will new crimes be introduced to countries that did not have them before.

The response to these transitions is the co-ordination of efforts in training, research and the publication of the findings in the fields of crime prevention and control.

It is expected that a recently created African Institute for the Prevention of Crime and the Treatment of Offenders, affiliated with the United Nations (UNAFRI), with Headquarters in Kampala, Uganda, will strengthen the efforts towards more effective international co-operation in the field of crime prevention and criminal justice.

Crime, especially in developing countries, is a very costly business. Scarce resources that would go for constructive work, or for the education of street children, or medical care is spent on efforts controlling crime by way of hiring large armies of police, prison and other criminal justice system personnel. It is obvious the higher the crime rate prevailing in a country, the higher the cost of processing the participants in crime as offenders as well as the victims; for the medical care of ten thousand victims of violence and the processing of the ten thousand offenders through courts and prisons, is not the same as processing one thousand victims and one thousand offenders. The more people involved in criminal situations, the higher the cost, not only in terms of funds, but also in human suffering.

It is, therefore, prudent to reduce the crime rate in order to accelerate economic development because crime costs money and less crime will reduce expenditure, thereby making funds available for more pressing economic activities.

Crime, just like large armies, has become very uneconomic, in the sense of squandering meagre resources that could be put to better use in other areas of human need. If crime is uneconomic at the national level, it is even more so on the individual family level. Consider the number of destitute children who are orphaned when their parents are killed and also the children who lack parental support because their parents are serving long or life prison sentences, and these number thousands in any single nation. In countries where law and order has broken down and given way to inter-tribal or inter-religious conflicts, the number of orphans, widows and old people who lack support runs into hundreds of thousands, and this, in some countries, still continues to be the case.

Prevention of Crime

Crime is an enormous problem for every country in Africa, just as it is for nearly all countries in the world; and as such, national leaders and their governments must be willing to commit not only state funds, but their personal efforts in order to reduce the volume of crime crimes.

On the international level, suggestion is made for co-operative efforts by police departments to work together in combatting crimes of an international nature, such as drug trafficking, illegal trade, kidnapping, smuggling and exportation of human beings for the purpose of sexual exploitation in brothels and also in commercial farming.

Proper control of ports and borders could be of greater value in the reduction of international crimes.

There is also great need for the exchange of information on the part of the police and other law enforcement agencies. This is important in the way of disseminating knowledge in the field of law enforcement and in the maintenance of law and order.

The co-operative effort should also be extended in the field of training judges, lawyers, magistrates, police and probation personnel, so as to give them a uniform perspective in the field of crime control. It is in this respect that the African Institute for the Prevention of Crime and the Treatment of Offenders (UNAFRI), could be of immense value in the co-ordination of training programmes for different categories of officers at various levels of operation, right from high court judges to clerical officers within the judiciary system or in other service departments.

The role of well-trained law enforcement personnel cannot be over-stated. The way the police, magistrates and judges handle the members of the public is both positively and negatively affected by the way the officials are trained. Training also is crucial not only in the collection of criminological data, but also in the analyses and interpretation of these data, and in the implementation of crime prevention policies.

Up until now, many countries in Africa have had to put up with inadequately trained personnel at all levels of the criminal justice system, which leads to the unsystematic collection of data and delays in the processing of court cases, whereby injustice is done to innocent persons resulting in the abuse of human rights.

The most important part of the prevention of crime falls within the domain of national governments. The national leaders in Africa need to be convinced that crime is a serious social, economic and political problem which calls for urgent attention.

When leaders are fully convinced that crime constitutes a serious problem, they should then proceed to draw up a comprehensive crime prevention programme[5] which should provide for:

a) Universal and compulsory education for all, for at least up to ten year's, in order to reduce illiteracy which reduces unemployability in a fast modernising society;

b) The reduction of unemployment among the youth;

c) The creation of employment opportunities through the expansion of the economy by establishing new industries and agricultural projects;

d) The eradication of poverty and all its offshoots of ignorance, disease, backwardness, tribalism, intolerance and man's inhumanity to man;

e) The decentralisation of government offices, businesses, industries, educational facilities and supportive programmes;

f) The reduction of the rate or urbanisation, and, at the same time, embarking on rural development programmes such as the upgrading of rural roads, electrification and provision of decent housing, recreation and water supply;

g) Reduction of corruption, especially among the top leaders and among the rank and file of the civil service, by increasing salaries, provision of amenities and attractive conditions of service;

h) Prompt investigation of crime, the arrest and prosecution of suspects by competent officials;

i) Short, sharp and shock prison sentences for the offenders. Short sentences make it possible for the offenders to get out of prison before the process of criminal hardening takes place within the prison setting. Short sentences make it possible for offenders to return home before their facilities begin to disintegrate due to the lack of support by the main bread winner;

j) More use of non-custodial penal sanctions such as fines, weekend prison, community labour in lieu of imprisonment and probation;

k) The abolition of capital punishment for all crimes, because it is cruel and unusual punishment which brutalisers society, stigmatises relatives of the offenders and does not help in the deterrence of crime. It should be substituted by a combination of imprisonment, fines and restitution to the victim's family;

l) The restoration and strengthening of family values through home improvements, social security, clearance of neighbourhoods, control

---

5 Mushanga T., Ibid, pp.190-201

of family violence and alcoholism and the reinforcement of social control in the field of child socialisation and in making people responsible for the welfare and safety of their relatives and neighbours.

In the selection of topics for the volume as well as the contributions, consideration was given to the need of balaancing topical issues in the field of criminological typologies, scholars and practitioners. In this regard, traditional crimes such as homicide and corruption were included, as well as new forms of criminality, like drug trafficking and drug abuse as well as the impact of rural-urban migration which, for all intents and purposes, must be considered as a recent dimension in the field of criminology in the African context.

Another attempt was made by balancing contributions by lingustic classification in terms of English and French speaking countries, as well as by region. The ideal was to obtain equal contributions from all the three regions of East, Southern and West Africa, but this proved difficult, as it was also difficult to obtain more contributions from female criminologists. In selecting contributions, special effort was made to reach the most experienced scholars, researchers and practitioners in the field of criminology and the administration of the criminal justice system. Nearly all the contributors are internationally renowned for their work in the field of African criminology as their contributions justly testify.

The last, but by no means least, and the most important item on the agenda for the prevention of crime in Africa, must be democracy. Democracy is not defined as freedom to arm and fight the government that one does not want in power irrespective of how it was constituted. Democracy must be defined as a system of government where the people have a say in the selection of the leaders, democracy must also mean that those who are not happy with the way things are done, must be listened to but without taking the law into their own hands (and this will happen when those in power do not listen).

Democracy will ensure peaceful coexistence within a country and between countries. A lot of people have perished in Africa just because of undemocratic methods in which leaders have gained power and in which they try to govern their countries. Conflicts over who does what, where and when within the political system and also over the allocation of resources, has led to the death of millions of people and to the misery of even greater numbers of people in Africa during the last 20 to 30 years since the independence of the majority of African countries.

Democracy itself is a very delicate crop that needs the right soil, the correct atmosphere and adequate rainfall in order to bear the fruits of liberty, freedom and plenty. But Africans must struggle to cultivate these conditions in order to reduce the amount of suffering of the African people.

From the time the Portuguese discovered Africa as a source of cheap labour way back in 1440, when the first batch of slaves were brought from West Africa and sold in Lagos, an ancient town in Portugal,[6] Africa has never known peace and tranquillity. It is estimated that 12 million people were transported from Africa during this period,[7] and this is said to be an under-estimation. some historians put the figure at between 30 to 50 million over a period of 450 years. The mass exodus of slaves that went on for four and a half centuries had left the continent bare of its human resources, was soon replaced by colonialism. The period of colonialism was twice interrupted by wars in which Africans lost their lives in hundreds and thousands. Then soon after independence, the African people found themselves left alone to settle their own affairs. This was something for which they had not been prepared. The majority of the leaders were novices and inexperienced in the political field and soon plunged their countries into political chaos from which a good number have still not managed to deliver themselves.

Africa, therefore, has been characterised by political violence for a very long time and it will require an enormous amount of political commitment to reduce violence in most African countries.

Now the continent is gripped by a new wave of political demands for multi-party politics after a whole generation of one-party dictatorships in some countries and military dictatorships in others. The multi-party movements. are threatening a new wave of violence, and if not handled carefully, may prove to be as destructive as the dictatorships they wish to replace.

I wish to express my gratitude to all our contributors to the volume from all parts of the continent both in the English and French speaking countries. Their contributions are of immense value to the development of criminology in Africa and also an addition to the body of criminological knowledge on the African continent. To all of them, I make only one request, and that is their continued quest for the prevention of crime in Africa.

---

6   Rogers A.J. 1961. *Africa's Gift to America*. Civil War Centennial Edition.
7   Everett S. 1978. *History of Slavery*. London. Bison Books Limited. London, p.6.

Lastly, but by no means least, I wish, on behalf of all the contributors, and indeed on my own behalf, to thank UNICRI's Director, Ugo Leone, Research Co-ordinator, Ugljesa Zvekic and in particular, Angela Patrignani, Associate Research Officer, for her tireless efforts and dedication to the production of this volume, without whom, I would not have been able to edit the volume on *Criminology in Africa*.

Kampala, September 1992 *Tibamanya mwene Mushanga*

TRADITIONAL, COLONIAL AND PRESENT-DAY ADMINISTRATION OF CRIMINAL JUSTICE

Leonard P. Shaidi*

1. Administration of criminal justice during the pre-colonial period

The present-day sub-Saharan African states were created by colonialists. Prior to colonial rule, this region consisted of different ethnic communities, representing varying historical stages of development, ranging from highly organized semi-feudal kingdoms to scattered stateless village communities. For example, while the Baganda had a well-organized kingdom and a highly-developed court structure which included a comprehensive appeal system, some communities, such as the Nyaturu in Tanzania were not centrally organized at the tribal level and their "judicial" institutions for settlements of disputes never extended beyond village or clan level.

Communities at the same level of development portrayed similar social features, in most cases with identical customs or laws, (Dundas, 1921:217). The social and political organization from clan to tribe and beyond signifies the level of development of any given pre-colonial community. In the more developed communities, the chief became more and more identified with the interests of the economically powerful class.

Diamond (1978) clearly indicated how the emergence of law arrived simultaneously with the emergence of a political society (i.e., the state). He has shown that, with the emergence of the state, custom which had no compulsive submission in primitive communal (classless) societies is transformed into customary law, the latter backed by coercive force (see also Engels, 1970:317; Hoebel, 1961:26-27). Of course, where the state is new and unstable, as in many pre-colonial communities, the distinction between custom and (customary) law is obscured. With the consolidation of state power, it becomes obvious how "customary laws" are imposed from the top, instead of developing from popular practice as in the case of customs. (Snyder, 1982).

Notwithstanding the differences in levels of development, certain generalizations can be made in respect of the conceptualization and treatment of crime in pre-colonial Africa.

---

* Head of the Department of Criminal and Civil Law, University of Dar-es-Salaam, Republic of Tanzania

In stateless communities, there was never a clear distinction between criminal and civil matters. "Judicial" proceedings were mostly inter-family, inter-clan or even inter-tribe. However, wherever state forms were developed, the individual became fully responsible for his actions.

With the emergence of the state, one would obviously expect that any acts, omissions or threats to state power would be punishable. Sir Henry Maine (1906:382) maintains that this was how the whole idea about "crime" came into being as a separate category from the more embracing term "delicta". Anthropological studies have clearly shown that in pre-colonial African states, treason was considered to be a very serious crime and in all such states, treason and espionage were punishable by death. In some communities a spy, when caught was killed together with all his close relatives, presumably as a deterrent measure (Cory, 1954:12).

Witchcraft is another offence which was invariably met with the death penalty. In some cases, when a witch was discovered, close relatives would be the first to attack him, thereby disassociating themselves from his evil deeds and sanctioning his death (Dundas, 1921:233).

On the other hand, different forms of homicide were considered reconcilable. Where reconciliation was not possible, the normal cause of action was a blood feud. The extent to which blood feuds were restricted depended in the main on the authority of the chief. In the Kilimanjaro area, Dundas (1924:282) discovered that where chiefs were less powerful, blood revenge was common, and where the chief was powerful there were fewer feuds. Generally speaking, the chief's intervention in the cases of homicide was for the purpose of reconciling the feuding parties rather than for merely punishing the culprit. They also favoured reconciliation (with compensation paid to the wronged parties), since this prevented frictions within the chiefdoms. Where compensation was to be paid, the blood money was usually contributed by the whole clan and was not appropriated by an individual, but was shared by all the members of the wronged clan.

Because of the indivisibility of the family's property interests, formal action involving members of the same family (and sometimes clan) could not be taken. Instead, a purification ceremony would be resorted to. An example of this from the Kavirondo is given by Wagner:

> "Thus, if a person commits adultery with one of his father's or brother's wives, the usual compensation of a heifer is not paid, as a father and his sons form a property-holding unit in which the payment of compensation by one member to another member would be pointless. If a person kills a member of his sub-clan, no compensation would be paid either ... , as they say

that the loss of life affects the whole sub-clan and not merely the immediate kinsmen." (1940:218)

If an offending kinsman was not repentant, the alternative to a purification ceremony was expulsion from the clan.

The low level of development of private property or its total absence in some cases, also signified the absence of notable offences against property. There were, however, some exceptions to this. In the Kilimanjaro area, where property differentiation had become notable, property offences also started to emerge, e.g., robbers caught red-handed were punished with death (Dundas, 1921:232). By the time of the German intervention in Kilimanjaro in the late nineteenth century, there was already a clearly worked out system of compensation or fines for common offences. The following sample is illustrative of this (Dundas, 1924:297):

Compensation orders for selected wrongs among the Chagga

Type of offence (or wrong):	Fine or compensation
1. Theft of stock	Double the number of animals stolen
2. Theft of honey out of a hive	1 bull and 1 goat
3. Crippling an arm, or leg or destroying an eye	2 cows and 2 goats
4. Wounding with a weapon	1 bull and 1 goat
5. Striking with the fist	2 goats

Equivalent developments existed in a few other chiefdoms for example, the Haya, Nyamwezi, Hehe, Sukuma to mention the larger ones. But it can clearly be seen that these property cases resemble our present day tort law rather than criminal law.

In the sense that, as a rule, pre-colonial law did not say "Thou shalt not" but "Thou shalt", Driberg (1928:65) argues that it did not create criminal offences, nor did it make criminals:

> " ... it directs how individuals and communities should behave towards each other. Its whole object is to maintain an equilibrium, and the penalties ... are directed, not against specific infractions, but to the restoration of this equilibrium ... The deterrent or purely penal theory does not enter into primitive law."

3

In the same vein, Clifford (1964:478) laid emphasis on the fact that the African concept of crime was "socially oriented". "A crime (or wrong) will be any act or omission having a detrimental effect on social relationships". That is why, for example, adultery featured prominently in "customary laws" as an offence. One colonial official in Tanganyika once remarked that:

> "The individualism of laws imposed by the European and the 'monism' of European judgements stupefy and bewilder the African brought up to different ideas. He is aghast that a clan member should be cut off from the tribal life for a period and be unable, say, to attend such an important event as an initiation ceremony or a marriage in the clan, or a planting festival. By his law a compensation would have met the case and the delinquent's work would not have been lost to the tribe. How efficient would be crime prevention - that ideal of administration - were it possible to accept the old tribal law and custom of communal punishment."

Collective responsibility which prevailed in pre-colonial African societies was also very significant in social control. It was the responsibility of every adult in the village to play mother or father roles in scolding, instructing, advising or rewarding children. This was reflected in the general use of immediate family terms (mother, father, brother, sister) to other villagers whether related or not. (Blakemore and Cooksey, 1981:17).

After a detailed study of the social and political organization of the Meru of northern Tanzania, Paul Puritt (1970) concluded that "a simple description of rules or norms is not sufficient to understand the processes of social control among the Meru". Gibbons (1936:81-82) impressed by the order and discipline existing in African societies thought that "to an African, good manners are of vital importance - much more than to a European". He correctly observed that "it is impossible to regard lightly ill-breeding. It strikes at the very root of their social inheritance and tribal homogeneity". The desire to stand well in *public opinion*, or put conversely, the fear of *public condemnation*, with its attendant consequences, contributed a great deal in ensuring social conformity in the pre-colonial Tanzanian communities. The success of such a system was dependent on the relative impartiality of public opinion and its unanimity, that is, the public opinion had to be really "public", i.e., reflecting a community which is *acting for itself as a whole* and not in defence of any factional interests. With the emergence of classes and class antagonism, especially in the colonial period, genuine public opinion disappeared. The opinion of the dominant class became public opinion, generally reflected in the laws, politics, religions and the educational system.

1.1   Conclusion

When we discuss pre-colonial African communities, it is crucial to remember that they were developing and not static. State structure and consolidation was taking place in different areas under different circumstances. Productive forces were developed and production was expanding and undergoing a transformation. It was, therefore, inevitable that even without colonialism, the social order could still have changed to fully-fledged feudalism and beyond. All indications clearly pointed to the inevitable stage where blood-ties could have been replaced by territorial ties; collective responsibility by individual responsibility; the family as the unit of justice and order by the state, and where feuds and compensation could have been replaced by punishment, even without colonial intervention.

In studying customary law, many anthropologists rightly warn against the dangers of crudely applying current Anglo-Saxon legal concepts to explain "primitive" legal orders (Hoebel, 1961; Dundas, 1921; Diamond, 1978; etc.). On a more general note, Hoebel (1961:20) warns that "in any approach to other people's law, thinking at all in traditional legal concepts tends to limit our perception of unfamiliar legal forms". If we apply the conventional Anglo-Saxon definition of crime as embodying three basic elements, i.e., 1) conduct (act or omission), 2) prohibited by the state and 3) punishable, we can say that very little of it existed in pre-colonial African communities. But for those anthropologists who have labelled every custom "law", (e.g. Malinowski, 1926), even the non-observance of the etiquette of a handshake would amount to a crime. Traditional dispute settlement proceedings which the Kikuyu of Kenya referred to as "Kiama" (similar in meaning to the Tanzania Chagga's "Kisanda"), literally meant "consultation" but the colonial invaders chose to label such proceedings as "trials" to suit their own desires (Dundas, 1921:220; Ng'maryo, 1981). Attempts to understand law as an historically determined category, reflecting material conditions existing in any given society, should rid researchers of the above misconceptions.

Finally, we contend that classless communities practiced the highest degree of democracy than any class society up to the present time. As Hoebel correctly observes:

> "If the more primitive societies are more lawless than the more
> civilized, it is not in the sense that they are *ipso facto* more

disorderly; quite the contrary. It is because they are more homogeneous; relations are more direct and intimate; interests are shared by all in a solid commonality; and there are fewer things to quarrel about. Because relations are more direct and intimate, the primary, informal mechanism of social control are more generally effective. Precisely as a society acquires a more complex culture and moves into civilization, opposite conditions come into play. Homogeneity gives way to heterogeneity. Common interests shrink in relation to special interests. Face-to-face relations exist not between all the members of the society but only among a progressively smaller proportion of them ... The need for explicit controls become increasingly greater. The paradox ... is that the more civilized man becomes, the greater is man's need for law and the more law he creates."(1961:293)

Put differently, the lower the level of complexity of society, the more emphasis will be placed in the dispute-settling process, based upon reconciliation; and the more complex the society, the more emphasis will be placed on rule enforcement (Chambliss and Seidman, 1971:25-26). At the same time, any talk of rule enforcement pre-supposes the existence of legitimate political and legal institutions capable of such enforcement. Herein lies the inevitability of state power at an historically determined level of development of human relations.

2. The colonial period

The colonial period in Africa may be roughly divided into three phases. The early period, marked by wars of conquest and resistance, the middle period, marked by the creation of institutions of law and order and the period preceding independence, marked by the consolidation of the colonial legal system.

The final decades of the nineteenth century were marked, in many parts of sub-Saharan Africa, by colonial wars of conquest and the people's resistance to colonial rule. In Tanganyika, the period between 1884 to 1907 was marked by instances of extreme violence and brutality exercised by the German colonizers, which may never be sufficiently documented. This brutality was not only committed by the state itself, but by all its agents from the settlers to the missionaries. Each individual European had unfettered powers to treat the "natives" in any way he pleased and this period clearly illustrates the practice of the state's coercive role by individual agents, more so than by state institutions. For its part, the state relied very much on punitive expeditions involving killing, burning houses and the properties of people who showed any form of opposition or resistance to its rule.

The process of centralizing and monopolizing coercive power by the state came after all manifestations of resistance had been ruthlessly crushed. In most parts of sub-Saharan Africa, this came after the First World War, and in Tanganyika, where the British succeeded the Germans after the war, they found an already pacified country.

As in their other colonies, the British introduced a *dual* structure in the administration of justice: subordinate courts which came under a high court and native courts. Most of the subordinate courts were manned by administrators and not professional magistrates and in Tanganyika, professional magistrates manned only first class subordinate courts. The native courts were manned by chiefs or headmen,[1] though the native courts were not under the high court, but placed under district and provincial administrations, with final appeals being made to the governor.[2] It was felt that the high court was not in a position to understand and consider sympathetically the chief's judicial role as an administrator would do.

The involvement of administrators in the judicial process has been one of the major weaknesses in the administration of justice in the colonies and is contrary to the well-established doctrine of the separation of powers. Bushe (then Assistant Legal Adviser in the Colonial Office) called this measure a "retrograde step in the colonial administration".

> 'The executive gives the law and administers it. Political officers adjudicate upon their own orders and, if need be, upon their own conduct. No court can control them, no lawyer is even allowed to watch them. A native may appeal from Caesar to Caesar, but is otherwise without redress. The result to my mind will be the complete subordination of law to policy ...We have built a sound proof wall round the administration of native justice and, since no echo can reach the outside world, the system of course 'works satisfactorily'."(Morris, 1972a:150)

It has been noted that convictions were generally higher in native courts and courts manned by administrators than those under professional magistrates and judges. (Read, 1972; Colonial Office, 1934). Even advocates were not happy with administrative officers as magistrates. They preferred to appear before their "learned" friends. In the early 1930s, one advocate complained that the administration of justice by administrative officers was

7

bound to be "irregular, slow, unjust, bad and uneconomical to the last degree".[3] Another one thought that to appear before an administrator's court, was "nothing short of an insult to advocates".[4]

The subordinate courts - descendants of the old consular courts originally established in East Africa to administer justice to British subjects - administered basically the established law. The bulk of the prosecutions, as far as Africans were concerned, came before the native courts. In practice, serious crime was dealt with by subordinate courts under the established law, while minor crime, especially if committed in rural areas, was dealt with by native courts applying customary law (Morris, 1970:10). Customary law was restructured, and in many cases distorted, to serve the colonizers' political and economic aspirations. Thus, to the British colonizers, the test for a valid customary rule was not based on its popular acceptance by the people, but whether it was not repugnant to the British concept of "justice and morality", or inconsistent with any "Order in Council or Ordinances".[5] Referring to Senegal, Snyder (1982:119) has correctly observed that customary law was "over dramatized, modified and institutionalized during the colonial period". The creation and institutionalization of customary laws during this period is of course best reflected in the creation of native or customary law courts, whose laws or procedure could hardly be compared with pre-colonial customs and practices of the people (see also DuBow, 1973:32). As Ghai remarked:

"In fact, these courts were not traditional ... Neither their procedure nor their personnel was traditional, and over the years an increasing proportion of the cases tried infractions of statutory rather than traditional law. Furthermore, the whole milieu in which they operated was alien to customary procedure."(1979:108)

The history of native courts clearly shows their gradual transformation "from simple customary tribunals into systematized courts of justice, with written records, court officers, and a procedure closely modelled on that prevailing in the magistrates' courts though in a simpler form" (Morris, 1972a:131-132). They succeeded in becoming effective apparatuses of the colonial state in the maintenance of law and order amongst the colonized peoples in both urban and rural areas. A senior colonial official remarked in the 1940s that:

"Many people think that the Native Courts, or rather those who function in them, are losing touch with the ordinary people who come to have their affairs settled by due process of law ... A more serious criticism of these men is that they are even losing the confidence of the ordinary peasant. It is said that their tendency to act as paid officials of Government, secured in their places by Government backing and no longer subject to the former sanctions to which an African chief was liable at the hands of his people if he did not comport himself well, is losing them much measure of popular support and acceptance ... "[6]

The judicial system of colonial Tanganyika was clearly racist in character. The most favoured people were the Europeans followed by Asians, and the most disadvantaged were the Africans. For example, juries were solely for Europeans, and legal representation, except for capital crimes, could only be afforded by the propertied classes (mainly Europeans and Asians); while the Africans were placed under Native Courts and courts of administrative officers without any safeguards (Ghai, 1979:105). With English as the official language of the subordinate courts, and many people speaking their ethnic languages other than Swahili, interpretations sometimes had to involve three languages (Colonial Office, 1934:45-46). Coupled with the technicalities of both procedural and substantive law, and without any legal representation, the conviction rate of the local people had to be high. Things were definitely much worse where the complainant or prosecutor was a European versus a black accused. In such cases, there was a strong desire to get a conviction since, as one European put it:

"In cases of failure the resulting loss of face is a serious handicap to the further preservation of discipline. There is also loss of face, but to a less serious degree, when light sentences are given."[7]

As the available evidence clearly shows, the administrators' concept of justice was both crude and racist. Their arguments for simplified rules of evidence and procedure, and the extensive use of corporal punishment, were clearly not in the interests of Africans. Even the Bushe Commission (Colonial Office, 1934:95-96), rejected the extensive use of corporal punishment, arguing that it was a misconception, that it was an effective mode of punishment *for Africans*. The Bushe Commission preferred to look at the issue from a *class* rather than a racial point of view. When the Bushe Commission was arguing that corporal punishment was degrading to "civilized" Africans (from a class point of view), the Governor of Uganda came forward with a tribal analysis of the issue, arguing that corporal punishment should not be restricted to just the Nilotic tribes where he had found it effective. (Morris, 1972:96)

It must, however, be admitted that the monitoring of affairs in the colonies by London sometimes played a useful function. The best example in this regard was in the administration of corporal punishment. In 1937, the Colonial Office sent a circular originally drafted in 1897, urging restricted use of corporal punishment in the colonies:

" ... if flogging becomes the rule and not the exception, there is apt to grow up a perverted public opinion satisfied with keeping order by the lash, as being apparently an effective and inexpensive method of enforcing discipline and opposed to sounder and healthier views as to deterrence and reform. Especially in this case when, as is inevitable in the tropical colonies, the offenders are for the most part of a different race and colour from those who are placed in a position to control and to punish them."[8]

The requirement that annual corporal punishment returns should be sent to the Secretary of State, made the Governor and his chief Secretary careful in making sure that figures should not be embarrassingly excessive.[9] Even the High Court tried to circumscribe the awarding of corporal punishment:

"Recourse to this type of punishment should generally only be had in cases in which the accused has been guilty of some act of considerable physical violence or of cruelty or viciousness ... Furthermore the magistrates should give his reasons for imposing a whipping."[10]

Nevertheless, statistics of corporal punishment awarded were misleading, since they did not include those awarded by native courts, and of course those ordered illegally by employers.

The crudeness of the system of the administration of justice in the colonies becomes even more apparent when compared with what was happening in the mother country. Pritt (1971:81), a progressive lawyer with considerable experience in the colonies, correctly observed that "the role of the law and the lawyers in the government of colonial territories ... is in truth just a crude reproduction of their role in the metropolitan countries". There were several pieces of legislation and administrative as well as judicial practices which could only be found in the colonies. For example, a

10

Collective Punishment Ordinance[11] empowered the Governor to impose a fine on "any inhabitants of any village, area or district or members of any tribe, sub-tribe or community" if after inquiry he is satisfied that they have harboured, colluded with or have failed to take all reasonable measures to prevent the escape of a criminal; or they have suppressed evidence in any criminal charge; or stolen property is traced to within the limits of their area. The only safeguard which seems to have restricted the wide use of the Ordinance was the requirement that punishments imposed under the Ordinance had to be reported to the Secretary of State for Colonies.

In Tanganyika, even a District Commissioner could order the removal of "undesirable natives" from one area to another where such natives had "no regular employment or other reputable means of livelihood"[12] although such an order was appellable to the Provincial Commissioner. This was as well as the Governor's power to *deport* any person "conducting himself so as to be dangerous to peace and good order" from one part of the territory to another.[13]

Bills of attainder which ceased to operate in England since the Bill of Rights of 1668, were used extensively in Africa (Seidman, 1969:64). In Ghana, for example, they were used against Prempeh the *Asantehene* (King) of Ashanti, including the royal family (ibid.). The so-called British "democratic traditions" were clearly for domestic consumption within Britain and had no place in the colonies.

In the Botswana case of *The King v. The Earl of Crewe, Ex parte Sekgome,*[14] Sekgome, who was a chief of a tribe in Botswana, was detained in custody by the British High Commissioner on the grounds that his detention was necessary for the preservation of peace within the Protectorate. On an application for a writ of habeas corpus to the Secretary of State, the Earl of Crewe, Vaughan Williams, L.J. upholding the ruling of a divisional court dismissing the application, remarked (see p.610) that although Britain was "a nation of liberty and justice", such a principle could not be extended to where "the Protectorate is over a country in which a few dominant civilized men have to control a great multitude of the semi-barbarous". Kennedy, L.J. delivering a separate judgment in the same case, defended the wide discretionary powers enjoyed by the white colonial officials in a more racist way. Construing the meaning of the phrase "for peace order and good government" (see p.627), he argued that the strict interpretation given in Britain should not be extended to the colonies "where, as in the case here, the trustee has to govern a large unsettled territory, peopled by lawless and warlike savages, who outnumber the European inhabitants by more than one hundred to one".

The screws were also tight on sedition laws and each colony had a list of banned publications and associations. In Zambia, Mainza Chona, the National Secretary of the United National Independence Party was convicted of sedition in 1961 (on the verge of independence), for issuing a press statement describing the evils of colonial rule and stating that "there was no justice whatever under colonial rule anywhere in the world" followed by some particulars of police brutality and magisterial bias.[15] The judge observed (see p.346) that "when the statement was written it was a seditious publication because it intended to bring into hatred or contempt, and to excite disaffection against the administration of justice in the territory, for the purpose of propagating the policy of the United National Independence Party". In order to silence him, the accused was sentenced to six months imprisonment with hard labour wholly suspended for three years, on condition that he should not be convicted of any offence related to public order or security or under any subsidiary legislation related to public order or security - "in order to give (him) an opportunity to behave responsibly and to develop into a mature citizen". (see p.258)

In Tanganyika, in 1958, Julius Nyerere was also tried and convicted of criminal libel and fined £150 for something which "no one would have even dreamed of prosecuting in England" (Pritt, 1971:127). Following the closure of some TANU branches, Nyerere had published in a TANU pamphlet, an article critical of some district commissioners, narrating how trouble seemed to coincide with such district commissioners wherever they went. One of the defence witnesses was a chief who had held that post for 32 years. On the first day of giving evidence, the government issued an order deposing him as chief "in the interests of peace, order and good government" and immediately deported him to another part of the country although he was still under examination as a witness (Pritt, 1966:181-188). The government was compelled to drop one count on which the chief's evidence was based, and Nyerere's trial continued "in a truncated form" until conviction (ibid.).

2.1   Conclusion

Although it has been asserted that the British colonialists wanted to leave the colonies with a strong legal system "in its British purity as the strongest safeguard against possible autocratic tendencies or the undermining of individual rights by future governments" (Morris, 1972:104), surely they must have realized that they were setting a standard which they themselves failed to achieve anywhere in Africa in the entire history of colonial rule. The whole issue looks ridiculous when a simple matter like training local personnel for the judiciary was a thorny issue during colonial rule. In 1946, the Attorney-General of Tanganyika, dismissing proposals originating from Kenya, that an elementary law course for Africans should be established at Makerere College in Uganda said: "A little knowledge, especially of law and especially by young Africans, is a dangerous and a useless thing".[16] The Attorney-General won the support of the Governor who remarked that native courts were best served by lay people: "I view with something akin to horror the invasion of the Native Courts by a number of half-trained lawyers" (ibid.). It was only in 1951, that the first two indigenous people were appointed as magistrates (for subordinate courts, third class), while a third was appointed in 1954.[17] The Bench, (as a symbol of colonial power) was jealously protected from being "polluted" by natives throughout colonial Africa. Tanganyika attained her Independence in 1961, with only one African advocate out of a hundred then practising in the country (Gower, 1967:117). Even Zimbabwe, which gained Independence in 1980, did so without a single qualified African judge, and had to recruit some from Tanzania and elsewhere to give a new face to a hitherto white dominated judiciary. Therefore, the colonial legal system was, at best, a pale reflection of what existed in the colonizing country and could not have been any better, since the whole concept of colonial rule can never be justified.

3. The administration of criminal justice during the post-colonial period

The post-independence Tanzanian legal system, like other structures of the state, was basically based on the concept of *continuity*. In the period immediately preceding independence, an Ordinance[18] was enacted which laid the legal foundation for such continuity. The jurisdiction of the High Court was to be "exercised in conformity with the written laws which are in force", and "in conformity with the substance of the common law, the doctrines of equity and the statutes of general application in force in England and ... with the powers vested in, and according to, the procedure and practice observed by and before courts of justice and justices of the peace in England". By and large, this provision was a replica of the 1920 Reception Clause, save for the change in dates. When the country attained a republican status in 1962, this position was reiterated, (i.e., the Continuity of Independence laws).[19] The first point to be noted, therefore, is that the independent government inherited the legal framework and the laws intact.

Again, the provisions in the 1961 Judicature and Application of Laws Ordinance on the position of customary law are identical to similar provisions in the 1920 Reception Clause. Section 9 reads:

"In all cases, civil and criminal, to which persons subject to native law and custom are parties, every court shall be guided by native law and custom so far as it is applicable and is not repugnant to justice and morality or inconsistent with any written law, and shall decide all such cases according to substantial justice without undue regard to technicalities of procedure and without undue delay."

This meant that customary law, both criminal and civil, continued to exist, subject to the abovementioned limitations. However, customary criminal law was finally abolished in 1963.[20] The demise of customary criminal law was accompanied by the unification of the courts system, giving rise to a one-tier structure from the primary court at the bottom to the High Court. Administrative Officers ceased to perform judicial functions and the adversary (accusatorial) system was therefore entrenched in the Primary Courts, as opposed to the dispute-solving system, partially founded on the pre-colonial societies. One significant thing to be noted in this regard is that, in discarding customary criminal law, the state displayed the confidence and comfort it had on the imported legal system, which effectively replaced customary law, even in the most remote parts of the republic. Consequently, the pre-colonial social structure was sufficiently transformed to accommodate capitalist institutions, though not necessarily to the same level of sophistication and competence as those existing in advanced capitalist nations.

The post-colonial judiciary is relatively free from direct political interference compared to other institutions. Two months before the Declaration of Independence, whilst opening the first Faculty (Law) of the then Dar-es-Salaam University College, Julius Nyerere, speaking as Prime Minister promised that:

"Our judiciary at every level must be independent of the executive arm of the State. Real freedom requires that any citizen feels confident that his case will be impartially judged ... "(Nyerere, 1966:131)

In 1963, whilst providing guidelines for a state commission appointed to consider the implementation of a party decision to establish a one-party state, he reiterated that "the Rule of Law and the Independence of the Judiciary shall be preserved" (Nyerere, 1966:261).

There are, however, notable limitations to the application of these concepts in Tanzania. In a state which preaches the concept of "party

14

supremacy", there has not been a well-defined application of this idea with respect to the concept of the independence of the judiciary. Theoretically, in capitalist societies, (both advanced and under-developed), the concept of party supremacy contradicts the concept of the independence of the judiciary, (as it does in the case of the supremacy of parliament); since ideally, the supremacy of parliament and the independence of the judiciary presupposes multi-party democracy. There are, therefore, some examples where party and government leaders in Tanzania, invoking the concept of party supremacy, have interfered with the functions of the judiciary.

There has been direct interference by some party functionaries in judicial work, especially at the regional level. Some regional party secretaries, invoking the concept of "party supremacy", have sought to exercise their personal "supremacy" over the judiciary in their areas. There are reports of party sittings which have, at times, constituted themselves into "courts", bypassing the judicial process in cases they are interested in (Mlawa, 1983). For example, in *Kivuyo and others v. Regional Police Commander*,[21] six people were arrested and their four vehicles and goods seized on suspicion of being involved in smuggling. Their case was handled by the Arusha Regional Defence and Security Committee which discussed the matter in camera in the absence of the persons involved, and without them being represented. On the recommendation of the Committee to the Prime Minister, the vehicles and goods were forfeited to the government (Kibuta, 1983).

Even more serious has been the total disregard of some court rulings by some party functionaries and the executive. In *R. v. Paul Masawe*,[22] the accused was acquitted by the court on a charge of attempting to export restricted goods. The court then ordered the restoration of the goods to the accused in question, together with the vehicle which was conveying them, which had been seized by the police. The regional party secretary, however, intervened and ordered the confiscation and eventual sale of the goods and vehicle and the government pocketed the proceeds. More commonplace is the re-detention, under the Preventive Detention Act, of people acquitted of criminal charges. An appeal judge remarked that "there are numerous cases in which the courts in criminal cases acquit the accused person but as he leaves the court room, he is immediately re-arrested on an order for preventive detention" (Kisanga, 1981).

These examples show that, although the concept of the independence of the judiciary is officially acknowledged, what actually happens is less than the actual interpretation of this concept. The state's claim to having an independent judiciary, of course, serves the same purpose as it does in advanced capitalist countries, i.e., to present the judiciary as a neutral institution devoid of any class or factional bias. The judiciary, and the legal system as a whole, being largely a replica of the Anglo-American system, employs similar forms of mystifications, to give an appearance of independence and neutrality. Again, like the law in developed capitalist countries, it transcends crude class interests, and under the prevailing conditions, there is no organized resistance to it. However, it would be wrong to say that it represents a genuine *consensus* between different classes, because this law was, in the first place, imposed by a colonial power. Although the same system was found to be useful by the new ruling class, the subordinate classes could only accept the arrangement from a position of weakness. Because post-colonial states are based on a very shaky foundation, coercion is more widely practiced compared to more stable developed countries.

During the colonial period, the ideology of nationalism (which cut across class lines) was employed as a clear alternative to colonial rule. In the post-colonial period, there has not been an equivalent unifying factor for challenging the existing order.

Political instability has tended to be a serious problem in most of post-colonial Africa. Many states, being aware of this fact, have taken measures and introduced harsh laws in the name of maintaining "law and order". Such measures have included the establishment of one-party politics, the introduction of preventive detention laws and the maintenance of the colonial deportation laws. In Tanzania, a Preventive Detention Act was introduced only a year after Independence.

The Preventive Detention Act empowers the President to detain indefinitely "any person ... conducting himself so as to be dangerous to peace and good order", or any person who is "acting in a manner prejudicial to the defence ... or security of the State".

Another unusual feature of the administration of criminal justice in post-colonial Tanzania, was the introduction of minimum sentences legislation. The Minimum Sentences Act was passed in 1963 at a time when the crime rate was relatively low and there was no social or economic crisis. It imposed minimum sentences, ranging from two years and mandatory corporal punishment for certain specified offences. Until mandatory corporal punishment was abolished in 1972, statistics of official corporal punishment were much higher than during the colonial period. Generally speaking, punishment became much harsher than it used to be. The mandatory minimum term of imprisonment is now 30 years in certain cases like armed robbery.

Attempts to use the criminal law to enhance production also features prominently in post-colonial Tanzania. There has been a tightening and expansion of vagrancy laws and a strict enforcement of by-laws which deal with agricultural production. The fact that the state plays a direct central role in promoting economic development, has resulted in the continuation (from the colonial period) of coercion as a necessary instrument of social policy. With an underdeveloped social structure, the state has no real incentives to offer in order to generate development. The dwindling prices of primary commodities, especially in times of recession, means that the peasants have to be *pushed* to increase the volume of their production in order to sustain the economies of the post-colonial states.

3.1   Conclusion

The colonization of Africa marked the imposition of capitalism on pre-capitalist social structures. Since this was usually met with resistance, coercion was both intensively and extensively used to pacify the indigenous population. Criminal law was of particular importance to the ruling class in transforming the pre-capitalist social structure into accommodating the capitalist notion of production. This also meant the undermining of the pre-colonial social order and the imposition of a new set of values. In the field of law, this was manifested by the disintegration and the contraction of customary law simultaneously with the consolidation and the expansion of the received (or statutory) law. It was the newly-independent government of Tanganyika, which in 1963, while abolishing customary criminal law, retained a provision in its Penal Code stating that the Common Law of England was one of the sources of Tanganyika's criminal law. In effect, Tanganyika's courts were explicitly becoming *custodes mores* with respect to the Common Law of England, and not the Customary Law of Tanganyika.

The process of transforming the social structure, through the imposition of capitalism, had three basic consequences. Firstly, it arrested and destroyed the natural development of the indigenous societies and their institutions. Pre-Colonial African societies were developed along the same path taken by more advanced societies. Colonialism marked the creation of dependency-relationships which has been the biggest stumbling block to the *development* of the post-colonial states. Secondly, laws were introduced "from above", clearly serving the interests of an alien ruling class and not reflecting the popular demands of the local inhabitants. Thirdly, the process of transformation witnessed the emergence of new forms of conduct defined as

17

criminal by the ruling class. The colonial legal system was, therefore, at best, a pale reflection of what existed in the ex-colonial power.

After Independence, the new indigenous ruling class (which developed during the colonial period) inherited the colonial state apparatuses intact. Since the social structure remained substantially the same, the nature, character and function of criminal law has more or less remained unchanged. Dependency is reflected even in the law, in the sense that the decisions made by English courts are of considerable value to our courts, and in many cases, both the judiciary and the legislature invariably adopt changes to the laws originating in England.

Notes

1 I shall not give a detailed description because I am concerned with basic features of general interest.
2 Tanganyika Native Courts Ordinance, No. 5 of 1929.
3 Tanzania National Archives (T.N.A.), File No. 19653. See also Morris 1972a:87.
4 T.N.A. File No. 21815.
5 See for example, Tanganyika Order in Council 1920, s. 17 commonly known as The Reception Clause.
6 T.N.A. File No. 33270.
7 T.N.A. File No. 50050.
8 T.N.A. File No. 11929.
9 T.N.A. File No. 16742.
10 T.N.A. File No. 25683.
11 No. 24 of 1921.
12 Townships (Removal of Undesirable Natives). Ordinance No. 6 of 1944; amended in 1953 (No. 14) to read undesirable *persons* instead of *natives*.
13 Deportation Ordinance No. 15 of 1921.
14 (1910) 2 K.B. 576.
15 R. v. Chona /1962/ R. & N.L.R. 344.
16 T.N.A. File No. 33270.
17 T.N.A. File No. 41755.
18 Judicature and Application of Laws Ordinance, No. 57 of 1961 (Cap. 453).
19 The Republic of Tanganyika (Consequential, etc. Provisions) Act, No. 2 of 1962.
20 Magistrates' Courts Act, 1963 (Cap. .537) s. 66
21 High Court (Arusha) , Misc. Civ. App. No. 22 of 1978 (unreported).
22 (1979) L.R.T. 18.

References

Blakemore K., Cooksey B. 1981. *A Sociology of Education for Africa.* London. George Allen and Unwin.

Chambliss W.J., Seidman R.R. 1971. *Law, Order and Power.* Reading (MA). Addison-Welsey Publishing Company.

Clifford W. 1964. *The African View of Crime.* British Journal of Criminology. 4, pp.477-486.

Colonial Office. 1934. *Report of the Commission of Inquiry into the Administration of Justice in Kenya, Uganda and the Tanganyika Territory in Criminal Matters and Correspondence Arising out of the Report.* London. Her Majesty's Stationery Office.

Cory H. 1954. *The Indigenous Political System of the Sukuma.* Dar-es-Salaam. The Eagle Press.

Diamond S. 1978. *The Rule of Law Versus the Order of Custom.* In: Reasons C.E., Rich R.M. (Eds.). "The Sociology of Law: A Conflict Perspective". Toronto. Butterworths. pp. 239-262.

Driberg J.H. 1928. *Primitive Law in Eastern Africa.* Africa. 1, pp.61-72.

DuBow F.L. 1973. *Justice for People: Justice and Politics in the Lower Courts of Tanzania.* Ph.D. dissertation. University of California.

Dundas C. 1921. *Native Laws of Some Bantu Tribes of East Africa.* Journal of the Royal Anthropological Institute. LI, pp.217-278.

---- . 1924. *Kilimanjaro and It's People.* London. H.F. & G, Witherby.

Engels F. 1970. *The Origin of the Family, Private Property and the State.* In: Marx K., Engels F. "Selected Works". Vol. 3. Moscow. Progress Publishers. pp.204-334.

Ghai Y.P. 1979. *Indirect Rule and the Search for Justice. Essays in East African Legal History.* International Journal of African Historical Studies. 9, pp.103-111.

Gibbons R.M. 1936. *African Good Manners.* Tanganyika Notes and Records. 1, pp.81-83.

Gower L.C.B. 1967. *Independent Africa: The Challenge of the Legal Profession.* Cambridge (MA). Harvard University Press.

Hoebel E.A. 1961. *The Law of Primitive Man.* Cambridge (MA). Harvard University Press.

Kibuta O. 1983. *Human Rights in Tanzania.* Mimeo.

Kisanga R.H. 1981. *The Role of the Legal Sector in National Development.* Mimeo.

Maine H.S. 1906. *Ancient Law.* London. John Murray.

Malinowski B. 1926. *Crime and Custom in Savage Society.* London. Routledge & Kegan Paul.

Mlawa G.F. 1983. *The Constitution of the United Republic of Tanzania: Proposed Changes.* Mimeo.

Morris H.F. 1970. *Some Perspectives of East African Legal History.* Uppsala. The Scandinavian Institute of African Studies.

---- . 1972. *English Law in East Africa: A Hardy Plant in an Alien Soil.* In: Morris H.F., Read J.S. "Indirect Rule and the Search for Justice". Oxford. Clarendan Press. pp. 73-108.

---- . 1972a. *Native Courts: A Connerstone of Indirect Rule.* In: Morris H.F., Read J.S., "Indirect Rule and the Search for Justice". Oxford. Clarendan Press. pp.131-166.

Ng'maryo E. 1981. *Bases of Compulsive Sanctions and Coercion.* Mimeo.

Nyerere J.K. 1966. *Freedom and Unity.* Dar-es-Salaam. Oxford University Press.

Pritt D.N. 1966. *The Defence Accuses.* London. Lawrence and Wishart.

---- . 1971. *Law and Politics in the Colonies.* London. Lawrence and Wishart.

Puritt P. 1970. *The Meru of Tanzania: A Study of their Social and Political Organization.* Ph. D. Thesis. Urbana. University of Illinois.

Read J.S. 1972. *The Search for Justice.* In: Morris H.F., Read J.S. "Indirect Rule and the Search for Justice". Oxford. Clarendan Press. pp. 167-212.

Revington T.M. 1937. *The Pain of Individualism.* Tanganyika Notes and Records. 3, pp.120-121.

Seidman R.B. 1969. *The Reception of English Law in Colonial Africa Revisited.* Eastern Africa Law Review. 2, pp.47-85.

Snyder F.G. 1982. *Colonialism and Legal Form: The Creation of Customary Law in Senegal.* In: Sumner C. (Ed.). "Crime, Justice and Underdevelopment". London. Heinemann. pp.90-121.

Wagner G. 1940. *The Political Organization of Bantu of Kavirondo.* In: Fortes M., Evans-Pritchard E. (Eds.). "African Political Systems". London. Oxford University Press. pp.197-236

VICTIMS OF CRIME AND THEIR RIGHTS

Ntanda Nsereko*

1. Introduction

A victim of crime is any person who suffers damage, loss or injury as a result of the criminal conduct perpetrated by another person. The victim may be a natural or juristic person. The natural person is an individual human being or a group of human beings. A juristic person, on the other hand, is an artificial or fictitious being which the law clothes with personality. It includes non-profit associations, companies, statutory corporations and governmental departments or agencies.

The damage, loss or injury suffered by the victim may be physical, mental, financial or social. For example, as a result of the criminal conduct, the victim may be physically or mentally incapacitated. His health may be impaired and his property may be lost, destroyed, or damaged. His professional and business interests may be ruined. His reputation and standing in the community may be shattered. His privacy rudely intruded upon, and his family's peace and quiet disturbed. His family's welfare may be dealt a heavy blow, particularly when he is the sole bread winner and he is killed, or his ability to support his family is partially or completely destroyed. In this respect, members of the victim's family may also be considered victims.

The rights of the victim as a human being, or as a citizen of a given country, are thus violated by the criminal, and yet, for the most part, he is innocent, going about his own business peacefully and lawfully.

Victims may be divided into two broad categories:

    a) victims of conventional crimes; and

    b) victims of crimes linked to the abuses of power.

Victims of conventional crimes are victims of crimes committed by "ordinary" criminals, sometimes referred to as "street" criminals.

Victims of crimes linked to the abuse of power, on the other hand, are victims of crimes (usually ordinary crimes such as assault, murder, theft, robbery, extortion, arson and malicious damage to property) committed by persons who wield power. Power in this context, means authority or

---

*   Head, Department of Law, University of Botswana, Gaborone, Botswana.

influence and this may be political, economic or social. It may, in turn, be private or public. It is considered public when it is vested, by whatever means, in one person or group of persons, to be exercised on behalf and for the good of the whole community. Public power with which we are primarily concerned here, is essential to the existence of an orderly community. When legitimately used, power can be blessing. It can be used to protect members of the public and their property. It can be used to vindicate the innocent and to punish the wrongdoer, and to promote peace, harmony, justice and happiness for all. It can also be used to create an environment within which individuals can exert their energies and faculties for self-fulfillment and development. However, when power is abused it becomes a curse, and its abuse means misusing it or using it illegally. It includes "(a) the use of power to avoid the imposition or application of legal sanctions or controls on certain behaviour, which may occur at high levels of the socio-economic and political order, and (b) its use to avoid the prosecution of offenders in high positions, even for ordinary offences" (United Nations, 1980a). What makes victimization linked to the abuse of power particularly evil and egregious, is the fact that it is perpetrated by persons whose duty it is to protect and defend the people that they victimize. These persons control the police, the crime investigation apparatus, the prosecutorial machinery and, sometimes, even the courts themselves. The crimes they commit are never investigated or prosecuted. Without the crimes they have committed being proved against them, it is technically impossible to talk of "victims of crime". The remedies that are normally available to victims of crime, such as compensation, may not be available to people who are injured by conduct which has not been judged to be criminal by the courts of law (Nsereko, 1983).

This chapter attempts to discuss the position of the victims of crime under both indigenous African law and custom and under present day criminal justice systems. Because of the vastness of the African continent and the diversity of the many legal systems in existence, the scope of the discussion will be limited to English-speaking African countries, and, even then, to those in the Eastern and Southern region.

2. Victims under indigenous law and custom

The criminal justice systems of many pre-colonial African societies focussed mainly on the victim rather than on the offender. Their primary aim was to vindicate the victim and his rights, and the sanctions that they imposed were aimed not so much at punishing the offender as to eliminate the consequences of the offence. They were, by and large, compensatory rather than punitive. They were intended to restore the victim to the position he was in prior to the commitment of the offence. This was, of course, limited to the extent to which money or property could solve the problem. Thus, according to a Tsonga saying, *Musasi wa nnadzu i Kuria*, i.e., the redemption of crime is restitution (Junod, 1961:31). When awarding compensation to a complainant against the accused, Botswana High Court Judge Corduff J., also stated that "traditionally, compensation of the aggrieved party was the accepted way of doing justice in Botswana ... "[1]

The payment of compensation to the victim by the offender involved an element of apology and atonement for the harm done to him. This helped, to some extent, to calm the ill feelings between the two parties and their respective families or social groups. The parties' families or social groups are mentioned because of the close affinity and cohesion that existed among members of traditional African families. Injury to a member of the family or social group, was often interpreted as injury to the rest of the family or social group. Conversely, an offence committed by a member of a social group against someone external to it was attributed to the whole group. This is the reason why families in many African communities were always willing and ready to come to the aid of a fellow member, pay compensation ordered against him and bail him out of trouble.[2] This is also the reason why clansmen in some African societies were very careful not to offend their clan for fear of forfeiting the clan's assistance in case of need.[3]

The widespread use of *dia*, or blood money, in some African societies, is further evidence of the solidarity within the traditional African family or social group. For example, in the traditional Somali society, each person must belong to a unit of close kinsmen varying in size between a few hundred and a few thousand males, called the *dia-paying group*. When a member of the group commits homicide, whether accidentally or intentionally, all the adult male members of his group are jointly and severally liable to pay *dia* or blood money to the deceased's group as compensation for the life of the murdered victim. The payment is apparently predicated on the Somali belief that "no man receives or pays compensation individually". The livestock of the members of the *dia-paying group* is also liable to confiscation if the debt remains unpaid (Somali Supreme Court, 1965:170; Contini, 1969:66; 1971:77; Cook, 1962:470). The payment of *dia* serves as a guarantee against revenge or inter-communal warfare which a homicide might otherwise provoke.

Even in societies where the concept of *dia* is unknown, compensation was always accepted by families of victims of homicides. This was true of the Baganda and Banyankole of Uganda (Roscoe, 1924:20; 1965:267), the Kikuyu of Kenya (Kenyatta, 1938:227-228), the Mashona and Ndebele of Zimbabwe (Mittlebeeler, 1976:163 and 193), to mention but a few.

It should, however, be pointed out that generally speaking, prisons did not exist in pre-colonial Africa and that the most common forms of punishment were execution, mutilation, stocks and corporal punishment. It is significant that families of homicide victims accepted compensation from the offender or his kinsman in lieu of having the offender executed. Compensation assured them of continued means of support and put an end to intra-family feuds and vendettas, whereas little, if any, would be gained from the death of the guilty person (Katende, 1967). It would only prolong and exacerbate intra-communal animosity, feuds and conflicts. Moreover, as modern penological knowledge demonstrates, the imposition of the death penalty on persons convicted of murder does not necessarily deter would be murderers; nor does its existence serve to lessen the incidence of murder or homicide generally.[4] It is no wonder therefore, that it has been abolished in many nations, particularly developed ones, with no consequential harm to those nations.[5] It is therefore untrue to say, as some writers have tended to imply, that pre-colonial Africa generally preferred compensation to "punishment", even in cases of murder, merely because Africans did not value life or were incapable of any "feeling of public sentiment", or a sense of social solidarity "capable of arousing the corporate ire of the community and expressing itself in some form of joint effort against disturbers of the social equilibrium" (Elias, 1956:110-129). This is far from the truth. As has been demonstrated, the institution of compensation had an intrinsic value. It is due to this value that it has been recommended for acceptance and adoption by Western nations. This is well exemplified by the European Convention on Compensation to Victims of Violent Crimes and by the United Nations Declaration of Basic Principles of Justice for Victims of Crime and the Abuse of Power, both of which emphasize compensation as a desirable goal for the criminal justice systems of all nations.

The advantage of compensation over imprisonment has been aptly explained by Chief Justice Hiemstra of Bophuthatswana in the case of *S vs. Change*. The learned Chief Justice was reviewing a case in which the accused, after being convicted of assault, was sentenced to a fine of R300 or, to 300 days imprisonment. Commenting on the sentence Hiemstra said:

> "It appears that this accused, who says he earns R90 per month in a mine was able to pay the fine of R150, and he was released. That is very satisfactory, because a man is kept out of prison, he can go back to his job and earn his wage and support himself and his family. This is much better than languishing in prison at State expense and to lose all his wages during the period and probably lose his job as well.

But there is a result which would have been even better. If the accused had paid the amount as compensation to the injured person, his punishment would have been more effective because he would symbolically have been apologizing to the man so grievously injured by him. The victim would have received some solace for his pain and suffering. All round justice would have been better done.

We are not saying that compensation can in all cases take the place of a prison sentence. Sometimes an accused person's conduct is so disgraceful that one feels that the community's sense of justice is not satisfied if he goes free by just paying a sum of money.

But in all cases where the option of a fine is given, the magistrate has already formed the opinion that the person need not go to prison if he can pay.

We therefore urge all magistrates, in every case where damage was done, to consider whether prison is necessary, and whether compensation would not be better."[6]

The other advantage of the indigenous African approach, is that it facilitated speedy and inexpensive justice to the victim, in consonance with the adage that "justice is sweetest when it is freshest". In this respect, a saying of the Baganda is also instructive. It goes thus: *Kantanyi kaggweerawo: kafumitabagenge w'akufumitira w'omweggiramu*, (i.e. a case or an offence is settled privately and swiftly: you pull out the spiky seeds of a plant called *kafumitabagenge* on the very spot where they stung you). It is for this reason that civil and criminal actions were more often than not assimilated in one and the same proceedings. Save in exceptionally serious offences, the prosecution was often conducted by the victim/complainant himself in his own name. Thus, writing of the Kikuyu, Jomo Kenyatta said:

"In the Gikuyu society all criminal cases are treated in the same way as civil cases. The chief aim in proceeding was to get compensation for the individual or group against whom the crime was committed. Since there was no imprisonment, the offenders were punished by being made to pay heavy fines to the *kiama* and compensation to right the wrong done" (Kenyatta, 1938:226).

This is, of course, not to say that indigenous African jurisprudence knew no distinction between crimes (wrongs against the community at large and calling for collective or community reaction), and torts or delicts (wrongs against individuals calling only for an individual or personal response). The distinction was there, albeit in varying degrees, in the various African societies (Cotran and Rubin, 1970:101).

Another noteworthy point about victims under indigenous criminal justice systems, is that they were cared for by the community. Social solidarity and the spirit of good neighbourliness was strong in African communities, which were mostly rural. When a person was attacked by criminals, or was exposed to any kind of danger and raised an alarm, all adult male members of the community were expected to respond and go to his rescue. They tracked down the criminal and made sure that he was brought to justice. When the victim's property was stolen, damaged or destroyed, members of the community made contributions toward replacing some of that property, at least the bare essentials. If his house was destroyed by an arsonist's fire, they erected another one in its place, albeit of a temporary nature. If he was killed, they provided material and psychological support to his dependents. It was a serious matter for a villager or member of the community not to respond to an alarm. Among the Baganda, it was considered a criminal offence, and it often resulted in the culprit being expelled from the village or being punished in some other way. Clans or kinship groups were also particularly helpful to their fellow clansmen, particularly those who fell victim to criminal conduct. The clan system may in this respect, be equated to social security systems that now exist in modern societies. It is for this reason, that it was considered extremely important for a member of a clan to remain in good standing with the rest of the clan.

3. Victims under contemporary criminal justice systems

The criminal justice systems to be found in the majority of African states today are those inherited from the former colonial powers. They are, by and large, Western European oriented. Their primary preoccupation is maintaining "the king's peace" or governmental authority. They pay little attention to, and do very little, if anything, for the victim, the person whose rights might have been so grievously violated. There are virtually no services for victims in the African countries under study. The victim's role in the justice system is marginal. As to his rights and welfare, he is more often than not left to his own devices.

3.1   Victim services

With the disintegration of the traditional African society, no other institution has been established that *adequately* protects individuals from crime or from the consequences of crime once they have become victims. Religious and other voluntary organisations do sometimes provide some material assistance of the type provided by the clan in the past. However, this usually comes too late and is often too meager and sporadic. Third-party insurance schemes for victims of car accidents benefit but a very tiny percentage of victims of crimes. Even so, far too few victims of car accidents are able to claim or to obtain insurance protection, and this is due mostly to their low educational level and to the unscrupulous practices and technicalities often indulged in by the insurance companies.

In modern society, the police force is the major social institution established to protect the community from crime. Generally speaking, because it is a "new" institution, its role is not always fully appreciated by many members of the public and even by the individuals who constitute it. The police are not often perceived as protectors or friends of the public at large. On the contrary, they are often perceived as enemies, fault finders, and intimidators to be avoided. The behaviour of some members of the police does sometimes confirm and perpetuate these unfortunate public perceptions of the police. Members of the police force are often considered by the general public as being arrogant, brutal and unfriendly. Therefore, out of fear for being doubly victimized, many victims of crime do not report crimes to, nor solicit the assistance of, the police. Victims of sexual attacks for example, are often reluctant to report the attacks to the police. The questioning they are subjected to whilst at the police station makes them appear as the offenders rather than the offended. Victims of other types of offences also often receive no police assistance as and when they need it. This is very often due to either inadequate training or lack of facilities such as transport, or is simply due to downright inefficiency, corruption or sheer lack of sensitivity towards the victims' needs.

For example, in one Ugandan case a detective constable testified in court as follows:

"On 9 November 1971, I went to visit my cousin Girisomu Dimu at Kibuli. He reported to me a robbery at his house and informed me about a report made at the Central Police Station, Kampala. He added that no action had been taken by the police till that time. On 10 November 1971 early in the morning Dimu's wife Alice led me to a house nearby and identified the accused to me as one of the assailants. Thereupon I arrested him."

This testimony evoked the following criticism from Wambuzi J,. as he then was:

"If this evidence is true and I have no reason to doubt it, then it means that if Dimu did not have a cousin in the Police Force his case may never have been dealt with. This is a matter of concern to the public who may require police assistance and who may not have cousins in the Police Force. It is our hope that those concerned will look into this matter and rectify."[7]

In some countries, the plight of victims is further exacerbated when the police and other security organisations are turned into actual instruments of oppression. Members of the police and other security organisations commit murder, torture, assault, abductions, robberies and arson in broad daylight. Nothing is done to them. Nothing can be done about them, as they are apparently beyond the reach of the law. Victims of their conduct have no recourse whatsoever at the national level. This was the situation in Uganda during the 1970s and 1980s (Amnesty International, 1978 and 1982; Lule, 1982).

3.2 The role of the victims in the justice system

The marginal role of the victims of crime in the criminal justice system under review, is attested to by the dominant role of the central state prosecuting authorities, be it the Attorney-General or the Director of Public Prosecutions. Section 51 (3) of the Constitution of Botswana is a typical example on this point. It states that:

"The Attorney-General shall have power in any case in which he considers it desirable so to do:
a) to institute and undertake criminal proceedings against any person before any court (other than court-martial) in respect of any offence alleged to have been committed by that person;
b) to take over and continue any such criminal proceedings that have been instituted or undertaken by any other person or authority; and

28

c) to discontinue at any stage before judgment is delivered any such criminal proceedings instituted or undertaken by himself or any other person or authority."[8]

The Attorney-General, therefore, has complete discretion as to whether criminal proceedings should be instituted or not. Whenever, in his view, it would be "contrary to public interest" to institute or to continue with any criminal proceedings, he does not institute or continue with them. In taking this decision, he does not need to, and in practice does not, consult or seek the consent of the victim of the crime in question. The court itself cannot force him to institute or to continue with any criminal proceedings[9]. Similarly, when he decides to discontinue any proceedings instituted by himself or by any other person or authority, he does not have to give any reason for this, either to the victim, or to the person that had instituted the proceedings, or to the court itself. It is enough for him to say that, in his view, it would not be in the public interest; whereupon, the court must close the case and discharge the accused forthwith.[10] Where the Attorney-General decides to institute or to continue with the proceedings, he does so in any way that seems proper to him. For example, he may divert the charges, or he may engage in plea bargaining with the accused, and agree to a charge of a lesser offence than that which had actually been committed. In doing all this, he needs not, and usually does not seek, the views of the victim of the crime.

The courts, too, do not seek the opinion of the victim on the mode of disposal or, in the case of a conviction, of the type of sentence imposed on the accused. Moreover, they sometimes exhibit a lack of sensitivity to the needs of the victim in certain types of cases. One glaring example is that of cases involving sexual attacks. Courts sometimes insist on trying these cases in public, which usually entails requiring the victim/complainant to narrate in public the embarrassing, humiliating and often gruesome details of the attacks.[11] Some courts, particularly those presided over by males, sometimes exhibit stereotyped prejudices in the course of the trial or in their judgments or when dealing with appeals in such cases. A good example is the Tanzania case of *R vs. Hiiti*. The accused was charged with rape and the victim was a married woman. The rape took place in the presence of other persons (although asleep at the time), and as a result of the attack the victim/complainant contracted gonorrhea. The accused was sentenced to 12 months imprisonment and 12 strokes of the lash. He was also ordered to pay the sum of Shillings 300/- as compensation to the victim/complainant. In the course of passing sentence, the trial magistrate remarked that:

"In this case, there exists some thoroughly foul breach of ... elementary decency as committed by the accused, and some mean injustice against PWI who came to contract gonorrhea as a result of the unlawful sexual intercourse committed ... One never knows of other more serious consequences [that] might befall the poor lady e.g., sterility."

On review, the Tanzania High Court reduced the sentence to 6 months imprisonment and 12 strokes of the lash, saying that:

"*The complainant was a married woman to whom sexual intercourse was a frequent, if not a weekly indulgence ... No* violence was inflicted on the complainant. As such, the learned District Magistrate could (*sic*) not have justifiably chosen to treat the accused so harshly."

The High Court also reduced the amount of compensation from Shillings 300/- to Shillings 50/- only, saying that on assessing it, the magistrate had been swayed by "emotionalism and moral indignation" rather than by law.[12]

According to the laws of many states where the Attorney-General or the Director of Public Prosecutions declines o prosecute, the victim himself may institute the proceedings in the name of the state or in his own name. The rationale for permitting these private prosecutions is the need to prevent victims from taking the law into their own hands. However, private prosecutions are not immune from the intervention of the public prosecuting authorities. For example, section 22 of the Botswana Criminal Procedure and Evidence Act provides as follows:

"In the case of prosecution at the instance of a private prosecutor, the Attorney-General or the local public prosecutor may apply by motion to any court before which the prosecution is pending to stop all further proceedings in the case, in order that the prosecution for the offence may be instituted or continued at the public instance and such court shall in every such case make an order in terms of the motion."

Once the Attorney-General or public prosecutor has taken over the case, there is nothing to stop him from terminating the case altogether. Indeed, the purpose of taking it over may have been to abort it. As established by the courts in England, the court cannot compel him to continue with the case, unless it can be proved that in deciding not to continue, he was actuated by malice or that he acted in bad faith.[13]

All in all then, the role of the victim in contemporary criminal justice systems is that of an informer, state or prosecution witness and observer. This is hardly surprising, since the primary focus under present day systems is on the accused, and not on the victim.

3.3   Sanctions

The sanctions that are imposed under the contemporary criminal justice systems are aimed at impressing upon the offender the need to abide by the law. They are imposed essentially for deterrent purposes. Lord Denning summed up the principle thus:

> "It is, I think, a principle of our law, that the punishment inflicted by a criminal court is personal to the offender ... In every criminal court the punishment is fixed having regard to the personal responsibility of the offender in respect of the offence, to the necessity of deterring him and others from doing the same thing again, to reform him ..."[14]

It is for this reason that so much money is spent on the offender: incarcerating and rehabilitating him and helping him become a responsible, productive and law-abiding citizen. This is justifiable. However, when it comes to the victim and his rights, he is very often advised to seek redress through the civil courts, because until very recently, victim compensation in criminal proceedings was not recognized under the laws of many Western European countries on which Africa's criminal justice systems are based. It should be noted, however, that redress through the civil courts is often fraught with procedural impediments which place it beyond the reach of the majority of victims. Filing fees, depending (in some countries) on the value of the subject matter of the suit, must be paid by the victim/plaintiff, prescription periods must be heeded, and many documents must be exchanged between the victim/plaintiff and the defendant. Numerous procedural technicalities, not intelligible to a lay person, also need to be observed. Yet the ordinary victim/plaintiff often cannot afford to hire a lawyer whose participation in the suit may be crucial. It should also be noted that while both the state and the legal profession may be willing, or obliged, to provide free legal assistance to indigent offenders, they are not too eager to do so, and often do not extend similar assistance to indigent victims trying to enforce their rights against criminal offenders. To these disadvantages should be added the fact that civil litigation tends to be protracted and costly. Moreover, the victim/plaintiff will have already spent considerable time and expense traveling to the police station to report the crime or to make statements, and to the court to give evidence at the criminal trial. In cases involving victimization linked to abuse of power, victims face problems of identifying the actual offender, especially when the victimization occurred in the course of an army or police operation. They also face the difficulty of gathering the necessary evidence to prove their claims, since in cases of this kind, usually the police do not carry out investigations or prepare reports which can be relied upon by the victim/plaintiff. Furthermore, since the offenders are almost invariably powerful persons, they may, and very often do destroy all traces of evidence of their criminal conduct, or may, by threats or bribes, prevent prospective witnesses coming forward to give evidence on behalf of the victim/plaintiff.

The end result is that victims often become discouraged and do not pursue their rights in the civil courts.

Nevertheless, many African countries have for some time attempted to graft indigenous notions of criminal justice to the present day law, and in deference to these indigenous notion, they provide for some form of compensation to victims of crime.

The countries under study follow two approaches to this matter; the first approach, followed by Kenya, Uganda and Zambia, is the one which provides for compensation out of fines. The other approach, followed by Botswana, Lesotho, Swaziland, Tanzania and Zimbabwe, provides for compensation directly from the accused irrespective of whether or not he has also been sentenced to pay a fine.

For example, section 177 (1) of the Zambian Criminal Procedure Code provides as follows:

> "Whenever any court imposes a fine, or confirms on appeal, revision or otherwise, a sentence of which a fine forms part, the court may, when passing judgment, order the whole or any part of the fine recovered to be applied:
> a) in defraying expenses properly incurred in the prosecution;
> b) in the payment to any person of compensation for any loss or injury caused by the offence, when substantial compensation is, in the opinion of the court, recoverable by civil suit."

By and large, provisions of this kind remain a dead letter of the law, either because of their extremely limited scope or because of the niggardly interpretation that the courts place on them.

In the first place, victims would not receive compensation for offences such as rape, which are not punishable by fines. Secondly, if in a given case, the trial court considers it inappropriate not to impose a fine, even if it has the option to do so, there would be no compensation. Compensation can only be paid out of a fine.[15] Thirdly, in determining the appropriate amount of the fine to impose, the courts must be guided solely by the financial situation of the accused and his ability to meet the fine. This being the case, then, the fines imposed tend to be woefully insufficient to adequately compensate the victim for the damage, loss or injury suffered as a result of the crime. In one Ugandan case, for example, the accused had pleaded guilty to ten counts of forgery and ten counts of obtaining by false pretences. On each of the ten counts of forgery, he was sentenced to two years imprisonment, all sentences to run concurrently. On each of the counts of obtaining by false pretences, he was sentenced to a fine of Shillings 1,4000/, a total of Shillings 14,000/-. It would appear that, in imposing these fines, the trial magistrate was influenced by the desire to create a sufficiently large fund from which compensation could be paid to the victims of the fraud. On appeal, the High Court set aside the sentences of fines, saying that they were based on wrong principles and laid down the following rules for the future guidance of the inferior courts:

(1) A criminal court never imposes a fine except as punishment;
(2) Regardless of any loss suffered by a victim of the crime, a criminal court must first make up its mind how much that fine should be;
(3) When the court has decided on the amount of fine, the court may order part or even the whole of the fine to be paid to the victim.
(4) The criminal court must not be made the means of helping people to recover debts.[16]

Fourthly, compensation is ordered only when a substantial amount would be recoverable by civil suit. Commenting on an identical provision in the Kenya Criminal Procedure Code, the Kenya Supreme Court stated:

"Section 175, sub-s. (1) (b) of the Criminal Procedure Code which authorizes compensation to be paid out of proceeds of a fine should be invoked in the clearest cases. That is to say that there should be no such order unless the right of compensation in a civil suit is clearly established."[17].

Moreover, recovery is limited to "substantial" compensation only. Victims who are not entitled to substantial compensation by civil suit are denied any recovery at all. There is no rational justification for this approach. The *raison d'être* for awarding compensation in criminal proceedings is to do justice to victims expeditiously and to obviate the need of instituting separate civil proceedings. To deny it to some of them merely because it is not substantial is to do them an injustice. As the Baganda and the Banyankole of Uganda say, *N'ow'emu akoomera* (that is to say, even the man with only one cow should have a right to take care of that cow: he is entitled to as much protection as the one with many cows).

Section 175 of the Zambian Criminal Procedure Code permits courts to award compensation to victims who have suffered "material loss or personal injury in consequence of the offence committed" irrespective of whether or not the offenders have also been sentenced to pay fines, provided that such compensation would be recoverable by that victim by civil suit. A proviso to the section nevertheless renders the provision nugatory when it insists that "in no case shall the amount or value of the compensation awarded exceed fifty kwacha." Section 31 of the Kenyan Penal Code, in identical terms with Section 32 and Section 31 of the Malawi and Tanzanian Penal Codes respectively, does not put any limit on the amount of compensation that the courts are empowered to award in similar circumstances. It provides thus:

> "Any person who is convicted of an offence may be adjudged to make compensation to any person injured by his offence. Any such compensation may be either in addition to or in substitution for any other punishment."

Nevertheless, however liberal the provision may appear, the courts have by interpretation, placed such severe restrictions on its application as to render it virtually worthless. For example, the Eastern Africa Court of Appeal in a case originating from Kenya quashed an order of a lower court awarding a substantial amount of compensation to a victim, saying that:

> "We are of the opinion that s. 31 of the Penal Code should only be used in the clearest of cases, *as when a person has suffered a comparatively minor physical injury: or has been deprived of property, or whose property has suffered damage, and such deprivation or damage is of readily ascertainable and comparatively small value. It should not, in our opinion, be used to award compensation in the nature of substantial damages normally recoverable in a civil suit.* "[18]

The only explanation that this writer can offer for this niggardly attitude, is the lack of appreciation on the part of a largely expatriate or foreign-trained bench of the philosophical norms that underlie the provision. Only in Tanzania have the courts allowed the plain meaning of the provision to take the normal course and remained undeterred in awarding substantial compensation to victims of crime who would otherwise have no remedy (Slattery, 1972:121; Brown, 1966:33)

Section 312 (1) of the Botswana Criminal Procedure and Evidence Act is a good example of the more liberal provisions on this point. It is substantially similar to those of Lesotho, Swaziland, Bophuthatswana and Zimbabwe. It provides as follows:

> "When any person has been convicted of an offence which has caused personal injury to some other person, or damage to, or loss of property belonging to some other person, the court trying the case may, after recording the conviction and upon the application of the injured party, forthwith award him compensation for such injury, damage or loss."

A salutary feature of this provision is that it imposes no limitations on the amount of compensation that the courts have power to award. The compensation may be substantial or nominal. The amount is not even limited to that which the courts have the power to award in civil cases. The courts are thus empowered to order compensation to the full extent of "the injury, damage or loss" suffered by the victim. This includes all the losses resulting directly or foreseeably from the offender's conduct. The Botswana case of *Ramakolwane Didlotlo and Another vs. the State* illustrates the types of losses that the offender is liable to amend. The accused were charged with and convicted of two offences: stealing and unlawfully defacing brands on six cows and five calves. Four of the cows and three of the calves were recovered and returned to the victim/complainant. The victim/complainant applied for compensation, which the court awarded him in the amount of P2,096.24, as itemized below:

1.	Value of the two missing cows and calves	P 1,200.00
2.	Transport costs incurred whilst searching for the beasts	P 244.24
3.	Transport costs incurred in recovering the beasts	P 184.00
4.	Reward for information which led to the recovery of the beasts	P 100.00
5.	Transport costs incurred in taking the beasts to court as exhibits	P 368.00
	Total	P 2,096.24

In answering the defence counsel's objection to the award in respect of the transport costs and the reward for the information that led to the recovery of the beasts, the trial magistrate said:

> "I accept the complainant's application for, and calculation of, compensation. To suggest that one cannot recover money spent on transport, on rewards or something else - recovering the cattle is, to me, startling. CPEA section 312, which provides for compensation, provides that compensation orders take effect as a civil judgment, and I accordingly - and in the absence of cited authority - interpret the word "damage" in that section in its civil law sense. It is my view that under section 312, compensation may be granted for all losses flowing directly and foreseeably from the theft, as, in a civil case, damages may be granted for all losses flowing directly and foreseeably from delict. Were that not so, the victim of a theft would be better off seeking not to recover his stolen property but recover the value thereof from the thief, which, with respect to the counsel, is obviously nonsensical."[19]

On appeal, the High Court upheld the magistrate's decision. In a similar Tanzanian case, the victim/complainant had spent Shillings 256/- to pay the expenses of persons who had searched for and recovered his stolen cattle. The Tanzanian High Court held that the victim/complainant was entitled to recover the sum from the offender.[20]

On the question of proof, the onus is on the victim/complainant to strictly and satisfactorily prove his claim for compensation. He may, for this purpose, rely on the evidence already presented at the trial, and he may also present fresh evidence on the matter. However, the accused must also be afforded an opportunity to be heard and to oppose the grant of compensation against him; or else the award would be a nullity for contravening rules of natural justice.[21]

Since victims are not represented at criminal trials and are invariably ignorant of the law and procedures, it is suggested that courts should be more willing than they are at present to assist them in proving their claims. For example, they should, in all appropriate cases, order inquiries and subpoena expert witnesses to testify in support of the victim/complainants' claims. They might also consider authorising prosecutors, particularly those who are lawyers, to assist the victims in presenting their claims. They should permit victims who are sufficiently affluent, to engage the services of lawyers of their own choice to represent them *amicus curiea* at the sentencing stage.

Regarding complicated cases, a Botswana judge remarked thus:

> "In cases where the calculation of compensation is complicated
> and cannot be done fairly and equitably without the assistance
> of the mechanism available in civil cases such as pleadings or
> discovery a court should decline to entertain such an application
> and leave a loser to his civil remedy."[22]

With due respect, this approach is neither just or not appropriate to the conditions prevailing in most of present-day Africa. Unlike Britain, where there are both civil and criminal courts presided over by specialized judges, there are no such courts in most of English speaking Africa. The same court, judge or magistrate invariably handles all civil and criminal matters brought to his court. It is, therefore, pointless to refer "complicated cases" to a civil court, since no such courts exist. In any case, it would be the same judge or magistrate who would hear the civil case. Furthermore, referring a case to a civil court would subvert the policies that underlie the compensatory provisions, i.e., to do justice to victims of crime in an expedient and inexpensive manner. What kind of justice would poor, uneducated victims receive from civil courts? None whatsoever, since they are more often than not unable to invoke their aid.

The courts, in some jurisdictions, decline to award compensation on account of the offender's lack of financial means to pay. It is believed that to order an impecunious offender to compensate his victim would be to force him to commit further crime in order to comply with the court order.[23] Other courts, in other jurisdictions, take the position that since compensation orders have the effect of a civil judgment, the offender's poverty should be no excuse for not making an order against him. As Chief Justice Hiemstra of Bophuthatswana stated:

> "Magistrates sometimes do not make such an order (i.e. for
> compensation),] because they believe the accused has no means
> of satisfying such an order. That is no reason for not making it.
> It has the effect of a civil judgment and if there are no assets to
> sell in execution, it is the complainant's misfortune."[24]

Echoing similar sentiments, Chief Justice Macdonald of Zimbabwe said:

> "A court ... does not have to be satisfied of the ability of an
> accused person to make restitution before making appropriate
> provision in its sentence for such an eventuality. Nothing is lost

by making appropriate provision for the possibility of restitution, even where the prospects of this appear to be remote."[25]

The making of a compensation order against an offender who, at the time of the order, is unable to pay has some advantages. In the first place, it brings home to the offender the message that crime does not pay, and in the second place, it obviates the need for the victim/complainant to institute fresh court proceedings. As long as he has the order, he can enforce it later on, when the offender appears to be more affluent.

Suspension of custodial sentences is one way of ensuring that the offender satisfies a compensation order made against him. First, the court determines an appropriate custodial sentence to impose. It then suspends the whole or a larger portion of the sentence for a reasonably long period of time, on condition that during the period of suspension, the offender does not commit a similar offence and that he pays compensation to the victim. If the offender violates any of the conditions of the suspension, the suspended portion of the sentence is reactivated and he is sent back to goal. The advantage of suspended sentences is that it enables the offender to stay out of prison, and to work and comply with the compensation order. Where, however, it appears that there is no reasonable likelihood of the offender being able to pay during the period of suspension, it is preferable that the payment of compensation to the victim is not made a condition of the suspension.

In minor offences, the accused need not be incarcerated or fined. Instead, he may be ordered only to compensate the victim, or to perform services for the victim, such as repairing damaged property, etc., if this is acceptable to the wronged person.

The last point to note concerning the compensation provisions in Botswana and other jurisdictions, is that the "injured party" himself must apply for compensation. The courts cannot order it *mero motu*. Furthermore, since the prosecutors are not acting on behalf of the victim, they too cannot apply for it. If the court were to in order to, such an order would be nullified.[26] However, since the courts serve a largely illiterate population, the judge and prosecutors alike, have a duty to advise the victims of their rights. As Chief Justice Dendy Young of Botswana counselled:

"This section (i.e. s. 312 of the Criminal Procedure and Evidence Act) usually provides a speedy and efficient means of obtaining compensation, and failure on the part of complainants to employ it, is very often due to ignorance of the procedure. It is only right that a judicial officer in a proper case remind complainants of their rights."[27]

4. Concluding remarks

Victimization necessarily involves the violation of the victim's fundamental rights and freedoms. Indigenous African law and custom, in dealing with the offender, was more concerned with vindicating the victim and his rights than with punishing the offender. Contemporary criminal justice systems, on the other hand, have tended to be more preoccupied with the offender and his rights than with the victim.

The rapid social changes and urbanization taking place all over Africa are leaving in their wake an ever increasing incidence of crime. This in turn, means the existence of more and more victims of crime, who must be protected from the consequences of crime. Failure to do so might inevitably result in a lessening of public confidence in the justice systems, and in the victims being tempted to take the law into their own hands, which will undoubtedly produce negative consequences.

As part of the effort to provide protection, there is a need to establish assistance services to take care of victims, particularly of violent crimes, as soon as possible after the attack. There is also a need to train and sensitize members of the police service, members of the medical profession, court personnel and others who deal with victims, and to inform them about the immediate needs of the victim. Victims must also be accorded a more meaningful and dignified role in the criminal justice system.

Finally, compensation for the victim remains the single most important mechanism of ensuring that justice is done. The United Nations Organization, through its Declaration of the Basic Principles of Justice for Victims of Crime and the Abuse of Power, has come out forthrightly in urging member states to ensure that compensation is an available sentencing option in criminal cases (United Nations, 1986). In this respect, it is urged that states review their laws with a view to achieving this goal. Judicial attitudes toward compensation in criminal cases must also change. This is the case, happily, in some countries. For example, Chief Justice Macdonald of Zimbabwe remarked in 1980 that:

> "The courts rightly attach greater weight to restitution now than in the past, and this being so, it is hoped that criminal courts will encourage restitution by making appropriate orders whenever there is the possibility that arrangements for it may conceivably be made."[28]

39

It is hoped that more and more courts in independent Africa will follow this advice. Compensation is in keeping with Africa's heritage It ensures expeditious and inexpensive justice.

Notes

1 See *Aupa Khasu v. The State*, Botswana High Court Crim. App. No.68 of 1984 (unreported).

2 See, for example the case of *Ahmed Mahamud vs. R.* (1959), East African Law Reports 1087. In this case elders of a Somali community in Kenya offered to pay compensation to the complainant in respect of an assault on him by Ahmed Mahamoud, the accused, who was a member of their community.

3 This is true of the Baganda of Uganda. One of their proverbs says that: *Omusango oguzzanga ku busenze n'otaguzza ku kika*, i.e. it is less risky to commit an offence against a community where you are just a settler than against your own clan.

4 For example in Botswana where the death penalty exists for murder, the High Court recorded 31 convictions of murder in 1986 as opposed to 14 in 1976.

5 A survey conducted by the United Nations in 1974 (United Nations, 1980) showed that of all states that responded to the survey 23 were "abolitionist", by law or practice, while 26 were "retentionist"

6 Bophuthatswana Law Reports (1980-81), 176.

7 Uganda High Court Crim. App. No. 437 of 1971 (unreported).

8 Similar provisions are found in other African Constitutions. For example, see section 26 (3) of the Constitution of Kenya; section 58 (2) of the Constitution of Malawi; section 72 (3) of the Constitution of Mauritius; section 160 (1) of the Constitution of Nigeria; section 97 (4) of the Constitution of the Seychelles; section 71 (2) of the 1966 Constitution of Uganda; section 58 (2) of the Constitution of Zambia; and section 76 (4) of the Constitution of Zimbabwe.

9 For example, see the South Africa case of *R. vs. Sikumba* (1953), 3 S.A. 125, particularly the opinion of De Villiers J. at p. 127D-E.

10 For example, see *In the Matter of a writ of Habeas Corpus and in the Matter of an Application by Joyce Lwebuga Wife of Eriabu Lwebuga an Unconvicted Prisoner at Njabule Prison*. Uganda High Court Misc. Cause No.11 of 1963 (unreported).

11 Although the laws of most states in the region require trials to be conducted in public, they make exceptions and authorize trials *in camera* "in the interests of defence, public safety, public order, public morality, the welfare of persons under the age of eighteen years or the protection of the private lives of persons concerned in the proceedings." See section 10 (11) of the Constitution of Botswana. Also see section 77 (11) of the Constitution of Kenya; section 10 (10) of the Constitution of Mauritius; section 33 (3) of the Constitution of Nigeria; section 12 (1) (a) of the Constitution of Uganda; section 58 (2) of the Constitution of Zambia; and section 20 (11) of the Constitution of Zimbabwe.

12 Crim. Rev. No. 14-A71. 1971. *Tanzania High Court Digest*, 142 (emphasis supplied).

13 For example see *Gouriet and Another vs. Attorney-Generaland Another* (1978), A.C. 435. *Raymond v. Attorney-General* (1982), 1 Q.B. 839.

14 In *Askey vs. Golden Wine Co. Ltd.* (1948), 2 *All. E. L. R.* 35.

15 For example in the Kenya case of *Terrah Mukidia v. Republic* (1966), East Africa Law Reports, 425, the Eastern Africa Court of Appeal quashed a compensation order on the ground, *inter alia*, that the accused had not been sentenced to a fine.

16 *Mehar Singh v. R.* (1936-51), 6 Uganda Law Reports 265.

17 *Ahamed Mahamoud v. R.* (1959), East Africa Law Reports 1087.

18 *Terrah Mukidia v. Republic* (1966), East Africa Law Reports 425, at 425, per Law, J.A. (emphasis supplied).

19 High Court Crim. App. No. 90 of 1985 (unreported).

20 *Semoloup s/o Melita vs R.* Crim App. No. 34-A67 (1967), High Court Digest, 230.

21 For example see *S. vs. Fitsane* (1984-87), Bophuthatswana Law Reports 335. Also see *Kyagonga vs. Uganda* (1973), East Africa Law Reports 486.

22 *Ramakolwane Ditloio & Another vs. State*, High Court Crim. App. No. 90 of 1985 (unreported).

23 For example see the following Botswana cases: *Elias Mogami Lepang Lekorwe vs. State*, High Court Crim. App. No. 99 of 1985 (unreported) and *Daniel Makhura vs. State*, High Court Crim. No. 172 of 1984 (unreported).

24 *S. vs. Manoko & Others*, Bophuthatswana Law Reports 152.

25 *Regina vs. Zindoga* (1981), Zimbabwe Law Reports 86.

26 For example see *State vs. Boy Ton* (1972), 1 Botswana Law Reports 42; *State vs. Gaontse Selawe*, H.C.Rev. Case No.465 of 1984 (unreported); *State vs Kerileng Mothobi*, H.C. Rev. Case No. 4 of 1985 (unreported); *S. vs. Bepela* (1977/79), Bophuthatswana Law Reports 13; *Rex vs. Mohopi Gadebe* (1926-53), High Commission Territories Law Reports 111; *Lemphane Lesoli v. Rex* (1974-75), Lesotho Law Reports 209.

27 *State vs. Mmipi* (1968-72), Botswana Law Reports 32. Also see *S. vs. Manoko & Others* (1977/79), Bophuthatswana Law Reports 152.

28 See *Regina vs. Zindoga* (1980), Zimbabwe Law Reports 86, at 88.

References

Amnesty International. 1978. *Human Rights in Uganda.*

----. 1982. *Human Rights Violations in Uganda*

Brown D. 1966. *The Award of Compensation in Criminal Cases in East Africa.* Journal of African Law.

Contini P. 1969. *The Somali Republic: An Experiment in Legal Integration.* London. Frank Cass and Company Ltd.

----. 1971. *The Evolution of Blood-Money for Homicide in Somalia.* Journal of African Law. 15.

Cook R.A. 1962. *Blood-Money and the Law of Homicide in the Sudan.* Sudan Law Journal.

Cotran E., Rubin N.N. (Eds.). 1970. *Readings in African Law.* London. Frank Cass and Company Ltd.

Elias T.O. 1956. *The Nature of African Customary Law.* Manchester. Manchester University Press.

Junod N.P. 1961. *Reform of Penal Systems in Africa.* East African Law Journal.

Katende J. W. 1967. *Why Were Punishments in Pre-European Africa Mainly Compensatory Rather than Punitive?.* Journal of the Denning Law Society. 2.

Kenyatta J. 1938. *Facing Mount Kenya.* London. Secker and Warburg.

Lule Y. 1982. *Human Rights Violations Under Obote.* Pasedena (CA). Munger Africana Notes. California Institute of Technology.

Mittlebeeler E. V. 1976. *African Custom and Western Law.* New York and London. Africana Publishing Company.

Nsereko D.D.N. 1983. *Group Victims of Crime and Other Illegal Acts Linked to Abuse of Public Power with Special Reference to Africa.* Paper submitted to the Interregional Preparatory Meeting for the Seventh United Nations Congress on the Prevention of Crime and the Treatment of Offenders. Ottawa, 9-13 July 1984.

Roscoe J. 1924. *The Banyankole.* Cambridge. Cambridge University Press.

---- . 1965. *The Baganda. Their Customs and Beliefs.* (2nd ed.). London. Frank Cass and Company Ltd.

Slattery B. 1972. *A Handbook on Sentencing with Particular Reference to Tanzania.* Nairobi. East African Literature Bureau.

Somali Supreme Court. 1965. *Hussein Hersi and Anor.v. Yusuf Deria Ali.* (Civil Appeal No. 2 of 1964). Journal of African Law.

United Nations. 1980. *Human Rights Questions: Capital Punishment.* Report of the Secretary-General. Document E/1980/9, 8 February.

---- . 1980a. *Crime and Abuse of Power: Offences and Offenders Beyond the Reach of the Law?* Working Paper prepared by the Secretariat United Nations Document A/CONF. 87/6.

---- . 1986. *Document. DP1/895.* August. 10 M.

LES DELAIS DANS L'ADMINISTRATION
DE LA JUSTICE CRIMINELLE DE MADAGASCAR

Andrée Ratovonony[*]

1. Introduction

"Le délai est le temps accordé pour faire une chose" nous dit le Petit Larousse.

Dans l'administration de la Justice, ce délai est d'une grande importance car, s'il permet d'assurer les droits de la défense et de garantir les libertés individuelles, il incite aussi à être prompt. En effet, il en est ainsi puisqu'au-delà du temps accordé, la prescription enraye toute action.

On dit que le titulaire d'un droit qui est demeuré trop longtemps inactif et ne l'a pas exercé en Justice pendant un certain délai, est déclaré irrecevable à agir par la Loi. Le délai est prescrit. Or, qui dit prescription, dit délai à l'expiration duquel l'action publique est éteinte contre le criminel ou le délinquant, ou au terme duquel le condamné est soustrait à l'éxécution de la peine.

De ce fait, le principe admis dans les sociétés modernes que, "une fois qu'un acte antisocial a été commis ou tenté, il importe que ce fait attire l'attention des autorités publiques, et que celles-ci marquent, par des moyens appropriés et efficaces, l'importance qu'elles attachent à ce que leurs prescriptions soient respectées et à ce que de nouvelles infractions soient évitées" (Rakotomanana, 1978:81) est mis en cause.

Beaucoup de justifications sont pourtant avancées pour expliquer cette prescription en matiere pénale: dans l'intérêt de la paix et de la tranquilité sociale, mieux vaut oublier l'infraction qu'en raviver le souvenir; la crainte et le remords dans lesquels a vécu le délinquant équivalent à un châtiment et que, ce serait trop punir que de punir deux fois; la négligence de la partie poursuivante à mettre en mouvement l'action publique ferait que la société perdrait son droit de punir parce qu'elle ne l'aurait pas exercé en temps utile. En réalité, il existe une raison particulière en faveur de la prescription de l'action publique, celle du dépérissement ou de la perte de la valeur des preuves à mesure que le temps s'écoule (Ratokomanana, 1978:114). En un

---

* Magistrat, Ministère de la Justice, Antananarive, Madagascar.

mot, une action exercée trop longtemps après la commission de l'infraction risquerait de provoquer une erreur judiciaire. Pour l'éviter, dans l'intérêt même de la justice répressive et, partant, de la société, le mieux est d'empêcher l'exercice de l'action publique.

Bien entendu, sur le terrain de l'utilité sociale, le temps ne saurait atténuer ni supprimer le danger que représente un criminel pour la société. On pourrait même se demander si l'impunité n'est pas un encouragement à persévérer dans la délinquance.

C'est donc à juste titre que, la prescription de l'action publique tout comme celle de la peine, a été critiquée par Beccaria ou Bentham. Les positivistes, pour leur part, en refusaient le bénéfice aux délinquants d'habitude ou par tendance. Quant à la Jurisprudence, elle subit la prescription plus qu'elle ne l'accepte, et en réduit la portée par divers procédés, notamment en reculant le point de départ ou en multipliant les causes d'interruption et de suspension du délai (Ratokomanana, 1978:115).

De la sorte, dans l'intérêt de la société, la procédure pénale doit assurer une répression prompte et certaine des infractions.

C'est dans ce souci que le législateur malgache, par l'Ordonnance n° 62 052 du 20 septembre 1962, a porté promulgation du Code de Procédure Pénale Malgache. Ce Code, bien que calqué sur le Code d'Instruction Criminelle de 1808, a apporté une réforme importante résultant de l'adoption d'un type accéléré de poursuite, organisé sous le nom "d'information sommaire" (art. 206 et suivants, art. 223 et suivants).

Il s'agit de l'extension d'une procédure connue jusqu'ici sous le nom de "procédure des flagrants délits". Elle est applicable à certains crimes flagrants (art. 178), aux délits flagrants et à certains délits non flagrants.

La caractéristique générale de cette procédure est qu'elle est entièrement conduite par les magistrats et les officiers du Ministère Public. Il n'y a ni intervention du juge d'instruction, ni transmission obligatoire du dossier à la Chambre d'accusation de la Cour d'Appel de Tananarive dont le ressort s'étend à tout le territoire de la République de Madagascar. Celle-ci n'intervient que si elle est saisie par la voie de l'appel ou de l'opposition, dans certains cas limitativement prévus.

Cette procédure permet de juger l'auteur d'un délit dans les vingt-quatre heures de son arrestation, ou trois jours après s'il l'exige, et de juger l'auteur d'un crime trois semaines environ après son arrestation, si une session de cour criminelle est ouverte.

En contrepartie, les mandats de dépôts décernés par les magistrats du parquet pour ce type de procédure ont une validité limitée à trois mois au maximum (durée qui, en cas de crime, peut être allongée jusqu'à la prochaine session de Cour Criminelle au moyen d'une "ordonnance de prise de corps").[1]

Le même souci d'assurer une répression prompte et certaine a conduit le législateur à instituer des règles de procédure pénale relatives à la Haute cour de justice, au Tribunal Militaire, aux juridictions appelées à juger les mineurs âgés de moins de 18 ans, aux infractions concernant les vols de boeufs, aux infractions économiques ou d'ordre économique, aux actes de banditisme (le phénomène "Dahalo"), c'est à dire des règles particulières. Concernant ces dernières, rares sont les personnes qui pensent que la Justice est une institution importante pour la réalisation des objectifs économiques dans un Etat. Or, pouvait-il y avoir une économie prospère dans un Etat où régnait l'insécurité et où la Justice était incapable de faire respecter les Lois d'organisation économique de la Nation? Conscient de cette vérité, le Ministère de la Justice a fait instaurer par le Pouvoir Révolutionnaire deux juridictions spécialisées pour lutter contre les fléaux économiques que sont les infractions économiques (ORD. 76.019 du 24.5.76) et le phénomène de banditisme (ORD. 77.068 du 30.9.77). Il s'agit des Tribunaux Spéciaux Economiques et des Tribunaux Criminels Spéciaux. Les Cours Criminelles Spéciales régissant les vols de boeufs étant un héritage de la 1ère République (ORD. 60.106 du 29.9.60).

Cette succession de textes touchant à l'Administration de la Justice Criminelle depuis le Code de Procédure Pénale Malgache (CPPM) du 20.9.62 révèle l'effort d'adaptation des textes aux réalités politique, économique et sociale du pays. Mais, combien difficile! En effet, la prétention de servir à la fois deux maîtres tyranniques et exclusifs (l'Etat et l'Homme) s'offre comme une gageure encore plus aiguë qu'ailleurs dans un pays en développement comme Madagascar.

Dans ces conditions, la question est de savoir si les délais (Lois de procédures, donc ayant pour but d'assurer les droits de la défense et de garantir les libertés individuelles) dans l'Administration de la Justice Criminelle sont respectés ou battus en brèche.

Cette question est d'autant plus importante dans la mesure où Madagascar a adhéré à la Déclaration Universelle des Droits de l'Homme, au Pacte des Nations Unies relatif aux droits civils et politiques, lesquels sont consacrés dans la constitution du 31.12.75. De plus, la nation malgache a toujours manifesté, quel que fut son mode d'organisation, sa volonté de s'ériger en "Etat de droit".

Ce problème sera exposé dans les chapitres suivants: "Situation actuelle" et "Moyens mis en oeuvre pour accélérer les procédures depuis 1975".

Le non-respect des délais apparaît aussi bien à la phase de l'instruction que de l'éxécution des décisions.

2. Situation actuelle

2.1 Dans la phase de l'instruction

2.1.1 En Information Sommaire

Comme il n'y a qu'une seule Cour d'Appel à Madagascar, sa compétence s'étend à tout le territoire de la République. Il est alors aisé d'imaginer l'importance du volume des dossiers qui lui sont soumis. Aussi, même en *Information Sommaire*, dans la majorité des cas les crimes traités suivant cette procédure, conformément à l'article 241 du CPPM qui dispose que le "Procureur Général, après avoir reçu le dossier de la procédure, est tenu de mettre l'affaire en état dans les meilleurs délais ... Il requiert, enfin, l'inscription de l'affaire au rôle de la prochaine session de la cour criminelle compétente", accusent un certain retard. Par exemple, le dossier du Tribunal d'Antalaha ouvert en Information Sommaire sous le n 659.RP/IS/87, relatif à un viol sur une mineure de moins de 15 ans (Art. 332), transmis au Procureur Général le 6.8.87, a fait l'objet d'une réquisition sur l'inscription de l'affaire au rôle de la prochaine session du 7.3.88 pour une session fixée à l'audience du 1.8.88.

2.1.2 En Instruction Préparatoire du 1er et du 2ème degré

Aux termes de l'article 304 du CPPM, "lorsqu'une procédure criminelle concerne des faits que la Loi punit de la peine de mort, ou des travaux forcés à perpétuité, ou de la déportation, le dossier en est transmis sans délai au Procureur Général après que le juge d'instruction ait rendu l'ordonnance prévue à l'article 290". C'est à dire l'ordonnance de transmission du dossier et un état des pièces à conviction, qui doivent être transmis sans délai à la Chambre d'accusation. Ici encore, il faut constater que les dispositions précitées sont loin d'être appliquées. Par exemple, pour le dossier d'Antalaha n° 363.RP/77 sous le n° JI.17.IP/CR/77 du Juge d'instruction, transmis au Procureur Général le 11.10.78, soumis à la Chambre d'accusation suivant réquisitoire en date du 1.8.79, l'acte d'accusation du Procureur Général porte la date du 16.11.82, et celle de la session de la Cour Criminelle, le 22.3.84.

Les dossiers d'Information Sommaire et d'Instruction Préparatoire n'ont pas encore fait l'objet d'une instruction à l'audience, à l'heure actuelle, pour renvoi à la prochaine session, pour citation des témoins et des parties civiles. Ce genre de motif de renvoi est très fréquent dans les procès pénaux étant donné qu'en général les Huissiers se heurtent, eux aussi, à des problèmes de crédit et de locomotion. Ils répugnent à aller au-delà de leur ressort.

2.2 Dans les suites des décisions pénales

2.2.1 De l'éxécution des décisions

L'établissement des pièces d'éxécution est quelque peu délaissé. Ceci est la conséquence du retard dans la dactylographie des jugements rendus (voir Tableau 1). Ainsi, pour la section de tribunal d'Analalava, aucune pièce d'éxécution n'a été établie depuis 1975. Pour celle de Morondava, les pièces d'éxécution n'ont été établies que pour 33 jugements rendus en 1978, pour 65 rendus en 1979 et pour 39 rendus en 1980. Concernant la juridiction de Morombe, les pièces d'éxécution n'ont pas été établies entre 1979 et octobre 1981 (Ministère de la Justice, 1986:5).

Ce retard est imputable, comme par le passé: à l'insuffisance de matériels (machine à écrire et ses accessoires, fournitures de bureau, imprimés, etc.); à l'insuffisance quantitative et qualitative du personnel d'éxécution, et à l'inaction des greffiers, favorisées par l'absence de suivi ... (Ministère de la Justice, 1986:49).

Au niveau des établissements pénitentiaires, ceux-ci ne disposent pas toujours des imprimés et des fournitures pour adresser au Ministère de la Justice les pièces périodiques réglementaires. Aussi, les gardiens chefs ne peuvent-ils plus, depuis plus de dix-huit mois, établir l'état mensuel des personnes détenues préventivement qui sont des documents de 20 à 30 pages pour les Maisons Centrales d'Antananarivo, Antsiranana, Fianarantsoa, Mahajanga, Toamasina et Toliary, Ce qui aboutit souvent à des détentions arbitraires parfois prolongées et auxquelles il n'est mis fin, la plupart du temps, que par les inspections effectuées sur place par des magistrats procédant à des visites dans les prisons. Douze établissements pénitentiaires ont été inspectés en 1986 (Ministère de la Justice, 1986:6-7).

2.2.2 Des voies de recours

Le rapport d'activités du Ministère de la Justice de 1986 a relevé que beaucoup d'affaires se trouvaient atteintes par la prescription. En cas de pourvoi en cassation, le retard fait que le demandeur a déjà purgé sa peine lorsque le dossier parvient-au greffe de la Cour Suprême (Ministère de la Justice, 1986:5).

Dans une note n° 547-MJ/DIRAJ du 29.4.86, Monsieur le Garde des Sceaux a diffusé un arrêt de la Chambre Administrative de la Cour Suprême ayant condamné l'Etat Malagasy, Ministère de la Justice, à payer 50.000 Fmg. à titre de dommages et intérêts à un justiciable, en réparation du préjudice subi par ce dernier, en raison du retard apporté à la communication du dossier d'appel correctionnel le concernant (Ministère de la Justice, 1986:5).

Une fois de plus, "dire le droit" paraît donc un travail intellectuel aisé pour le profane - ce qui n'est déjà pas exact - mais le faire respecter, ce qui est son objectif, est un travail matériel considérable. Il ne faut pas, en conséquence, s'étonner que des milliers de décisions (voir Tableau 2), ne soient pas exécutées; que les agents du Trésor ne recouvrent qu'un infime pourcentage des amendes prononcées; qu'en 1980, sur plus de 21.000 détenus, moins de la moitié (41,43%) a été passée en jugement. Un tel état de chose nous permet de dire que "la lenteur de la Justice équivaut à la suppression de la Justice" (Charles, 1964:33).

Le remède radical serait un accroissement proportionnel aux charges, du personnel, du matériel et des crédits. En effet, le nombre de personnes qui rendent les décisions croit, mais les décisions tendent de plus en plus à demeurer lettre morte car "l'intendance ne suit pas". Une autre solution serait la décentralisation de la Justice conformément au Livre Rouge[2], et la mise en place d'une nouvelle structure.

En effet, depuis 1975 (avènement de la Seconde République), les deux objectifs fondamentaux de la Charte de la Révolution Socialiste Malgache en matière de Justice sont: rapprocher la Justice des justiciables; rénover l'organisation des juridictions spéciales.

3. Moyens mis en oeuvre pour accélérer les procédures

3.1 Rapprocher la justice des justiciables

Si au lendemain de l'Indépendance, l'encadrement judiciaire d'une population dépassant 5.000.000 d'habitants répartie sur 590.000 kilomètres carrés a pu être assuré au moyen de six Tribunaux et vingt-cinq sections de Tribunal, actuellement, les efforts du Pouvoir Révolutionnaire pour réaliser son premier objectif - rapprocher la Justice des justiciables - ont été couronnés de succès avec la création de six tribunaux de Première Instance. En effet, dans certains domaines, les procédures sont plus longues et plus onéreuses devant les Tribunaux de Section où un magistrat du Ministère Public n'est pas spécialement affecté, puisque les dossiers doivent être communiqués au Procureur de la République du Tribunal de Première Instance de rattachement siègeant au chef lieu du Faritany.[3] Aussi, dans un but de simplification et d'accélération des procédures, les Tribunaux de Section des anciens chefs lieux de Préfecture ont été érigés en 1976 en Tribunaux de Première Instance. Il s'agit des Tribunaux d'Antalaha, de Maintirano, d'Ambatondrazaka, d'Antsirabe, de Farafangana, de Tolagnaro.

Cette promotion de Tribunaux de Section de Première classe en Tribunaux de Première Instance de 2ème classe s'est accompagnée naturellement de l'extension des bâtiments du Palais de Justice existants qui étaient trop exigus.

Actuellement, les Tribunaux de Première Instance sont au nombre de 12 et les Tribunaux de Section de 19 pour 10.908.900 habitants.[4]

Les perspectives pour la période de 1984-1988 ont été les suivantes: en application de l'article 86 de la Constitution relative à la Cour Suprême, et dans le cadre de la politique de rapprochement de la justice des justiciables, pour la période de 1984-1988, les efforts de la Chancellerie ont été orientés principalement vers la réalisation de trois objectifs, en admettant qu'elle obtienne les moyens financiers indispensables:

- la mise en place de la formation de contrôle de la Cour Suprême, dans l'administration de la Justice (projet réalisé depuis 1985);
- la construction des Cours d'Appel des Faritany, dans les cinq autres Faritany de Madagascar. Il a été prévu, dans un premier temps, la construction des Cours d'Appel de Fianarantsoa et de Mahajanga et, dans un second temps, des trois autres. La construction des deux premières est déjà faite à l'heure actuelle, mais les Cours en question ne sont pas encore opérationnelles, faute de crédits;
- la construction des Tribunaux de Section de Moramanga, d'Ampanihy-Ouest et de Mitsinjo. Mais jusqu'à présent, les Sections n'ont même pas encore vu la pose de leur première pierre.

3.2 Rénovation de l'organisation des juridictions spéciales

3.2.1 Les Tribunaux Spéciaux Economiques (T.S.E.)

Il a été constaté que le retard mis au règlement des dossiers se trouvait surtout à la phase de l'instruction. Par exemple, au 31.12.86, 7.050 affaires étaient en instance dans les cabinets d'instruction et, beaucoup d'affaires se trouvaient atteintes par la prescription (cas d'Ambatondrasaka). Ceci est dû, comme par le passé, à la lenteur excessive des parquets à prendre leur réquisition aux fins de réglement et la lenteur, non moins excessive, de la Chambre d'Accusation à statuer sur les demandes d'appel en matière de liberté provisoire et à retourner les dossiers pour continuation de l'instruction (Ministère de la Justice, 1986:5).

Dans chaque chef-lieu de Faritany, les tribunaux Spéciaux Economiques ont été créés pour lutter contre cette lenteur dans les juridictions de droit commun.

Le Pouvoir Révolutionnaire a fondé beaucoup d'espoir sur la création de ces tribunaux. Mais, force est de constater que les résultats escomptés sont loin d'être atteints.

En effet, l'efficacité des Tribunaux Spéciaux Economiques reposait sur:
- la simplification et, partant, sur la rapidité de la procédure. Il en est ainsi car on a pensé que, par suite des pénuries chroniques de toutes sortes dont souffrent les parquets, il y a lieu de lancer les citations, une fois l'enquête préliminaire terminée, directement par l'agent verbalisateur pour l'audience qu'il a lui-même fixée, sauf l'assignation à prévenu (art. 32 nouveau de l'ORD. 76.019). C'est le magistrat du Ministère public qui délivre cette assignation (art. 37 nouveau). Le Juge d'Instruction et la Chambre d'Accusation n'interviennent donc plus ici. La seule voie de recours, exception faite de l'opposition, est le pourvoi en cassation.
- la sévérité des peines par l'effet de l'exemplarité, la présence de l'agent verbalisateur au banc du Ministère Public et des assesseurs élus au siège étant considérée comme décisive.

Cependant, tel n'est pas le cas:
- D'abord, les affaires sont très souvent renvoyées à cause de l'absence à l'audience des agents verbalisateurs qui vont soutenir l'accusation avant le réquisitoire du Ministère Public, et des assesseurs fonctionnaires;
- Ensuite, le Tribunal Spécial Economique étant une juridiction collégiale (3 assesseurs siègeant avec le Président), il y a une dilution de responsabilité, les élus sont, semble-t-il, beaucoup plus facilement influençables et, en conséquence, les peines sont beaucoup plus douces que devant les juridictions de droit commun.

3.2.2 Les Tribunaux Criminels Spéciaux

Ils sont chargés de juger les infractions commises ou les personnes mêlées aux opérations de banditisme (vol de boeufs, meurtre, détention ou consommation de rongony - chanvre indien - détention ou consommation de toaka gasy - boisson alcoolique de fabrication locale).

L'objectif de célérité de la procédure en ce domaine n'est pas atteint du fait de l'insuffisance du nombre de magistrats (le Président du T.C.S. doit avoir au moins le rang de Conseiller à la Cour d'Appel ou de Substitut Général près ladite Cour) et de la disparité des endroits où s'effectuent les opérations contre le banditisme. Toutefois, il est certain que les lourdes peines infligées aux coupables ont eu un effet éminemment positif (Ministère de la Justice, 1984-1988). Ce qui n'a pas été le cas pour les Tribunaux Spéciaux Economiques, comme nous l'avons signalé auparavant. Ces derniers ont rencontré des problèmes en raison de la mauvaise qualification des infractions par les agents verbalisateurs et de l'insuffisance des charges relevées à l'encontre des prévenus par ces mêmes agents, et étant donné que le magistrat du Ministère Public n'a pas le pouvoir de classer sans suite en la matière, le Tribunal Spécial Economique en est saisi. A la suite de nombreux cas de ce genre, ces juridictions se sont déclarées incompétentes et ont prononcé la relaxe (voir Tableau 3).

La lecture de ce tableau révèle que l'objectif d'exemplarité ne semble pas être atteint.

Si l'on se réfère à la période antérieure à la création des Tribunaux Criminels Spéciaux et des Tribunaux Economiques Spéciaux plus particulièrement, on constate que le nombre de décisions de relaxe prononcées par les Tribunaux Correctionnels était moins important tant en ce qui concerne les matières purement correctionnelles que pour celles se rapportant à l'ordre économique (voir Tableau 4).

Eu égard à ces observations, il s'avère que ce n'est pas en creant des juridictions spéciales ou une procédure particulière y afférent que l'impératif d'exemplarité peut être atteint.

Le principe du double degré de juridiction qui est considéré comme une garantie de bonne Justice en ce sens qu'il permet l'examen de la même cause par deux juridictions hiérachisées l'une à l'autre, est ici supprimé et ceci représente une entorse au développement du droit. En effet, jusqu'à présent, au niveau des décisions des T.S.E., il est impossible de mettre à jour une jurisprudence constante au sens propre du terme. Ainsi, la Commission juridique de 1979, qui a voulu écarter de la compétence de ce T.S.E., les crimes de sang et l'atteinte à la sûreté de l'Etat, (infractions connexes) ne pouvait se baser sur une analyse jurisprudentielle.

Il s'avère, dès lors, nécessaire de tenter d'unifier la jurisprudence par une certaine unité d'interprétation réalisée par les juges de la Cour d'Appel. Ne serait-il pas alors fondamental de revenir au principe du double degré de juridiction? Le même souci se retrouve en ce qui concerne le Tribunal Criminel Spécial, du moins sur ce principe.

Deux autres problèmes se posent: en premier lieu, la qualité d'assesseur ne met pas le "représentant du peuple" à l'abri de l'impartialité ni de l'erreur dans l'appréciation des faits. Dans ce dernier cas, la Cour Suprême reste impuissante car elle n'est juge qu'au point de vue du droit. Or, dans la plupart des cas, les parties forment pourvoi en cassation en pensant pouvoir remédier aux erreurs d'appréciation des faits devant la Cour Suprême. Celle-ci se limite à appliquer l'article 373 CPPM, aux termes duquel les juges décident d'après leur intime conviction, les moyens qui tendent à mettre en cause les conditions de fait souverainement appréciées par les juges de fond sont irrecevables et non fondés.

De cette première constatation, il semble que les parties devraient donc subir les conséquences d'une décision qu'elles croyaient avoir été basée sur des faits mal appréciés de telle manière que la décision attaquée revêtait un caractère arbitraire.

En second lieu, il importe de rétablir le déséquilibre créé par l'organisation de la mise en mouvement et l'exercice de l'action publique, par ordonnance n° 76.019. En effet, le Ministère Public s'est vu dépourvu de ces prérogatives et des pouvoirs exorbitants ont été attribués aux agents verbalisateurs. Ces derniers peuvent, non seulement mettre en mouvement l'action publique mais ils l'exercent aussi. Sur le plan théorique, cela fait apparaître une contradiction qui risque de porter atteinte à l'ordonnancement juridique existant. En se référant aux termes de l'article 150 CPPM, le Ministère Public comprend: le Procureur Général près de la Cour d'Appel, les Avocats Généraux et les Susbtituts Généraux, les Procureurs de la République et leurs Substituts, les Officiers du Ministère Public. L'Officier de Police Judiciaire, l'Agent verbalisateur, ne figurent pas parmi les membres du Ministère Public. Il y a alors lieu de se poser la question de savoir si les erreurs de qualification signalées auparavant ne sont pas commises volontairement ou involontairement, par méconnaissance des règles ou par usage abusif des pouvoirs qui leur ont été attribués.

Pour pallier à ce problème, il convient tout simplement de remettre entre les mains du Ministère Public ces pouvoirs, voire de supprimer purement et simplement les Tribunaux Spéciaux Economiques.

La lutte contre la recrudescence du banditisme doit se faire au niveau de l'augmentation de l'effectif des Forces de l'ordre et de la Zandarmariam-pirenena (Gendarmerie) ainsi que sur la prise de conscience civique et morale de tout un chacun.

Il n'y a donc pas lieu de supprimer quant à eux les Tribunaux Criminels Spéciaux. Une refonte de l'ordonnance n° 77.068 du 30.9.77, relative aux pouvoirs des agents verbalisateurs est seule nécessaire.

4. Conclusion[5]

Le maximum a été fait, on le pense, pour accélérer les procédures devant les juridictions malgaches.

Le législateur les a dotées non seulement d'une institution originale, le système de l'Information Sommaire, mais aussi d'un foisonnement de juridictions *sui generis* comme la Haute Cour de Justice, le Tribunal Militaire, les Juridictions pour les mineurs de moins de 18 ans, les Cours Criminelles Spéciales, les Tribunaux Spéciaux Economiques et les Tribunaux Criminels Spéciaux sans parler des autres procédures d'urgence non exposées dans notre étude (le renvoi direct). D'une façon plus approfondie, voir l'article 238 CPPM pour ce qui concerne l'information sommaire, l'article 291 CPPM pour l'Instruction, et l'article 63 de la Loi 61 013 du 19.7.61 pour la procédure d'urgence, ainsi que, à titre d'information, l'article 11 de l'ordonnance 82 019 du 11.8.82.

Si la Justice continue à être lente, si les détenus ne sont pas condamnés dans un délai raisonnable et si les prisons regorgent de personnes attendant un jugement problématique, si les décisions ne sont pas éxécutées et restent lettre morte, ce n'est pas dans les procédures qu'il faut rechercher l'origine du mal, mais plutôt dans l'insuffisance du personnel, de moyen et de crédits (Ramanitra, 1968:449). La pénurie de ces moyens affecte le fonctionnement même des rouages de l'Administration de la Justice en général, au détriment des justiciables et de l'Etat lui-même.

Tables

Tableau 1[6]

Juridiction	Jugements restant a coucher
Manakara	1.110
Ambositra	4.294
Analalava	2.445
Port-Bergé	815
Ihosy	2.922
Antsiranana	5.249
Fianarantsoa	2.480
Morombe	2.000
Antalaha	3.939

Tableau 2

Instances aux sièges au 31.12.88

Juridiction	Criminelles en cours d'instance	Correctionnelles
Antananarivo	1.440	743
Antsiranana	826	104
Fianarantsoa	639	162
Mahajanga	295	310
Toamasina	491	177
Toliara	213	1.013
TOTAL	3.904	2.509

Tableau 3

Analyse des décisions rendues par les tribunaux spéciaux économiques

Années	Nombre d'affaires jugées	Décisions de relaxe	Décisions d'incompétence	Peine maximale d'emprisonnement de 1 à 5 ans
1978	3.679	653	98	
1979	5.413	1.729	65	1.025
1980	4.391	1.729	65	1.034
1981	4.374	2.352	20	886
1982	3.901	2.102	0	685
1984	2.749	1.578	78	559
1985	2.355	1.278	99	682
1986	2.980	1.300	57	566
1987	2.366	1.804	139	660

Tableau 4

Années	Nombre d'affaires à traiter par le parquet	Nombre d'affaires jugées par les tribunaux	Nombre de relaxes	Nombre d'affaires économiques	Nombre de relaxes en matière économique
1966	30.276	16.107	2.435	4.721	429
1967	36.892	18.077	2.737	5.249	683
1968	39.444	19.779	3.476	5.865	826
1970	45.668	20.803	3.871	5.423	1.070
1972	49.524	17.799	3.932	4.060	961
1973	53.715	19.284	3.575	3.598	1.052
1974	61.595	21.319	4.732	4.059	1.181
1975	65.595	23.167	6.201	3.769	1.420
1977	82.774	24.480	6.516	2.936	1.221

Notes

1 Exposé des motifs de l'ORD. 62.052 du 20.9.62 (1974: 8-9) de Procédure Pénale Malgache. Librairie de Madagascar.
2 Charte de la Révolution Socialiste Malgache dite "Le Livre Rouge" du 26 août 1975, par le Président Didier Ratsiraka.
3 Nouvelle structure administrative remplaçant l'ancienne Province.
   Depuis l'avènement de la Seconde République, l'organisation territoriale et administrative héritée de l'époque coloniale s'est effondrée à Madagascar. Communes, cantons, sous-préfectures, Préfectures et Provinces se sont effacés. A leur place se sont érigées les collectivités décentralisées schématiquement représentées par une forme pyramidale dont la base est constituée par le Fokontany, et le sommet par le Faritany, les deux échelons intermédiaires étant le Firaisampokontany (association de plusieurs Fokontany) et le Fivondronampokontany (regroupement de plusieurs Firaisampokontany). Le nombre de Firaisana, de Fivondronana et de Faritany est respectivement de 1.250, 110 et 6.
4 Renseignement recueilli auprès du Ministère de la Population, de la Condition Sociale de la Jeunessse et des Sports, en décembre 1989.
5 Voir Indrianjafy G.T.I. Rapport d'activités du Ministère de la Justice de Madagascar, 1980:13-14)
6 Ce retard dans la frappe des jugements entraîne trois conséquences néfastes: l'établissement des pièces d'éxécution est retardé d'autant; les justiciables ne peuvent pas se faire délivrer des grosses aux fins d'éxécution; les affaires ayant fait l'objet d'appel ou de pourvoi en cassation restent en souffrance dans les greffes.

Références bibliographiques

Bouzat P.B., Pinatel J.P. 1963. *Traité de Droit Pénal et de Criminologie*. Paris. Librairie Dalloz.
Charles R.C. 1964. *La Justice en France*. Paris. PUF.
Indrianjafy G.T.I. 1980. *Rapport d'activités du Ministère de la Justice de Madagascar*.
Ministère de la Justice. 1984-1988. *Rapports d'Activités*.
Rakotomanana H.R. 1978. *Procédure Pénale*. Antananarivo. Université de Madagascar. Filière Droit.
----- . 1981. *Notions de Droit Pénal Général*. Antananarivo. Centre Malgache de Promotion du Livre.
Ralahiarivony R.R. 1989. *Le Banditisme dans les Milieux Ruraux et Urbains*. Inédit. Antsirabe. Ecole Nationale Supérieure de Police Malgache. Mémoire de fin de Stage.
Ramanitra V.R. 1968. *Revue de Droit des Pays d'Afrique. Numéro spécial Madagascar*. Paris. Penant, La Documentation Africaine.
Sambson G.S. 1984. *Rapport d'Activités du Ministère de la Justice de Madagascar. Perspectives pour la période de 1984 à 1988*.

TWENTY YEARS OF STATE VIOLENCE IN UGANDA

Tibamanya mwene Mushanga[*]

"The world chuckled, Africans applauded, and Ugandans died at the rate of 100 to 150 a day", (Lamb, 1985:88)

1. Background

Uganda, as we know it today, is an amalgamation of formerly independent small kingdoms and tribal groups of people that lived under various political systems of native government, usually organized around a paramount chief of the tribe or clan. The British imposed what they called a Protectorate over these people in 1894. In Buganda, the central province from which the country takes its name, the British found a well-developed and organized system of government under a king known as the Kabaka. The country was divided into territorial chiefdoms, there was a judicial system with appellate courts, and a chief judge. Other departments of government consisted of the parliament, the army, the fire brigade, works, transport and all sorts of craftsmen that were required to keep the machinery of the state functioning.

After he had visited Kenya and Uganda in 1908, Winston Churchill wrote:

"The East African Protectorate - present-day Kenya - is a country of the highest interest to the colonialist, the traveller, or the sportsman. But the Kingdom of Uganda is a fairy tale. You climb up a railway instead of a beanstalk, and at the end, there is a wonderful new world. The scenery is different, the vegetation is different, the climate is different, and most of all, the people are different from anything elsewhere to be seen in the whole of Africa. Instead of the breezy uplands we enter a tropical garden. In the place of naked, painted savages, clashing their spears and gibbering in chorus to their tribal chiefs, a complete and elaborate polity is presented. Under a dynastic

---

[*] Professor of Sociology and Criminology at Makerere University in Uganda and at Nairobi University in Kenya; presently the Ugandan High Commissioner to Canada.

king, with a parliament, and a powerful federal system, an amiable, clothed, polite, and intelligent race dwell together in an organized monarchy upon the rich domain between the Victoria and Albert Lakes .... There is a court, there are regents and ministers and nobles, there is a regular system of native law and tribunals; there is discipline, there is industry, there is culture, there is peace. In fact, I ask myself whether there is any other spot in the whole earth where the dreams and hopes of the negrophile, so often mocked by results and stubborn facts, have ever attained such a happy realization" (in Hansen and Twaddle, 1988:4).

When the British established their colonial rule, they found an already existing and functioning system of government and sought to interfere with it as little as possible. They adopted a system of administration that they referred to as "Indirect Rule", whereby they established their rule through the existing native system.

Uganda is a well-endowed country with natural resources and with adequate and reliable rainfall; the land is fertile and the climate is good. Cash crops such as coffee, tea and cotton as well as other food crops such as bananas, maize, millet, beans and peas, which constitute the diet of the people, are grown with little effort; cattle, goats and sheep are kept in large numbers.

At the time of Independence in 1962, Makerere University ranked among the best universities in East and Central Africa; it was the Harvard of Africa (Lamb, 1985:89). The graduates of this University included teachers, doctors, lawyers, veterinarians, social scientists, economists, researchers, poets, civil servants and politicians. The civil service, the police and the postal services were ranked the best in the region. At the time the country attained its Independence, unlike other African countries, it did not lack manpower; if anything, there was soon to be unemployed university graduates.

During the first three or four years of Independence, the country continued to enjoy peace and political stability. The economic system and other developmental infrastructures continued to function normally and the association with Kenya and Tanzania in what was called the East African Community which ran the ports, airways, railways, and the postal system was doing very well (Dodge and Raundalen, 1987:16).

The seeds of political discord and economic ruin began to sprout through sectarian politics based on religion, tribes, ethnicity and sometimes on regions. Ill feeling began to appear between the Bantu people of south, west and east Uganda and the Nilotics and Sudanic people of the north and north-east, and also between Catholics and Protestants, and these divisions were to characterize the socio-economic and political trends in Uganda to the present day. In 1966 a political crisis erupted in the country precipitated by Milton Obote's quest for absolute power which led to a clash with the President, Sir Edward Mutesa, who was also the Kabaka of Buganda. Obote sent his army, under the command of Idi Amin, to storm the Palace of the King of Buganda, the President fled into exile to London, where he died in 1969. From then on, violence, torture and genocide became the main characteristics of Ugandan society.

2. Torture

The two decades between 1966 and 1986 will go down in the history of East Africa as a period in which the people of Uganda suffered death, brutality, torture, degradation, imprisonment and terrorism as a whole at the hands of state security personnel. At the time of the collapse of Milton Obote's Uganda Peoples' Congress (UPC) Administration in July 1985, the general population had already been hardened in its attitude towards violent deaths as a result of recurrent encounters with violence in their daily lives. Hardly a day passed without people hearing about or witnessing the death of a friend, acquaintance or fellow worker.

Dr. George Kanyeihamba, Uganda's Attorney-General and Minister of Justice, wrote about a British medical doctor, Nick Metcalfe of Manchester, who upon his return from a visit to Uganda at the invitation of the Government of Uganda, wrote to British ministers on 15 May 1985:

"I dearly loved the country and the people from its many different tribes. However, I grieve very much for the gross abuse of human rights that is going on in Uganda. My main concern here is not the restriction of basic liberties but mass murder. Uganda reflects the problems facing all 'African countries, the collapse of democratic government ... but it is an exception on the scale of not only killing of political opponents but the mass murder of innocent people. From my experience in Uganda, the Obote regime is guilty of all the crimes of Amin ... I base this on having worked in one area for a year and subsequently working and travelling around a majority of the country" (Hansen and Twaddle, 1988:75-76).

Another doctor, probably a Frenchman, was reported by La Croix, a French newspaper, to have stated that:

> "What was new for me, wasn't the poverty or the violence, but the daily and accepted terror. Ugandans live by the day and their only hope is that they survive ... When, in 1980, Milton Obote returned to power aided by Tanzanians, it was believed that Uganda would emerge from the nightmare into which Idi Amin had plunged it. Four years later, the opinion finds that the country is sinking deeper, into murderous chaos" (Hansen and Twaddle, 1988:75).

All-in-all, it is estimated that by the time this carnage came to an end in January 1986, when the National Resistance Movement came to power under the leadership of Mr. Yoweri Kaguta Museveni, almost one million people had lost their lives, and hundreds of thousands were living in exile in neighbouring countries notably the Sudan, Kenya and Zaire, and as far away as the United Kingdom and the United States of America (Hansen and Twaddle, 1988:239-253; The People's Struggle, No.1, January 1987, p.5).

From the west of the country, to the Central Region, from the south to the east, innocent people were taken from their homes, offices or at road blocks and "disappeared". Others were briefly held at military posts that had mushroomed all over the country as collecting centres for what the party and military officials called "anti-government elements and guerrillas".

In many cases, the victims were collected at night and taken to the camps for torture and interrogation. At these camps they were either shot dead or hatched to death by their captors; their bodies were then either left in the bush or buried in very shallow mass graves. In some cases, after interrogation and torture, the inmates of a prison, detention camp or torture centre were issued with sledge hammers and the victims were lined up in a single row. The first in line was ordered to hit the next in line on the head with the sledge hammer. This was then passed on from one person to the next until the last man, who was then either shot or sledge-hammered by the captors. In many cases, the use of the sword or the sledge hammer was preferred to shooting because it was more economical and did not cause the unnecessary rumours that were aroused by the sound of gunshots. Torture centres sprung up practically in every administrative division in the country, especially at the district level. In the capital of Kampala, torture and murder centres were set up in all the military barracks at Makindye, Lubiri, Kireka, Mbuya, Bugolobi and at the Maximum Security Prison of Luzira. Nearly all the police stations in and around the capital were also torture and murder centres: Naguru Central Police Station, Wandegeya, Jinja Road Police Station, Kawempe, Kibuye and Old Kampala to mention but a few.

Murder and torture centres were also improvised in residential quarters and in government hotels. Room 211 in Nile Mansion (now the Nile Hotel) was notorious as a torture chamber (High Court of Uganda, 1987:3), and it is reported that hundreds of people died in this beautiful hotel which the military elites and their political bosses had turned into their abode and working offices. One hotel worker told of how he had been mopping up the floor on the ground floor when the dead body of a man came rolling down the staircase. He had been killed in the corridor of the first floor and his murderer had just pushed the body down. Residents on the upper floors of this hotel were very often awakened in the early hours of the morning by the screams and cries of people being tortured.

The centre of all these acts of inhumanity was the State Research Centre at Nakasero, right in the middle of the city. What this place was intended for is not clear but it ended up by becoming the most dreaded butcher centre in the country; for very few inmates ever returned alive from this death centre. At peak periods, killings were being carried out by soldiers, party youth wingers and other officials almost all over the country with the exception of those in inaccessible regions and islands; but with Kampala and other smaller towns in the central regions witnessing more murders than outlying and remote towns.

2.1 Case reports of torture

Rape provided entertainment and amusement for the intoxicated soldiers. Old women, young girls and all were very often victims of rape and in many cases this preceded torture and murder. Eridadi Mulira, a prominent Ugandan and an advocate for human rights, wrote in April 1984:

> "Reports came from everywhere of acts of armed people attacking villages, raping wives in front of their husbands, mothers in front of their children, and children in front of their parents. School girls no longer feel safe to go to school" (1984:2).

In some cases of this nature, sadism was demonstrated by the use of objects on human beings. For example, coke bottles or green bananas were inserted into women vaginas. In one case, a prominent politician was being subjected to beating and torture. He pleaded to be allowed to speak to the head of state by telephone to explain his case. His torturer took a sword and

61

cut off his penis, pushed it into his mouth and told him to call the head of state through that "telephone." This politician was eventually killed, his body tied onto a long rope behind a Land Rover and driven through the streets, to the great shock of the spectators who were helpless to intervene. The following four cases were recorded by Amnesty International and will give the reader a general picture of the abuse of power and the violation of human rights leading to torture and murder.

Case A: Female, aged 56

"A's" account of events was as follows: in July 1982, three Land Rovers carrying uniformed soldiers came to "A's" house. The soldiers beat her husband severely and took him away. She does not know where he was taken and has not seen or heard of him since. The soldiers looted her house and told her that her husband was being taken because he and her sons were involved in anti-government guerrilla activities. The husband, who was a farmer and businessman, was a member of the Democratic Party. The sons were not at home at the time and were not arrested.

"A" was not herself assaulted on that day, but the next day the soldiers returned and took her to Makindye Barracks telling her that her husband wanted to speak to her. She was not beaten on the journey. On arrival at Makindye, she was put into a large room containing many prisoners, guarded by many soldiers; there were men, women, young women and youths. The guards said that the youths were "guerrilla leaders". There were over 50 people held in the room, including some school children. There were corpses and pools of blood and urine on the floor and the whole place was filled with smoke. She had been detained early in the morning and her torture began soon after she arrived. During the day that she was there, she saw other prisoners being subjected to various forms of ill-treatment.

"A" had her hands tied behind her back and a rubber tire was set alight above her. The burning material fell onto her scalp, face, arms and chest. In addition, some corrosive liquid was thrown over her. She thinks it was acid, as it caused the skin to peel off. After one day in custody she managed to escape from Makindye and was taken to a hospital.

However, soldiers came to the hospital and began robbing, beating and raping the patients - even those on intravenous transfusions. Some were killed. She escaped again and was taken to another hospital, where she stayed for about a month. Skin grafts were taken from her thigh and abdomen. She then heard that the army was searching the hospitals, so it was arranged for her to be smuggled out of the country. She has not heard of her husband or children since the time of her arrest.

Case B: Female, aged 21

"B's" account of events was as follows: in February 1984, while she was still attending school, uniformed soldiers came to "B's" house in Land Rovers one night to look for her *fiancé*. He was a soldier who had been arrested with the help of friends. She had heard nothing of him since the time of his arrest. The soldiers took her from her home to Makindye Barracks in Kampala. She was beaten on the way and was put in a room at the barracks in which there were other women, men and youths, but no children. There was no toilet or bucket, but there was a tap. They had to sleep on the floor and no food was provided, apart from that brought by friends of some of the prisoners, which was shared. Many people died, mainly of starvation but also from injuries.

She remained at Makindye for a month and was continually maltreated. Soldiers beat her with their fists, sticks and pangas (machetes), and also kicked her. Her skin was not lacerated and did not bleed, but she was badly bruised. Her toes were beaten with the butt of a pistol and she lost a big toe-nail. She was burned "all over" but especially on the legs, with what seems to have been a paraffin or butane gas flame, possibly a blow lamp. Her legs were tied together while this was done. Sometimes, the guards put a rope round her waist "for fun" and she was pushed backwards and forwards, causing abrasions on her waist. She was threatened with execution and saw others who died from torture and from lack of food.

"B" was repeatedly raped by many different soldiers. Many other women were raped in her presence. Some women were killed during rape. She became pregnant, but has no idea who the father of the child was. She remained in Makindye for a month and then was moved to Kireka Barracks, where she was told that "they didn't really know how to torture at Makindye", as she had not revealed her *fiancé*'s whereabouts. She was beaten at Kireka, but implied that this was not as severe as at Makindye. She remained in Kireka for four months until she was able to escape and flee the country.

Case C: Male, aged 32

"C's" account of events was as follows: "C" worked as a salesman of evangelical books. On January 1984, he was visiting a house to sell books. The owner of the house, the managing director of a company in Kampala, was politically active and apparently suspected of collaborating with armed opponents of the government. While he was at this house, soldiers in army uniform arrived in a Land Rover and lorry and began shooting at the door.

There were five people in the house at the time. Two tried to run away but were shot dead. The others, including "C", hid under the beds but were dragged out.

A woman preparing breakfast had the fire she was cooking on tipped over her; she was burned and he thinks she may have died. The soldiers (including two men without uniform) searched the house for ammunition but did not find any.

"C" was accused of being connected with the household, in spite of his protestations that he only happened to be there to sell Christian books. He was accused of being a money collector for the guerrillas. He was beaten and punched in the house. He was then forced to carry the two corpses out onto a lorry. Another Land Rover arrived and took the bodies away. The men captured in the house were then driven by lorry to Kireka Barracks but, just before arrival, the lorry stopped near a railway line where there were bushes. They were taken from the lorry and questioned, and it was suggested that they should admit to being armed. The prisoners agreed to confess to save their lives. At the gates of the barracks, they were beaten again by a group of soldiers, beaten "terribly for one hour". "C" was hit across the head with the butt of a rifle. They were then put into a small room of about five square metres, where they were questioned by an army officer. He called another man to interrogate the owner of the house, who denied that he was a guerrilla. They accused "C" of being a spy and alleged that he had been followed from house to house and that he had been collecting money to finance the guerrillas. More soldiers and another officer came and he and three other prisoners were thrown into another bare room, with blood on the floor. They were beaten with bars and sticks, especially on the arms and knees, and thrown against the walls several times. By now he was bleeding from the nose and mouth and could no longer hear properly. He was ordered to lie down and was trodden and stamped upon by soldiers wearing army boots. He thinks that this went on for about five hours.

Next day, they were taken out one by one, and "C" was the first. His interrogation and torture began in the morning and a written statement was prepared with a "confession" and he was told to sign it, as it alleged that he was involved in spying and assisting people who were fighting the government. He refused and was badly beaten again.

He was then asked if he knew his own body-weight. Then a copper weight of about 5 or 6 kilograms was hung to his penis and testicles with thin string and he was forced to walk around the room ten times with a guard. This episode lasted for about 15 minutes while the whole interrogation took about three hours. He eventually signed the confession and was returned to his cell at about 1 p.m. The cell was very cramped since it now contained eight people in it, instead of four. A man who had been present when they arrived had died and the owner of the house, who developed severe diarrhea, died on the third day. A few hours later, another man died. There was no toilet or bucket in the room and faeces everywhere. They were given food on the third day, consisting of posho (maize meal porridge) which had not been properly cooked and meat which was rotten. They had to eat the meat in the presence of the soldiers or be tortured again. "C" was vomiting but the soldiers tried to stop him from being sick, and wanted him to eat his own vomit. The other prisoners developed diarrhea.

During his third day in the cell, he was forced to lie down, while soldiers walked on his chest. He was kicked in the right hip, which is still painful and was pushed or dragged on the rough cement floor and forced to crawl on it, at half-hourly periods, thus grazing his hands and elbows and making them bleed. He was then forced to lie on his back and look up at the sun. He was also burned on the right heel with a heated metal bar and stabbed with a knife in the right thigh, made to walk barefoot over broken bottles, which cut the soles of his feet, then forced to eat more food, causing him to vomit. Another man died at about 6 p.m. that day and another at 7 p.m.: both bodies were left in the cell. At midnight, the cell was opened and they were taken out and put onto a lorry containing many other dead bodies. The engine had broken down and the prisoners were ordered to move the bodies onto another truck. Some were beaten as they were too ill and weak to help and five were left unconscious in the cell. "C" was told to go to a "big room near the gate". He refused, saying that he had not been ordered to go there by an officer. He was stabbed in the right arm with a bayonet, but ran back to his original cell.

On the fourth day he was questioned by an officer and was able to establish that he was, indeed, a salesman of religious books, after which he was eleased from the barracks. However, some time later on the same day, soldiers came to his home to arrest him again. He escaped but later learned that his wife had been arrested and that she had died in custody at Kireka Barracks.

Case D: Male, aged 26

"D's" account of events was as follows: in June 1982, while at his place of business, selling spare parts for cars, uniformed soldiers arrived in a Land Rover with two plain-clothed men who were either members of the Criminal Investigation Department (CID) or military intelligence. They took him to Makindye Barracks, which was only two kilometres away. On the way, they beat him badly with their fists. Upon arrival, he was beaten all the way to the cell with canes and batons. The "cell" was a large room like a go-down (store) with about 200 men in it, where he was kept for a fortnight.

The room was dark, and had only a small ventilator near the roof with no toilet or bucket and just a primitive toilet outside: to use this the prisoners had to shout for a guard, who would then beat them for wanting to use it. The only drinking water was a tap near the toilet and the prisoners had to sleep on the floor. The cell was very crowded and the prisoners were taken outside for interrogation and for food. This was supplied irregularly, and sometimes they were given nothing for two days, unless the guards were bribed.

"D" was accused of providing supplies to armed opposition groups. His business activities had involved him in trading in Nairobi, Kenya and it was because of this that he became suspect. He was accused of passing on information and his interrogators wanted to know about his finances. When they could not make out a case against him due to lack of evidence, they wanted him to pay a bribe for his release. Each time the guards changed shift, roll-call was made and indiscriminate beating took place while the guards ordered the men to explain why they were in prison. The guards were usually drunk and beat them indiscriminately with their rifle-butts. Some prisoners died. "D" saw "pink stuff" coming from their heads, presumably brain tissue. At other times, the guards used hammers to hit people on the head. This always happened at night, especially if the soldiers were drunk. He personally saw men being killed in this way and helped to remove dead bodies. People were huddled together, some fainting. He saw fractured jaws and eyes being gauged out by the guards.

After two weeks, he managed to call and bribe one of the soldiers and gave (or promised to give) him a small amount of money to contact his business associates. The latter raised 1,500,000 Ugandan shillings (about £ 2,000) which was paid to an officer and he was released and returned to his home, where he found his family unhurt. At the end of 1982 he was arrested again. He had just closed his shop at 6 p.m. and returned home, when seven soldiers came from Lubiri Barracks and attacked his house. They began shooting and breaking the windows. The front door was made of steel and was bolted. While he was fumbling with the bolts, bullets were fired at it and something from the door hit his head. When it was opened, he was forced to lie on the floor and they began beating him. He was told not to raise his head which was bleeding and one soldier remained to guard him while the others ransacked the house. He was struck on the back of the head with a pistol or gun-butt and lost consciousness. His family were away at a relative's house but the soldiers beat a servant who they found in the house. Clothes, shoes and other items were looted and put into the Land Rover. "D" was then taken to Lubiri Barracks and put in a cell where he remained until the following morning. He was then taken before an adjutant to explain his case. He pleaded that he knew nothing, so the officer ordered him to be beaten again. He received four strokes of a cane on his buttocks whilst lying on the ground. He was returned to his cell and this episode was repeated twice. He complained about his head injury and an officer came but no medical aid was given. The officer said that his case was very serious since he was financing the guerrilla movement.

The next day, he was taken to a first aid centre and treated by an orderly, who shaved his head and put some powder and plaster on the wound, which was dressed several times. He remained alone in his cell for about a month. His family did not know where he was and he was given no further explanations. The barracks were only 200 metres from his shop but he was not allowed any visitors. He knew a number of soldiers and succeeded in sending a message to his friends and relatives, who raised a ransom of 500,000 Ugandan shillings. This was unofficial, so he was released secretly at night and taken to his home (Amnesty International, 1985).

The victims of these episodes of violence can be grouped into several broad categories. Under Amin, victims tended to be those who opposed him or whom he imagined were opposed to his administration, or who disapproved of the policy of killing human beings. Under this system, the suspect was usually a well-known man and well-established in his profession or business. In numerous other cases, the victims were leading intellectuals, academics, professionals and prominent businessmen.

The victim was usually taken at night and members of his family left undisturbed. On reaching the military barracks, the victim was taken to the commanding officer for a very brief interview. The fate of the unfortunate victim was determined there and then. The commanding officer could order the victim to be "taken away", that is to silence, i.e. execute him; he could be ordered to be kept in the local prison or detention centre, pending further investigation.

When the decision of the commanding officer was to keep the detainee at the local station, this meant that his relatives now had a chance to come to his rescue by paying ransom money, which varied from case to case and from time to time. Under this practice, it was rare for a person who had been traced by his relatives to the military barracks to disappear. Those who were to "disappear" were usually never traced. So under Amin, before being killed, one had to be involved in anti-Amin activities or suspected of being anti-Amin.

But there were numerous other cases which resulted from personal conflicts that had nothing to do with the Amin administration. With the breakdown of law and order, soldiers, policemen and politicians engaged in settling old scores by all available means. Old scores were settled and rivalry and clan conflicts were resolved through violence; as were conflicts over women, land or debts.

Under Obote's fascist regime and especially under what has come to be known as Obote II, that is from 1981 to 1985, the victims tended to be his real or imagined opponents. They were generally members of political parties other than his own Uganda Peoples' Congress, and members of the Bantu tribes.

Thus, we find that Obote's victims, or victims of Obote's administration, were mainly drawn from the Southern Bantu tribes and in particular the Buganda for whom Obote seems to have had a congenital dislike in addition to his well-known "Bantuphobia". The persecution and terrorization of the people was carried out by members of the armed forces, the majority of whom were recruited from the Northern tribes of Nile-Hamitic people of Acholi, Lango, Teso and the West Nile Districts. The members of the police and prison forces were also drawn from the same districts and are also known to have participated in this exercise. Over and above this were the Uganda Peoples' Congress Youth Wingers who acted as the eyes and ears of the party. The Youth Wingers were to be found everywhere; in villages and in schools where they were known as the National Union of Students of Uganda (NUSU). In schools and colleges the NUSU were required to control and report not only on the activities of teachers and instructors, but also of fellow students. At Makerere University, many of these Youth Wingers were issued with hand guns which they kept with them all the time ready for use. Some UPC lecturers at Makerere University also carried guns, as did some of the senior priests in the country.

At the national level, there was an organization known as the National Security Agency or NASA whose function was a combination of intelligence gathering, protection of the President and overlooking the activities of youth wing and party members in general and, above all, keeping an eye on opposition groups. It was to NASA that reports of anti-governmental activities were made, and it was from NASA chiefs that orders for arrests, torture, disappearance and detention were received. The members of this terrorist group were secretly trained in communist countries, i.e., North Korea, Cuba, East Germany and the Soviet Union, and some had not received any training at all. They were given basic instructions on how to use a gun and how to disarm and immobilize an opponent without the use of a weapon. In some districts, such as Ankole, Toro and Busoga, the local NASA men were even more powerful than the local District Commissioners. In Ankole and Buganda, NASA leaders were the law itself; they took orders from nobody and reported to nobody except the Minister of State for Security in the Office of the President.

One major characteristic that distinguished the regimes of Obote and Amin and which the people in Uganda were very much aware of, was that under the Amin regime, the unfortunate victim was taken and killed but his family left alone, whereas in the case of Obote II, the victim's family also disappeared or was killed. This was especially true in the case of people from Buganda and the Luwere, Mpigi and Mukone Districts, where whole families were wiped out and their homes looted of all belongings such as money, clothing, beds, doors, tables and then set on fire.

This led to "internal" exile, for example, people abandoned their homes in the affected areas and sought security in the anonymity offered by the city and distant towns. It is estimated that about 300,000 people were living in internal exile from Luwero alone, and most of these were living in Kampala or the towns of Masaka and Mubende. It has also been said that, under Amin, if one kept a low profile, avoided conspicuous living and did not mix with members of the security forces, one would survive; this was not so under Obote II, because of the widespread intelligence network.

The two fascist regimes also differed in another aspect. The top members of the leadership of the National Security Agency (NASA) had received some training; for example, Mr. Chris Rwakasisi, the then Minister of State in charge of NASA, had spent some six years in the Soviet Union; Mr. Serwano Kabogorwa, who handled army intelligence was trained in Baku; Mr. Edward Buregyeya, the right-hand man of Chris Rwakasisi, was also trained in Russia. In contrast, the leaders of the State Research Bureau (SRB) of Idi Amin were generally semi-literate. Obote also recruited the Bantu into NASA to infiltrate Bantu communities, while Amin had depended upon Nubians who could not communicate because of language problems and were easily identifiable because of their ethnic and tribal characteristics. Under Obote II, it was the people one knew, in most cases from the same area, who carried out spying, identification, arrest and torture, whereas under Amin, nearly all those involved were usually outsiders. The violence under Obote II is said to have been more vicious because it was perpetrated by people who were known to their victims. For example, the number of people who were arrested in Mbarara and eventually killed at Kireka near Kampala were arrested by people who were known in and around Mbarara (High Court of Uganda, 1987).

3. The Banyarwanda

Another example of the misuse of power and the violation of human rights is the case of the Banyarwanda people. Some people of South-West Uganda have very close linguistic, cultural and socio-economic links with the people in the Republic of Rwanda. In some cases, the international line dividing the two countries goes through villages and separates clans and even families.

In the 1960s, there was ethnic violence in Rwanda which led to hundreds of thousands of people crossing the border into Uganda, where they settled. These are the Tutsi, who ruled Rwanda for centuries until they were ousted in the 1960s.

When, in 1981, anti-government movements spear-headed mainly by Mr. Museveni and elements of his Uganda Patriotic Movement, started the struggle, some of the young men and women of Rwandese origin also joined because they were already assimilated into Ugandan society. This did not please the administration in Kampala, and as a result, in 1982, the ruling party issued orders to evict all people of Rwandese origin and force them to return to Rwanda. The majority of these people, that is all those who were thirty years old or under, did not even speak Kinyarwanda. They were forced out of their homes and villages, they were beaten and tortured and driven away leaving behind their cattle, money and household effects and were not allowed to take any belongings with them. The sick, the old, the lame, and young were all marched to the border of Rwanda and forced to cross into camps where they remained until the National Resistance Movement took power in Kampala and allowed them to cross back into Uganda.

Dr. Louise Pirouet writes that there was good reason to believe that the eviction of the Banyarwanda was planned over a long period of time and that it was carried out at the instigation of the central government. When the exercise started, Obote was conveniently out of the country, but on his return he issued a statement on 29 October 1982, in which he disclaimed the involvement of the central government and concluded by saying:

"I want to assure the Chairman, Counsellors, Ugandans and the rest of the world that there was no Government approval, scheme or decision for the persons of Rwandese origin to be uprooted from amidst the Ugandan population. I also want to assure all the rest of the country as well as the world, that the Government of Uganda will not pursue such policy."

But only a week after the President had made his statement, the Chairman of Mbarra District Council addressed the Counsellors, county and sub-county chiefs, saying:

"I summoned you to inform you that the battle to collect and return the refugees to their places is over, and to thank you for the work you have done ... What remains now is to scrutinize refugees that might have stayed behind and rid villages of refugees ... I am glad to tell you that our exercise was performed perfectly well even if there were sporadic incidents which did not please us, e.g. our two youths and one policeman were killed ... This is not negligible. The good thing is that we won the battle through the blood of our friends above. Let us observe a minute of silence in their remembrance ... Go and preach the gospel and inform the people that we have won the battle. Let them follow as we know our destination and we have already started seeing sunshine there ... I am warning everyone to avoid the property of the Banyarwanda ... Be patient and the District Council will determine a way for you to share these properties ... to dispel all rumours and loose talk, the President's speech from the start to the end does not state that refugees and aliens should return to the lands they occupied." (Hansen and Twaddle, 1988:244-245).

This exercise was carried out by people from Ankole and three elements helped the UPC in their decision. One was that the majority of the people who had come from Rwanda were members of the Roman Catholic Church and as such, were unlikely to have any sympathy from the UPC Government in Kampala because of its religious bias. The reason is that in Ugandan politics, political parties were originally organized along religious lines. Roman Catholics were told to belong to the Democratic Party, which had very strong ties with the Catholic Church which had been imported into Uganda from Europe in the early 1950s. Whereas the members of the Protestant Church were organized to join the Uganda People's Congress. In some areas, rebellious Catholics joined the UPC, but these were the exception rather than the rule. On the other hand, Protestants who joined the Democratic Party were those who sensed some uneasiness or were being discriminated against within the Party because of their tribal background. For example, the Bahima of East Ankole and Western Masaka joined the Catholic Democratic Party almost *en-masse*, not because they were convinced of its sound programme or because of its enlightened leadership, but because of the way they had been treated by the UPC leaders in Ankole.

The second point which influenced the UPC leaders' decision to expel people of Rwandan origin, was that the majority of these people were ethnically related to the Bahima who, as a group, had embraced the Democratic Party and more so, a group from which Mr. Museveni came, the man the UPC had declared to be the State Enemy Number One.

The third element that led to the eviction of people of Rwandan origin was greed and envy. Corruption had engulfed the entire government; government bureaucracy was in a shambles due to corruption, nepotism and religious sectarianism. In this kind of situation, the party members in Ankole, especially those who held no party or government posts from which they could enrich themselves through corruption, found the Banyarwanda an easy prey since the latter had acquired considerable material wealth in terms of herds of cattle, businesses, shops and large tracts of land. The party activists were determined to evict the Banyarwanda in order to take over their property, since they, the Banyarwanda, had come with nothing and were to go back as they came. This was a repetition of Amin's expulsion of Asians a decade earlier, and of Obote's eviction of Kenyans during his first administration.

The Obote II Government had arranged to hold elections towards the end of 1985; in their wise judgment, the party leaders in Ankole calculated that if they removed as many Democratic Party supporters as possible, the chances of their winning in this district would improve considerably. What followed this decision was one of the most sordid episodes in the history of independent Uganda. Thousands of people - men, women and children - were forced by Youth Wingers of the UPC and soldiers to leave their homes and flee to Rwanda.

Many who were forced to return to Rwanda had settled in Uganda in the 1960s and were now very old men and women, many were men and women in their early twenties, but the majority were in their teens, and had never been to Rwanda and, furthermore, could not even speak the language. They had attended schools in Uganda, had been brought up according to the traditions of the local people in Uganda and suddenly found themselves being forced, at gun point, to cross the Kagera River and enter Rwanda, where they were definitely not welcome.

Hundreds died on the way, and those who managed to cross the border were kept in refugee camps. Meanwhile, the looted property of this people was divided among the UPC functionaries. This included cattle, goats, household goods which the owners could not carry with them, such as beds, iron sheets taken off the houses etc. There was a wide outcry, but the UPC insisted on expelling the people. Banana plantations and gardens of the people expelled were shared among local UPC members, some of whom began to move into the houses of the departed owners and this, of course, was a bonanza for local party militants. What is more surprising is that people who had no trace of Rwandan origin, but who were known or suspected of being sympathetic towards the anti-UPC struggle, were also expelled from Nshara, Isingiro, Rwampara and Kashari Counties of Mbarara District. It is estimated that as many as 30,000 families, which is almost a quarter of a million people, were affected in a relatively short period of time (Hansen and Twaddle, 1988:239-253).

Finally, another characteristic that differentiated the two regimes was that, whereas under Obote not a single person was publicly executed by a firing squad, this was instead frequently practiced by Idi Amin. Suspected guerrillas or bandits as they were called, were driven back to their home towns, their relatives were forced to witness the executions and priests were ordered to come and say prayers for the souls of the victims.

These executions were carried out after brief trials by military tribunals, presided over by semi-literate brigadiers, where the defendants had no right to legal representation or right of appeal to civilian courts (Republic of Uganda, 1977).

During Amin's reign of terror, many senior persons from both the armed forces and the general public lost their lives. These included the Vice Chancellor of Makerere University, very prominent surgeons at Mulago Hospital; the Anglican Archbishop of Kampala, Cabinet Ministers, the Chief Justice of the Republic, professors, businessmen, traders and retired civil servants. All-in-all, 500,000 people died during a period of 99 months, compared to 300,000 who died under Obote II, during a period of 55 months. (Hansen and Twaddle, 1988:250). Under Amin, 168 people were killed each day compared to 182 under Obote II, and both these figures are world records in that they are the highest ever recorded during peace time (Mushanga, 1988:24-25; see also Lamb, 1985:88).

4. The roots of violence

Uganda had started off very well on her road to independence on 9 October 1969. Elections were held through an agreement made between Obote's UPC and the Kabaka Yekka (KY), a locally organized party in Buganda that aimed at safeguarding the Bugandan Monarchy. Previously, Obote's UPC and Benedicto Kiwanuka's DP had very poor support in Buganda, but with the above-mentioned agreement, the UPC, under Obote, was able to form a Government with the support of the members of the

Kabaka Yekka, who were indirectly elected to the Parliament by the Bugandan Parliament or the Lukiko. In Buganda alone, the people also elected members to their Regional Parliament in Mengo which, in turn, elected members to the National Assembly in Kampala. In this way, UPC plus KY members were able to constitute the majority in the National Assembly.

The Independence Constitution had provided for the retention of the Kingdoms in Buganda, Ankole, Toro and Bunyoro and a year after independence, the King of Buganda, Sir Edward Mutesa II, was elected the First President of Uganda and Mr. Milton Obote was his Prime Minister. This arrangement seemed to have been a reasonable one under the circumstances, but there were, however, major problems that needed serious attention. One of these was the question of the "lost counties." These were counties which had been annexed by Britain to Buganda for the role the Kabaka played during the British struggle against Kabalega, the King of Bunyoro. The Bunyoro people wanted these lands returned to them and the London Independence Constitutional Conference agreed that a referendum be held in those counties to decide their future, in other words, whether they should remain in Buganda or be returned to Bunyoro. Sir Edward Mutesa, as the Kabaka of Buganda, was in favour of retention, while Obote was willing to abide by the results of the referendum. The results showed that of the three counties in which the referendum was held, only one opted to remain in Buganda. It is said that Mutesa, in his capacity as President of the Republic, refused to sign the papers of transfer of the territory, thereby creating a political crisis. The crisis sparked off a violent encounter between Obote's central government forces and the Kabaka's guards at his Palace at Mengo. This was in May 1966.

At this time, President Mutesa was staying at his Palace at Mengo just outside of Kampala when Amin, then Chief of the Army, on Obote's orders, attacked the Kabaka's Palace with heavy machine gun fire. Many people were killed, the Palace was burnt, and the President fled the country and went into exile to London where, as stated earlier, he died in November 1969. Soon after the Lubiri incident, Obote abrogated the Constitution and declared himself President. He abolished the Kingdoms as well as the Constitutional Heads of Districts that he himself had created. Violence began to spread and at Nakulabye, a small township just outside Kampala, several people were gunned down for no apparent reason and their bodies left in the open for all to see. The army became more visible, more mobile and more hostile towards the civilian population, and anti-Buganda feelings began to be expressed by those in positions of power. Obote became more and more alienated from the people, the UPC leaders became more arrogant, corruption became widespread, the Lango from the North began to refer to themselves as Princes from the North, harassment of the non-UPC members and especially the Democratic Party from Buganda continued, arrests became more frequent and road blocks were set up in most parts of the country as political power began to slip away from politicians to the soldiers. The end of Obote's rule was approaching very fast as anti-government elements began to surface such as when an attempt on Obote's life was made at Lugogo in 1970.

On 25 January 1971, Idi Amin staged a *coup d'état* while Obote was in Singapore and Kampala went wild with people dancing in the streets, not so much as to welcome Amin, but for the removal of Obote from power. As every one was to discover, the assumption of power by Amin was a continuation of Obote's policy of state terrorism which went on for eight long years (Lamb, 1985:88-90).

During the first year of the Amin administration, things appeared to go well. Amin appointed senior professionals, men with wide experience from various walks of life, as his ministers. But as soon as he began to learn more about his new role and about the individuals who surrounded him, he began interfering in the administration of ministries by attacking senior civil servants. Furthermore, his soldiers became unruly, undisciplined and hostile towards the general public. In the meantime, people began to disappear in and around Kampala. More and more people were being rounded up and taken to military barracks where they were detained for no reason, during which time they were harassed, beaten and tortured. By 1973, the security situation in the country had deteriorated considerably; violence had already spread through the army, the police force and Amin's secret agents, called the State Research Bureau.

During this period, the group that was targeted was the ethnic tribes of people from whom Obote originated and from where he recruited his armed forces; they were the Acholi and Lango tribes. Amin's fear was that since these men were of Obote's ethnic group and had been recruited by him, they were therefore his supporters. Amin then began to recruit into the army members of his Kakwa group and since the Kakwa are in a very small minority, he had to recruit from members of the same tribe from neighbouring Sudan, i.e., the Nubians. The killing of the Acholi and Lango people continued, especially in the army. Dead bodies were to be seen on streets, garbage heaps, in forests and at road blocks. The killings and disappearances of people increased as pressure mounted against the regime.

In 1979 Amin fled the country, his regime was overthrown and his soldiers forced out of Uganda into Sudan, but the violence did not disappear. The majority of the fighting forces who returned from exile to oust Amin were Obote's former soldiers who had previously fled the country at the time when Amin came to power. Also returning, were those who had fled from Amin during the hunt for the Acholi and Lango tribes. As soon as these men entered Uganda, they embarked on a policy of revenge against the people of the West Nile and Madi districts from where Amin drew most of his soldiers. The hunt for the Lugbara, Madi and Kakwa tribes was intense, many people died and hundreds of thousands went into exile.

Violence continued throughout the administrations of Presidents Yusufu Lule and Godfrey Binaisa, and under the Military Commission headed by Paulo Muwanga.

In December 1980, elections were held and Obote's UPC was declared victorious, despite overwhelming evidence of vote rigging. Obote, without a Constitution, and therefore without the Mandate of the people, was forced upon the people of Uganda by President Julius Nyerere of Tanzania. Furthermore, Paulo Muwanga, who had also not been elected to Parliament, was declared the Vice President of Uganda.

This fact is important when trying to understand the extent and nature of the violence carried out during the Obote II regime, since part of the explanation lies in the political process that was established immediately after the December elections in 1980.

With Obote back in the State House, political oppression, robbery with menace, rape, looting, wanton mass murders, disappearances, general insecurity and economic depression took a new turn for the worse. Not long after taking office, Obote plunged the country into the worst economic abyss it had been in since the arrival of the colonialists eighty years before. The hunt for members of the Uganda Patriotic Movement, a political movement that had been founded by Yoweri Museveni in 1980, was mounted. This Movement contested the 1980 elections, and only one of its candidates was elected. Elsewhere, the votes were either stolen or reversed in favour of the UPC. The hunt intensified soon after Museveni, together with twenty-six others, was determined to rid Uganda of injustice, corruption and above all, to put a stop to genocide.

In February 1981, two months after the elections, Museveni, in an effort to declare war on the new regime, attacked a military unit. The Government responded by unleashing heavily armed and enraged soldiers into the Luwero, Mubende and Mpigi Districts to rid the areas of guerrillas. As time went by, violence, looting, torture and murders spread throughout the country. The more the Government became aware that it couldn't eradicate its opponents, the more desperate it became and it sought the solution in what was called the "scorched-earth policy" proposed by North Korean military advisers.

According to this policy, whole families or villages of suspects or of people suspected of being sympathetic towards the anti-government agents were destroyed - men, women and children were killed, their belongings taken, and their homes razed by fire. While this was continuing in the central region of the country, the rounding-up of Museveni's supporters continued, arrests were made, people detained, interrogated, tortured and many killed at all the military barracks or police stations.

Road blocks were erected on almost all the major roads and stationed at every few miles. Business, trade and agricultural production were reduced to the minimum, corruption and bribery became rampant and smuggling became the main venue of international trade; coffee, cattle, gold, hides and skins and fish were smuggled out of the country in exchange for clothing, sugar, etc. Robbery with violence, especially of motor vehicles, became acute, the taking of hostages and demanding of ransom money by soldiers became more frequent and many other forms of criminal activity was widespread.

The social services were in a disastrous condition, and by the time the regime of violence ended, everything had almost ground to a halt. Most roads had become impassable, pot-holes were everywhere, bridges that had been washed away had not been repaired. Coffee, tea and cotton factories were in ruins and coffee and tea plantations were overgrown and no longer productive; schools were without equipment, with no chalk or exercise books; teachers and other civil servants went for months without pay; magistrates and police officers had no paper on which to write; hospitals were without drugs, bandages or syringes; salaries were very low and the standard of living very poor. In short, life in Uganda had almost surpassed the Hobbesian state of nature where life was brutish, nasty and short.

Perhaps the most important point to consider in greater detail is the role of illegal and deviant activities played in the economic and social survival by the people of Uganda. This is deemed to be very important in view of the fact that the entire socio-economic and political system had broken down, as was law and order, but yet, the Ugandan people continued to exhibit more resilience, fortitude and a determination to survive. David Lamb states that:

"The worse things became in Uganda, the more adaptable and accepting the Ugandans seemed to become. If there was no food in the stores, they picked fruit and ate it steamed, mashed bananas, which are served with local spices and are known as Matoke. If the phones didn't work, they did their business in person. If friends and relatives died for making ill-chosen comments, they became silent. If there was no public transport to get them to their city jobs, they walked. They did so without complaint or apparent anger. "Shauri ya Mungu," they said - Swahili for "It's God's will." ... They had learnt the art of Survival" (1985:90).

It is also important to note that in spite of these economic problems and the spread of violence, some parts of the country actually made gigantic progress in structural and commercial development. In these areas, building construction intensified and expanded beyond any level ever known before. This is said to have been made possible, through smuggling and "magendo" or illicit trading. Goods which were in great demand in neighbouring countries, such as coffee, beans, cattle, hides and skins, petrol, diesel and Kerosene were smuggled out of the country and sold at enormous profit and with the profit earned, the smugglers bought the required materials for building construction. Again, when one considers the fate of civil servants or any other wage earner, one begins to wonder just to what extent these salary earners became involved in illegal conduct in order to survive, since inflation was so high. For example, the salary of a middle-ranking civil servant was between 7,000 to 10,000 shillings per month (US$1 = 150 shillings at the official rate, but 300 to 450 shillings on the black market), and that would not have bought one meal in a hotel, and one had to work for an entire year to be able to pay for one night in a relatively cheap hotel.

In January 1986, the National Resistance Movement ushered in a new era of peace, reconstruction, rehabilitation and social progress, together with the rule of law, respect for human rights and peaceful co-existence with neighbouring countries.

5. The causes of the crisis

As one writer has rightly observed, no African state is a smoothly functioning democracy, but all these one-party dictatorships are not in turmoil of tyranny, anarchy and almost economic ruin (Hansen and Twaddle, 1988).

Uganda presents a unique case of a country that found itself in the grip of chaos, violence, economic collapse and decay. To explain this state of affairs, we must consider, among other things, four major factors that could have contributed to this crisis.

The first one is the history of the country. As noted earlier, Uganda as we know it now was unified by the British. They grouped together some of the most highly organized states with what the British anthropologists called "Tribes without rulers". This grouping was, from the beginning, characterized by dissension, mistrust and inequality. The Southern Bantu live in an area that is naturally endowed with good soil, rainfall and an abundance of water in rivers and lakes. They were also favoured by the British who recruited them into the civil service and other privileged white-collar jobs while the northern Nilotics, who hail from a semi-arid land with little resources, were recruited into the army, the police force and the prison service. The end result of this arrangement was to create a class society with the rich Bantu in the south, and the poor Nilotics in the north. This is sometimes termed tribalism simply because the people involved happen to belong to the Bantu and non-Bantu groups of people. In reality, the conflict is more economic than tribal, ethnic or linguistic. The Bantu, and especially the Buganda, resisted any attempt at assimilation with Nilotics unless they were in a position of control and this conflicting situation led to envy and rivalry.

Secondly, there was conflict between the traditional rulers, the Kings of Buganda, Ankole, Toro and Bunyoro (all in the south and west) who sought to maintain their traditional power over their subjects while the new political party leaders sought to establish a more democratic form of government in which power was to be derived from the masses. Political parties were a new wine that was quite unsuitable for centuries. The competition between traditional kings and political leaders led to a show of strength at Mengo Palace when Obote's soldiers, led by Idi Amin, stormed the King's Palace forcing him into exile.

The third element in the creation of the political crisis is what was repeatedly referred to by Museveni as political bankruptcy. One writer in fact stated that in a 1981 newsletter of the National Resistance Movement, Museveni:

> " ... argued that one of the reasons Uganda finds itself in the present political mess is because at Independence, men of low level of modern education, including school drop-outs like Obote found themselves at the head of the state affairs although Uganda had the best trained (elite) in sub-Saharan Africa" (Hansen and Twaddle, 1988:208).

This also applied to Amin, Paulo Muwanga and Tito Okello.

Fourthly, there was fear and insecurity because people who have tasted power in Third World Countries, found themselves in the grip of fear of losing it. The fear is psychological, economic and physical. The psychological part of it is related to the history of the people where power was traditionally handed over from father to son, and the new African leaders also tended to want the power handed over to their descendants, if not family descendants, then political ones. This, too, may explain the prolonged stay in power of such leaders who no longer enjoy the support of the majority of the people. The economic aspect of this fear is the dread of reverting to pre-leadership times when such men had no defined source of income and no professional skills to fall back on. The physical aspect of fear is related to the conduct of these leaders while in office. Those who engaged in acts of violence and abuse of power and violated human rights, feared revenge from members of the general public whom the leaders might have mistreated while in office.

Lastly, there is the quest for self-aggrandizement through the personality cult that leads to an abnormal or neurotic desire for fame. This can be seen in the way that Third World leaders adorn themselves with titles of doctor, general, and so on. Amin called himself the Conqueror of the British Empire or CBE and Bokassa crowned himself Emperor of the Central African Republic while many others acquired the titles of "Life President", the Light, the Saviour and the Teacher.

6. Conclusion

The people of sub-Saharan Africa, from Kenya in the East to Senegal in the West, are making genuine efforts to fight against the declared enemies of Africa, namely poverty, disease and ignorance. They have, since the time of independence, which is roughly one generation ago, been able to expand educational opportunities which has resulted in the high literacy rates, as in the case of Tanzania.

They have also developed infrastructures in many fields of human endeavour and political adjustments are being introduced to modernize the political systems by allowing multi-party methods, as against the single-party dictatorships. These changes are taking place in many countries such as Zambia, Zaire, the Congo and other African states.

What remains to be accomplished in Africa, South of the Sahara, is to develop a political system of government that will ensure the rule of law, respect for human rights, the eradication of corruption and, above all, the creation of a socio-economic and political atmosphere, that will minimize the rise to power of self-appointed dictators that have come to characterize this region of Africa since the advent of political independence. Because, I believe, that it is the socio-economic and political system that makes it possible for dictators to emerge on political scenes in Africa and in the Third World in general.

References

Amnesty International. 1985. *Uganda: Evidence of Torture*. London.
----. 1986. *Report*. London. pp.106-110.
Churchill W.S. 1908. *My African Journey*. London.
Dodge P., Raundalen M. (Eds.). 1987. *War, Violence and Children in Uganda*. Oslo. Norwegian University Press.
Hansen H.B., Twaddle M. (Eds.). 1988. *Uganda Now: Between Decay and Development*. London and Nairobi. East African Studies, Heinemann.
High Court of Uganda. 1987. *Criminal Session No. 17*. Kampala.
Lamb D. 1985. *The Africans*. London. Methuen.
Mulira Eridadi Medadi K. 1984. *The Uganda Tragedy and the Way Out*. The New Century. 1:71.
Mushanga T. 1988. *Crime and Deviance: An Introduction to Criminology*. (2nd edition). Nairobi. Kenya Literature Bureau.
Republic of Uganda. 1977. *Proceedings of the Treason Trial By The Military Tribunal*. Kampala.

CORRUPTION IN AFRICA:
A CASE STUDY OF NIGERIA

Adedokun A. Adeyemi[*]

1. Introduction: the meaning and scope of corruption

For a very long time, corruption has been recognized as a major problem in the developing world, where it has become a cankerworm, reaching the dimensions of an epidemic in the body politic of the various nations of Africa. Respective governments in the various jurisdictions have continually expressed alarm at the situation and have repeatedly disclosed their respective intentions to combat corruption. In Nigeria, various governments have expressed and demonstrated such intentions[1]. The present Federal Military Government has also joined its predecessors in recognizing the problem of the corruption epidemic and has also declared its determination to combat it[2].

It is recognized that corruption is the "most pervading and amorphous of all (crimes, which) acts as a catalyst to all the other (crimes)" (Adeyemi, 1990:110). Yet it is restricted to the improper giving and receiving of gratification to and by a public official of any category in order to perform or refrain from performing certain acts in the course of his official duties[3], excepting the extension of the offence from agents in connection with their principals' affairs or businesses[4].

This emphasis on public sector probity does not seem to recognize the complementarity of both the public and private sectors of the same integral society, in the light of which we should know that the "attitudes and habits in one sector are bound to affect and influence attitudes and habits in the other sector. Therefore, if we attempt to clean up the Public Sector ... without correspondingly doing the same for the Private Sector, the cankerworm will continuously be contaminating the Public Sector, with the attendant continuation of corrupt habits, in as much as it is impossible to insulate the Public Sector from the Private Sector. Hence, the two must be cleansed together... It is, therefore, clear that unless the same degree of probity is maintained for the Private Sector, we may be electing people to direct and

---

* Former Member of the United Nations Committee on Crime Prevention and Control and Head of the Department of Public Law, University of Lagos, Nigeria.

control the Public Institutions which we are cleaning, who themselves have no inculcation of probity whatsoever. The result will be that there will be no political will to effect probity seriously in the public institutions." (Adeyemi, 1979:6). This prophecy was amply fulfilled by the various civilian administrations of 1979-1983 in Nigeria, which were respectively characterised by graft and endemic corruption. Then the federal government failed to enact the necessary enabling law to establish the Code of Conduct Tribunal and Bureau, as provided for in the 1979 Constitution. It even failed to effect the constitutionally enjoined general declaration of assets by public officers outside the ranks of ministerial appointees. It is therefore clear that the offence of *corruption* must be defined to cover behaviour in both the private and the public sectors, in as much as probity in both sectors is essential to a healthy society. In this regard, it must cover all categories of persons: of high, medium or low status.

Also, in line with the dynamic activism of Bairamian J. (as he then was) in the case of *Biobaku v. Police*[5], where his Lordship defined the word 'corruptly' as meaning 'improperly', and then proceeded to define 'impropriety' as the receiving or offering of *some benefit* as a reward or inducement to sway or deflect the receiver from the honest and impartial discharge of his duties[6], we should define the offence beyond mere financial considerations, to cover such areas as the demanding or receiving of sexual favours, conferment of titles or appointments (including promotions) to offices, admission into clubs, societies or institutions, with a view to swaying or deflecting another person, particularly the receiver, from the honest and impartial discharge of any duties which are imposed upon him by law. Thus expressed, the offence of corruption will also cover all possible cases of abuse of office. But, of course, this might make the offence too broad, and even vague.

2. The extent of corruption in Nigeria

"When you can measure what you are speaking about and express it in numbers, you know something about it, but when you cannot measure it, when you cannot express it in numbers, your knowledge is of a meagre and unsatisfactory kind." (Kelvin, 1955: frontispiece)

Can we really measure the magnitude of corruption and express it is numbers? The answer is yes and no. We can do so because we have official statistical records of incidents of offences of corruption known and recorded as 'Bribery and Corruption' (see Tables 1 and 2 below). Yet the quantum of recorded incidents of 'Bribery and Corruption' is so disparate with the actual magnitude of the incidence of these offences that no one will accept the recorded figures as the true records of 'Bribery and Corruption' offences actually committed in Nigeria. The differences between the two, otherwise known as the 'dark figure', must be definitely large. This is why the answer to the question posed above must also be a negative one.

I explained this twelve years ago with reference to the nature of the offence of corruption as an offence of low reportability (Adeyemi, 1979:1-4). The factors responsible for this low reportability include the fact that corruption is a victimless offence, in which both the offender and the 'victim' (if he can be so called) are criminally responsible for the crime, and this inevitably inhibits the reportability of the offence of corruption. Incidental to this is the fact that the offence will be reported only when the provider of the bribe fails to effect the deal. If it is accepted, as should be the case, that most of the corrupt dealings are in fact implemented, since corruption would not flourish otherwise, it must then follow that only a small fraction of the deals fail to be implemented and are therefore reportable. A much smaller fraction ever becomes known to unsuccessful competitors and an even smaller proportion ever gets reported. It becomes clear then that corruption is destined to remain an offence of very low reportability. Again, feelings of shame and scandal, as distinct from fear of prosecution, also contribute to the magnitude of the 'dark figure' in corruption cases; so do fears of reprisal, as well as lack of confidence in the system of criminal justice administration which may itself be ridden with corruption. Hence, the attitude sometimes is: *'Why report Corruption to Corruption?"* Corruption within the criminal justice system will tend to encourage the corruption offender to exert the maximum pressure on the criminal justice personnel. It must be realised that this type of offender, by the very nature of his offence, is a very corrupt person and is more likely, than any other ordinary offender such as an assaulter or thief, to attempt to bribe any member of the criminal justice personnel in charge of his matter. He is, for this purpose, usually shameless and brave, almost to the point of being daring. Lastly, the scarcity of the recorded incidents of 'Bribery and Corruption' offences is also due to the scope of the offence created in our criminal laws, which have sought to define them mainly with reference to the conduct of public officers. This has left the Nigerian private sector with the impression that their country's laws permit them to be corrupt. Such a situation, as stated earlier, should not be allowed to continue in Nigeria or, indeed, in any other country. We should create the crime of corruption which should encompass the conduct of all citizens, both in the public and private sectors. No citizen should be allowed to feel that he is free to engage in corrupt practices with impunity.

Faced with the discovery of low police figures during the 1979 exercise, I then collected the figures from the now defunct Corrupt Practices Investigation Bureau. This, in contrast to the figures of 1,108 crimes known to the police in 1978, recorded 3,000 cases of bribery and corruption known to the Bureau. The police recorded 1,034 true cases, compared to 500 true cases reported by the Bureau in the same year. It would therefore seem that the police figures were higher than those recorded by the Bureau. This can probably be explained by the greater familiarity, on the part of the average citizen when making his complaints, with the police and the location of police stations than with any special investigating body and its offices.

It seems to me that, by its very nature, little information will be provided on corruption by the objective victimisation and self-reporting surveys that are normally used to fill in the gap of the 'dark figure' as much as possible. Hence, Odekunle was forced to suggest some ten methods for collecting information on the 'dark figure' of corruption (Odekunle, 1986:40-41). It seems to me, however, that some of the methods which he suggested may be more consistent with the functions of the police and intelligence officers than with those of a researcher (e.g. methods C and F). Some may be dangerous to the life of a researcher (methods C and H and, in part, E and G), whereas others may not yield accurate information (e.g. method A is to enable a disappointed crook vent his spleen and envy on a successful rival: whilst the value of gossips should not be over-rated in respect of method G); yet again, some may be so expensive as to pose the ethical problems of how a researcher may be able to justify his use of research funds for such purposes, such as where he goes to join clubs "for the purpose of meeting and associating with public or corporate officials and becoming, over time, intimated with their practices" (method H). As long as these problems are borne in mind, there is no doubt about a need to augment officially recorded data, as Odekunle has recognized. This increase, however, should only be used for interpreting and supplementing the officially recorded information.

Having recognized the need for this increase, the available crime statistics for 'Bribery and Corruption' can now be examined as indicators of the trends over time. These are contained in Table 1.

In order to assess the periodic consistency of the data, I computed the figures on the basis of four-year overlapping periods, the resultant data of which is contained in Table 2.

Table 1 and its related graph provide very interesting results, namely, that the corruption figures and their rates are roughly consistent with each other, both in pattern and trend; and that they reflect the strictness or laxity of the government in power in relation to probity in public life.

Hence, there were steady, low increases during the era covered by the second military regime in Nigeria (1967-1975), known as the Gowon Era. The successive era, namely that, of the Mohammed/Obasanjo Regime, showed sharp and high increases between 1975 and 1977, when both the figures and the rates reached their peak, and at which time the regime embarked upon what can be termed a 'Probity in Public Life Drive', which included the setting up of the Corrupt Practices Investigation Bureau and the retrenchment of corrupt and inefficient officials from the public service. But with the commencement of the 'Transition to Civil Rule' Programme in 1978 until the end of the military era in 1979, the figures continued to decline. This decline can be explained on the ground that the military had already commenced its process of disengagement from government, and had set in motion the necessary machinery for a civilian take-over. This, of course, meant that its probity drive noose had begun to slacken. The figures further declined with the advent of the civilian administration between 1979 and 1981, after which they broke the trend and rose slightly in 1982, apparently as a result of the complaint, contained in the President's New Year Message, about the endemism of corruption in the country at that time[7]. The figures fell again in 1983.

However, with the return of the military to government on 31 December, 1983 (that is, the Buhari/Idiagbon Regime), there was another sharp rise in the figures in 1984. That regime is remembered today mainly for its draconian laws and strict anti-corruption drive. However, with the ousting of that regime by the present military regime (the Babangida Regime), which proclaimed the observance of human rights to be the cornerstone of its administration, Nigerians appeared to have perceived the regime as being synonymous with a relaxation of the drive towards probity. Consequently, the figures have continued to decline. In fact, the 1989 figures declined further to 301; whilst only 177 incidents were recorded for the first three quarters of 1990 (January to September); figures for the last quarter (October to December) were unavailable at the time of writing.

The data contained in Table 2 also confirm the trend revealed by Table 1 and its related graph. The Gowon Era, covering the 1967-1970 and the 1971-1974 periods, showed a modest increase. The sharpest increase was registered during the Mohammed/Obasanjo Regime of 1975-1978, during which period the offence reached its peak. The civilian regime of 1979-1982 showed a sizeable decline in the figures. The military intervention which occurred during the next period of 1983-1986 showed yet another increase: whilst the humanist era of the Babangida Military Administration (1987-1988) recorded a sharp decrease.

This particular trend can be interpreted to mean that the offence of corruption gets reported to a greater extent whenever the public perceive the demonstration of a serious intention or will on the part of the government of the day to control and contain it. On the other hand, it gets reported to a lesser degree whenever the public perceive laxity in the attitude of the government of the day towards its control and containment. Hence, we can safely formulate the hypothesis that 'Recorded incidents of corruption are high whenever Government demonstrates an intention to control it.'

3. Causes of corruption in Nigeria

A developing society undergoes widespread multi-faceted transformations. These transformations involve the importation of foreign value systems, without the corresponding implantation of the conventions, customs and institutional framework within which they are based and with which they work. Such rootlessness generally leads to political, economic and administrative inefficiency which, in turn, leads to inadequacy or scarcity of goods and services. Such inadequacy or scarcity tends to turn the acquisition of such goods or access to such services into special privileges, rather than normal entitlements. The result is that people become quite prepared to buy the favour of having access to these goods and services.

Within this context, it is necessary to consider the impact of the system of polygamy. In terms of the upbringing of children and the socialisation process, polygamy results in imbalanced relationships between children and their parents. In particular, children are mostly in contact with their mothers, with little contact with their fathers, during the critical formative years of childhood. Children of monogamous marriages enjoy much greater contact with their fathers, both in terms of duration and quality, during the critical formative years of childhood. Consequently, without physical separation, as in cases of death or divorce, the child in the polygamous home suffers some amount of paternal deprivation which can, if serious enough, result in emotional insecurity and instability[8] (Andry, 1960; Grygier, et Al., 1969). Most of our present functionaries are products of such homes, and probably suffer from emotional insecurity and instability. Such a situation will tend to produce exaggerated fears for the future in the sufferer. The result is that they develop a strong propensity to acquire wealth to satisfy these fears. The strength of their fears is matched by the strength of their propensity, and results in the corresponding size of illicit wealth acquisition.

When a person with such a psychological/personality make-up is put in a position of opportunity, faced with the temptations offered by those wishing to buy their way out of the consequences of the inadequacy or scarcity of goods and services, the probability is that such a functionary will easily succumb to the temptation. This will be more so where the functionary is in the first generation of educated people in his family, if not actually the first person. Here, his mental culture conflicts (Sellin, 1938), aided by the general societal anomie (Durkheim, 1960), would enable him, on a differential association basis, to give priority to conduct norms in vogue with those of his type in society (peer groups) in an intense manner, where his contact with such peer group behaviour is frequent and of a long duration (Sutherland, 1960:chap.4). He has no contrarily established home norms to refer to inasmuch as the imported norms have tended to make him dissociate himself from his illiterate parents' norms, thereby losing the strength of the home's socialised inhibiting mechanisms (Andreski, 1968). Such people become innovators in the Mertonian sense, and take bribes to perform their official duties (Merton, 1938). They may even embezzle their employers' funds. On the other hand, parental or family normative reference is easier and more normal, in this regard, for those functionaries who belong to the second, third, fourth, or successive generations of educated people in their respective families. There is usually no normative conflict between them and their families, except for the problems of the generation gap which is common to all families. Here, maintenance of the family name becomes more dominant than the acquisition of wealth. This is because the fear for the future becomes less pronounced since his family has not been traditionally poor. This is more so if he is also of monogamous parentage.

Besides the criminogenic factors referred to above, the excessive financial burden attendant upon the responsibility of a well-placed African family man is also recognized as a strong factor in the etiology of corruption. Among other things, such a person is expected to "help to pay for the education of the children of his poorer relatives, ... provide feasts and to defray the costs of (family and community ceremonies, including) funerals ... As he cannot meet such extensive obligations out of his salary he is compelled to squeeze bribes, embezzle public funds, take rake-offs and so on." (Andreski, 1968:102). Corruption, therefore, can be regarded as a logical product of the transitional socio-economic situation, with the psychological and emotional make-up of the present functionaries.

In summary, rapid socio-cultural, socio-economic, socio-political and demographic changes have taken and are still taking place in Nigeria, which is still a largely rural community although steadily and rapidly urbanising, and a recently traditional society that is currently grappling with modernity and its attendant technological traditions. It is also a largely communal society grappling with the individualism which it has been labouring, through constitutional means, to impose upon itself. The resultant anomic situation has to be inefficiency and consequent inadequacy or scarcity of goods and services, as well as problems of emotional insecurity, now confounded by the mass retrenchment of workers in both the public and private sectors. These predisposing factors are aided by differential association, mental culture conflict and finally, by the precipitating factors of opportunity, temptation and greed. The situation has been further complicated by a combination of the demands of the extended family system (which is a crystallisation of our communal welfare which, however, has not been replaced by state welfare by the now emergent state), the economic recession and aspects of the implementation of the consequential structural adjustment programme. Further, there is the unwholesome nepotistic implementation of the 'Federal Character' provisions of the Constitution, which has resulted in the creation of a regime, in appointments and promotions, which tends to smack of favouritism on the one hand, and discrimination on the other. The disenchantment caused by this dethronement of considerations of merit and efficiency in federal appointments, and that of lack of job security arising from the numerous mass retrenchment exercises carried out by the military within the public service, have led to lack of dedication to duty, widespread indiscipline, lack of commitment to the country and the development of egoism which disregards, in varying measures, national interests - a negation of patriotism. Also, it has led to incompetence in policy formulation, and both incompetence and inefficiency in policy implementation. Finally, the previous lack of the necessary political will to combat corruption has remained a serious factor in the perpetration of corruption.

Additional to these causative factors is the downright disregard for, and outright sabotage of, the Nigerian national interests by foreigners who operate, associate or deal with our national economy. Whilst their Nigerian collaborators are guilty of heinous crimes, we should not forget that these foreigners always behave as if they have a mission to subjugate our economy to their home states' economies or, at least, to a level which will enable them to continue the exploitation of the Nigerian economy. This is the external arm which fuels the problem of corruption in Nigeria; and it has helped to create the 'Nigerian price' in virtually everything, ranging from contract costs, to goods, and also services. The 'Nigerian price' is much higher than the price operable anywhere else, and for any other place in the world.

4. The socio-economic and socio-cultural costs of corruption

Corruption has now become a major factor contributing to our present state of underdevelopment, which itself implies the lack of capacity to develop. This, in turn, implies not only a state of underdevelopment, but the absence of a mental attitude that is willing to develop. That absence itself becomes a refusal to develop when the often incompetent public official comes to appreciate the problems of shortage of goods and services caused by the inefficient performance of the economy controlled by him. He is then faced with a level of demand which far exceeds the possible supplies under his control. The result is that he then develops the appropriate machinery to satisfy the acute demands of the public, based on the instrumentality of gratification for himself and those other colleagues who are in a position to take decisions about whose needs are to be satisfied. The result is that the economy, very much influenced by government decisions and actions in the developing countries, does not depend on efficient productivity to develop, but rather on bribes and favouritism. Consequently, incompetence, inefficiency and graft become entrenched characteristics within the body politic of the society. These are definitely stultifying factors in the socio-economic development of any country.

What worsens matters is the fact that corruption also leads to direct attacks on the economy. The public officials, in order to obtain a kick-back of some ten to twenty per cent, collude with suppliers and contractors to inflate the contract costs by as much as one hundred to four hundred per cent. This is a very outrageous situation, which is capable of decelerating the pace of socio-economic development by fifty to ninety per cent. The consequences are the rapid depletion of the public treasury, without much to be shown for it, the resultant shortage of foreign exchange holdings, the consequential depression of the economy, leading to inflationary trends and unemployment, drastically reduced gross national product and *per capita* income.

Worse still, having been emboldened by the encouragement of the public official, the supplier/contractor now decides on a pricing base which is, in fact, two to three times more than the actual price, even before considering any allowance for kick-backs. This practice has now resulted in the creation of the 'Nigerian price' for everything. One wonders whether it is not now time for Nigeria to give serious thought to halting the situation whereby she pays four to ten times the amount paid for goods and services by some other African and third world countries, although we know that developing countries usually pay more for such goods and services than do the developed countries. Bound with this is the fact that Nigeria receives second-hand or obsolete machinery for the exorbitant prices she pays. The result is that, very often, projects executed at such criminally high costs function only for a short period of time before they cease to function. Examples abound in the area of our telecommunications systems. Some such equipment never even reached a functioning stage. Two famous cases include the Federal Aerostat Balloon Telecommunications Project, and the Waste Disposal System of the Lagos State, both of which projects were undertaken during the 1976-1979 Military Administration.

Socially and culturally, corruption has become deleterious to, and sometimes downright destructive of the Nigerian ethos, to the extent that its pervasiveness seems to have engendered the feeling, in an ever expanding circle of citizens, that wealth, including that obtained by crooked and corrupt means, is all that matters[9]. The moral values normally guiding the Nigerian national behaviour appear to be losing their hold on an increasing number of citizens[10]. This shift from observance of our cultural ethos to reverence for wealth and materials[11] is leading to a weakening of respect for probity and, even, law and order. Hence, the infusion of corruption into the political scene leading to electoral malpractice, including rigged elections, which led to the military *coup d'etats* of 1966 and 1983; whilst allegation of the corruption, inefficiency and ineptitude of a military administration led to the *coup d'état* of 1975; whereas allegations of lack of respect for human rights and the development of the fascist tendencies led to the *coup d'état* of 1985[12]. The shift to materialism has also led to the development of economic crimes[13] on a large scale. This development has now extended into the realms of drug trafficking, in response to the economic hardships and trading restrictions created by the Economic Structural Adjustment Programme currently being implemented by the present military administration to engender economic self-reliance and self-sufficiency. The situation has not been helped at all by the realisation that the efficiency of the criminal justice system to deal with the problem is being somewhat hampered by corruption. In particular, officials of the 'first contact' agencies (i.e. the police, the customs, and the Drug Law Enforcement Agency) are exposed to the highest danger of contamination. The police and customs officials are known to be contaminated. In fact, the two agencies have publicly declared so and have on occasions announced their plans to clean up the corruption in their respective ranks and files. Also, a major corruption scandal has recently rocked the newly-created National Drug Law Enforcement Agency. There have even been allegations of corruption in the judiciary, although it still remains the relatively cleanest of the criminal justice agencies in Nigeria.

It becomes clear, therefore, that corruption is a cankerworm in the fabric of the Nigerian body politic, which must be excised most urgently. The Nigerian Federal Government recognized this urgency when, in April 1989, it set up a National Committee on Corruption and Other Economic Crimes in Nigeria[14]. That Committee submitted its report to the President of the

Federal Republic of Nigeria in September 1990, together with a comprehensive draft legislation for the setting up of the necessary machinery for combatting corruption.

5. Strategies for combatting corruption

As already emphasized, the problem of corruption must be institutionally attacked in both the public and private sectors of society. Both sectors must be cleansed simultaneously, if the bane of corruption is ever to be successfully controlled. Accordingly, there is a need to create a Code of Conduct for Nigerians working in the private sector, parallel to that which exists for public officials. For acceptability, this should be called a 'Code of Business Ethics'. The bulk of the money used for the corruption of public officials comes from the private sector. Hence, the public sector operators will be spared the temptation if the private sector operators can be so controlled.

Broadly, strategies for combating corruption should be examined under the *preventive* and *interventionist* perspectives.

5.1 Preventive perspective

The perspective of prevention envisages the enthronement of a normative regime which will be antithetical to the thriving of corruption and other economic crimes. This will encompass the establishment and nurturing of the necessary political will to combat them, in particular the establishment of a normative order which will inculcate in every Nigerian the knowledge that he is likely to be caught, and when caught, will have to face the consequences. He must also be made aware of the fact that nobody is above the law. The perspective should then seek to establish an efficient society in which there will be full, meaningful and imaginative utilisation of the skilled and technological manpower available in Nigeria, and in which merit and excellence shall always be the target. Again, the perspective should establish, maintain and nurture social justice where the society must provide ample opportunities to all for orderly self-actualisation and realisation; where the citizens will be assured security of employment, easy access to such necessities of life as food, shelter, clothing, education and health. Communal welfare should become the paramount business of governments and the State of Nigeria. This was our past, and it should be resuscitated and pursued vigorously, with such modifications as are dictated by the conditions of modernity. However, this is not to advocate for socialism in the Marxian sense since this, in the Nigerian society, would lead to a greater entrenchment of corruption. We can all recall the corruption attendant upon state controls of the commanding heights of the economy in this country. Other examples on the African Continent should provide a further lesson to us. The perspective should again endeavour to entrench human rights; and citizens' entitlements should no longer be viewed only as privileges. A society in which people can express their views legitimately, without state oppression, will always pose a danger to corrupt practices. Finally, we should seek to be more indigenous, but at the same time ingenious, in our developmental processes in all social, economic, political and technological aspects. Politics and technology need not disrupt our culture. In fact, political arrangements must take account of the ethos of the people if it is to be understood by, and acceptable to the community; with regard to technology, we should avoid over-sophistication. We should endeavour to develop and/or embrace technology which we can afford, maintain or innovate. Once we can produce something ourselves, we shall be able to determine its course, price-wise, quantity-wise, quality-wise, and so on. Again, we will be better enabled to monitor and combat economic crime.

A happy and contented citizenry is always dedicated, patriotic and relatively more honest, as well as more amenable to the maintenance of discipline in society. The Nigerian citizen will have less incentive to collaborate with a foreigner to ruin his own patrimony and the heritage of his children if the socio-economic order of his country provides him with a sense of really belonging to the community, as well as a sense that the country is seriously catering for his needs.

5.2   Interventionist perspective

The perspective of intervention envisages both formal intervention by the appropriate state agencies and informal intervention by the citizenry and their organisations. The two approaches should be utilised.

5.2.1 Informal intervention

This can be achieved through public education, enlightenment and mobilisation. Citizens should be made particularly aware of the social and economic costs of corruption to the community. Special efforts should be made to find adequate local examples which the citizenry can recognize, and which can be utilised to demonstrate the deleterious effects of corruption on a particular community. Also, the entrenchment of human rights will make the citizens feel stronger to challenge the malpractice in question whenever they come across it; they will also be encouraged to report the situation to the authorities. Of course, it is envisaged that the strategies suggested under the preceding subsection would have been vigorously pursued along with the interventionist strategies. Furthermore, such education will enable the majority of our citizens to recognize corruption as a crime and also enable them to realise that they have a right to complain in each instance of corruption that comes to their notice.

Efforts should also be directed at the full utilisation and mobilisation of the various existing social, cultural and religious organisations and societies. A commitment to the control of corruption and economic crimes should also become a mandatory part of the manifestoes of the two political parties which have been registered in the country. These bodies should be encouraged to inculcate values antithetical to the commission and/or condonation of corruption. Above all, the primary and secondary institutions should establish curricula for the teaching of Nigerian children along these lines, thereby ensuring that they are made to imbibe the type of mores envisaged above.

5.2.2 Formal intervention

This can and should involve a two-pronged set of strategies, namely, of an administrative and legal nature.

a) *Administrative Strategies* - Apart from the strategies envisaged under prevention, it is essential that programmes for the prevention of corruption and other economic crimes be incorporated in the regular programmes of the various Nigerian governments - at the federal, state and local government levels. For this purpose, a Monitoring and Evaluation Unit should be established in each ministry or department, as the case may be. These units should prepare Quarterly Situation Assessment Reports which should be submitted quarterly to the Office of the President, Governor or Chairman, as the case may be. A copy of each report should be mandatorily forwarded to the National Assembly, State Assembly or Local Government Council, as well as to the office of the appropriate body set up to combat corruption. Interference with, or obstruction of the work of these units by any other authority outside the units should be criminalised, as should any obstruction or interference with the quarterly report. The units should be established, sustained, and funded from a consolidated fund established by the National Assembly, State Legislature, or Local Government Council.

These bodies should have the power to request any of the units to investigate and submit a report to them on any matter whatsoever, and should also be empowered to make improvements in the format, make additions to the sub-heads for the reports, or add items which will bring specificity to the reports. The President, Governor or Chairman of a Local Government Council, as well as ministers, commissioners and supervisory councillors, should also have the power to request such investigations and reports. However, any reports should be distributed in the same way as the quarterly reports. These Reports of Special Investigations shall only be in addition to, but not a substitution for, the regular quarterly reports of the units.

Additionally, every citizen should be obliged to declare his assets periodically, say every four or five years. After all, this is only a step further from the legal duty of every citizen to file his tax returns annually. The aim of such a declaration is to make the monitoring of wealth easier for the country, particularly where there is an allegation that a particular citizen is corrupt, or that he is adopting a lifestyle which is far above his legitimate means. Such monitoring will discourage the embracing of corrupt practices by the citizens.

b) *Legal Interventionist Strategies* - Broadly, these will encompass the legal definition of corruption to enable its effective control, the establishment of the investigative machinery, and the adoption of criminal justice procedures, including criminal trials and the prescription of appropriate penal sanctions.

5.2.3 Legal conceptualisation/definition of corruption

Care should be taken to delineate scrupulously the ambit of the offence. An over-ambitious amorphous definition of it will not make it easy to control. It will make people ignore the law, as being too ideal for the citizenry to comply with. Consequently, for a more pragmatic and effective approach, corruption should be defined with reference to impropriety involved in the offering, giving, acceptance or receipt of a benefit or advantage. Accordingly, it is proposed to accept the conceptualisation of corruption as the offering, giving, conferring or agreeing to confer, or soliciting acceptance or agreement to accept "any gratification whatever, whether pecuniary or otherwise, other than lawful remuneration... or... any valuable thing without consideration or for consideration which he knows to be inadequate". The beneficiary of any such unlawful gratification or valuable object without any adequate consideration shall be guilty of the offence of corruption[15].

5.2.4   The investigative machinery

In order to effectively combat the massive problem of corruption in Nigeria, a complete departure from the traditional procedures of the criminal process is required. Without necessarily closing the door to the ultimate invocation of the criminal process, but only using it as a last resort, corruption should be dealt with mainly by the investigative procedure.

For this purpose, a national Anti-Corruption Commission should be established. This commission should function on the basis of investigations by its sole commissioners, who will investigate matters following complaints by citizens, or as a result of the discovery of discrepancies in declarations, or between declarations and known assets. Here, a sole commissioner should be empowered to investigate the matter, to determine whether or not there is a *prima facie* case of corruption. In particular, the commissioner should be empowered to investigate a matter when the matter originates from a situation of obvious disparity between a person's assets and his known and verifiable legitimate income or his observable standard of living, or from a complaint about this from another citizen. The commissioner should first secretly investigate the person's assets or income. If there is a notable disparity between the known legitimate income and the verified assets, the commission should order the freezing of the person's assets. The latter should then be required first to file a statement on his assets (including his income and expenses) and, thereafter, to established the legitimacy of his acquisition of the assets. If he succeeds, the assets should be released to him. But if he fails, all those assets for which the legitimacy of the acquisition cannot be establish, should be forfeited to the state. The person should then be ordered to pay a fine to the state of a sum equal to one-third of his legitimate assets. If he fails to do so, he should be referred to a criminal court and, if found guilty, subjected to the regular penal sanctions such as imprisonment and/or a fine, together with the confiscation of all the illegitimately acquired assets. Where appropriate, restitution should be ordered, particularly in cases of embezzlement. All decisions of the commission or the Criminal Court should be subject to the normal processes of appeal to the Court of Appeal, and thence to the Supreme Court, in order to ensure compliance with due process[16].

The aim of these proposals is to eliminate corruption, the allurement of unjust enrichment. The proposals promoting compliance with due process will aid ready international co operation by foreign countries in proceedings for extradition. The offence of corruption should be specifically included in extradition treaties.

5.2.5   Criminal justice machinery

This should be the ultimate reference point for any person found *prima facie* corrupt through the investigative machinery. Such a person should be referred to the Criminal Court for trial in a normal way. If found guilty, the offender should be subjected to any of the following sanctions:

1. Restitution/restoration;
2. Personal reparations, wherever and whenever appropriate;
3. Forfeiture/confiscation;
4. Fine;
5. Community Service; and
6. Imprisonment.

It is only necessary to point out that effective deterrence for any crime depends, not on the severity of the penalty, but on the chances of the offender being caught and dealt with under the law. Accordingly, it must be pointed out once again that our salvation from corruption and economic crimes does not rest upon draconian punishments, but upon the establishment of a regime which will ensure the bringing to justice of offenders, and which will entrench the culture that nobody is above the law. Scientific evidence and experience have shown, and still show, that draconian sanctions only enrich the relevant enforcement officials, rather than solving the problem. We can readily cite smuggling and drug trafficking. The pattern, distribution and trends of offences are not often influenced by the severity of punishment (Adeyemi, 1990a:296-303).

To enable the establishment of a regime which will assure the bringing of an offender to justice and entrench the culture that nobody is above the law, the operation of the investigative procedure has been given to an Independent Commission Against Corruption (I.C.A.C.), along the lines of the Hong Kong Commission, as well as the creation of licensed private investigators, along the lines of private investigators in America[17].

6. Conclusion

This chapter has attempted to delimit the exact scope of corruption, assess its trends, examine the factors that have fuelled it, as well as the procedures and sanctions for combatting it.

It must be stressed that the major problem with the rampancy of corruption in Nigeria has been the fact that there has been no previous political will to combat it. Perhaps the time has now come for that will to be manifested in concrete action. It is hoped that the Nigerian Government will implement the Report of the National Committee on Corruption and Other Economic Crimes submitted to it in September 1990, and promulgate the appropriate laws to put the necessary anti-corruption machineries in place as soon as possible.

On the positive side, efforts should be made to improve the efficient performance of our political, social, economic and administrative systems, in order to ensure the availability and adequacy of goods and services and, consequently, reduce the consumers' desire to buy them at any cost. Nigerian citizens should be able to claim these as of right. Also, to ensure efficiency, competence is indispensable to the proper utilisation of our available manpower. Consequently, just as we should know that a tailor cannot perform a carpenter's job, and vice versa, we should ensure henceforth that our respective services are manned by appropriately competent people. Mediocrity should be dislodged from all facets of the Nigerian body politic, and merit and competence entrenched in its place. Otherwise, we shall be wasting both our time and our country's future. Corruption will always thrive in any community in which incompetence and mediocrity reign supreme.

Tables

Table 1   Bribery and Corruption in Nigeria 1967 - 1988[*]

Years	Bribery and Corruption		Annual Percentage increase/decrease		Their percentage share of total criminality	
	Figures	Rates per 100,000 pop.	Figures	Rates per 100,000 pop.	In figures	In rates per 100,000 pop.
1967	252	0.41	--	--	0.45%	0.45%
1968	277	0.44	+9.92%	+7.32%	0.48%	0.48%
1969	305	0.48	+10.11%	+9.09%	0.43%	0.44%
1970	340	0.52	+11.48%	+8.33%	0.30%	0.30%
1971	416	0.62	+22.35%	+19.23%	0.30%	0.30%
1972	515	0.74	+23.80%	+19.35%	0.35%	0.35%
1973	586	0.83	+13.79%	+12.16%	0.38%	0.38%
1974	678	0.93	+15.70%	+12.05%	0.37%	0.37%
1975	721	0.97	+6.34%	+4.30%	0.37%	0.37%
1976	1,008	1.32	+39.81%	+36.08%	0.47%	0.47%
1977	1,114	1.43	+10.52%	+8.33%	0.50%	0.51%
1978	1,043	1.29	-6.37%	-9.79%	0.47%	0.47%
1979	890	1.07	-14.67%	-17.05%	0.43%	0.44%
1980	656	0.76	-26.29%	-28.97%	0.31%	0.31%
1981	431	0.49	-34.30%	-35.53%	0.16%	0.17%
1982	513	0.56	+19.03%	+14.29%	0.18%	0.19%
1983	483	0.51	-5.85%	-8.93%	0.15%	0.16%
1984	1,085	1.11	+124.64%	+117.65%	0.29%	0.29%
1985	804	0.77	-25.90%	-30.63%	0.23%	0.23%
1986	588	0.55	-26.87%	-28.57%	0.20%	0.20%
1987	439	0.39	-25.34%	-29.09%	0.16%	0.16%
1988	324	0.28	-26.20%	-28.21%	0.10%	0.10%

[*]   The figures and rates in this Table are plotted in the Graph below and have been compiled from the
Statistics contained in the Annual Reports of the Nigerian Police Force and the figures supplied by
the Force, which are not yet published

Bribery and corruption offences 1967-1988: figures and rates

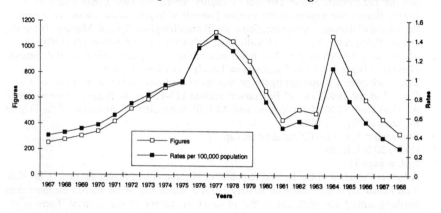

Table 2 Mean averages for bribery and corruption comptued on the basis of a 4 year overlapping period*

	Bribery and corruption		Annual percentage increases/decreases		Their percentage share of total criminality	
	Figures	Rates per 100,000 pop.	Figures	Rates per 100,000 pop.	in figures	in rates per 100,000 pop.
1967-1970	294	0.46	--	--	0.42%	0.42%
1971-1974	549	0.78	+86.74%	+69.57%	0.35%	0.35%
1975-1978	972	1.25	+77.05%	+60.26%	0.45%	0.46%
1979-1982	623	0.72	-35.91%	-42.40%	0.27%	0.28%
1983-1986	740	0.74	+18.78%	+2.78%	0.22%	0.22%
1987-1988	382	0.34	-48.38%	-54.05%	0.13%	0.13%
Total average for 1971-1988	683	0.81			0.30%	0.30%
Overall total average for 1967-1988	612	0.75			0.32%	0.33%

* The computations in this Tabel have been calculated from the data contained in Table 1 above. The overall periodic increases for 1967-1988 were actually computed on the figures for 1968-1988, since there was increase/decrease recorded for 1967 due to the non-availability of the figure for 1966.

Notes

1 See the 1957 Foster-Sutton Tribunal of Inquiry report; the 1962 Coker Commission of Inquiry Report; the Reports of the various Tribunal of Inquiry of the 1960s; the purges of the Murtala/Obasanjo Administrations; the Buhari/Idiagbon Special Military Tribunals, and the Babangida's Aguda and Uwafo Review Panels of the 1985/1986 era in Nigeria.

2 The opening Speech of President Babangida at the First-Ever Conference of Attorneys-General of Nigeria, delivered at Abuja on Tuesday, October 11, 1988.

3 This is adequately illustrated by the provisions of Sections 98-115 of the Criminal Code, Cap. 77 of the 1990 Laws of Federation; Section 115-121 of the Penal Code, Cap. 89 of the 1963 Laws of Northern Nigeria; and the Fifth Schedule to Constitution of the Federal Republic of Nigeria, 1989.

4 See Section 494 of the Criminal Code, cap. 77.

5 (1951) 20 N.L.R. 30.

6 Ibid. at page 31.

7 A former President of the Federal Republic of Nigeria, Alhaji Shehu Shagari, in his New Year Broadcast to the Nation on January 1, 1982, lamented: "What worries me more than anything among our problems is that of moral decadence in our country. There is the problem of bribery, corruption, lack of dedication to duty, dishonesty and all such vices."

8 However, this impact of polygamy is where it is transplanted from its natural rural habitat to the urban centres.

9 In fact, the National Committee on Corruption and Other Economic Crimes, at the inception of its work, found corruption to be so pervading as to have "become a way of life". See pp. 3-4 of its Report. At page. 6, it found the level of corruption "alarming".

10 See note 7.

11 The Attorney-General and Minister of Justice of the Federal Republic of Nigeria, Prince Bola Ajibola, SAN, K.B.E., in his address to the National Committee on Corruption and Other Economic Crimes in Nigeria, at its Inauguration on April 3, 1989, observed, *inter alia*: "In our acquisitive society, many people are rated in terms of what they own and what they are. Social climbing based on illicit wealth is not frowned upon. Public office is regarded as a vehicle for acquiring wealth and unbridled affluence and not as a merited avenue for rendering invaluable service to the Nation for our collective good".

12 The Military Administration ousted in 1985 was, however, on record as being extremely tough with regard to corruption. The then Head of State, in his maiden broadcast on January 1, 1984 was categorical in declaring that his New "Administration will not tolerate fraud, corruption, squandermania, abuse of office or graft ..."

13 The major characteristic of economic crime has been stated to be "its tendency to undermine the national economy, particularly in a developing country which, in turn, often results in the impoverishment in the quality of life of the citizenry of the country...". (Adeyemi, 1990:99).

14 The present Author was a member of that Committee, and was also its Criminological Consultant.

15 The ideas are embodied in the Draft Legislation which the National Committee on Corruption and Other Economic Crimes submitted to the Government in September, 1990, as part of its Report.

16 Compare the Provisions of Section 13-18 of the Prevention of Bribery Ordinance, Cap. 201 of the Laws of Hong Kong, 1974, as amended, and the Independence Commission Against Corruption Ordinance, 1974, Cap. 204, ibid. See also, the Corrupt and Illegal Practices Ordinance. The Hong Kong Anti-Corruption Legislations and Machineries have

also been copied, with various modifications, by some other African countries, like Ethiopia, Tanzania, Zambia and Zimbabwe.

17 These are contained in Chapters II and III of the Draft Legislation on Corruption and Economic Crimes, currently being considered for promulgation by the Nigeria Government.

References

Adeyemi A.A. 1979. *An Appraisal of the Corrupt Practices Decree No. 38 of 1975.* Unpublished paper delivered at the Valedictory Evaluation Workshop on "The Role of the Corrupt Practices Investigation Bureau Under a Presidential System". August.

---- . 1990. *Economic Crime in a Developing Society.* In: Yemi Osinbayo (Ed.). "Towards a Better Administration of Justice in Nigeria". Lagos. Nigerian Federal Ministry of Justice. Law Review Series. Vol.4, pp.98-114.

---- . 1990a. *Death Penalty in Nigeria: Criminological Perspectives.* In: Awa Kalu, Yemi Osinbajo (Eds.). In: "Narcotics Law and Policy in Nigeria". Lagos. Nigerian Federal Ministry of Justice. Law Review Series. Vol.8, pp.280-314.

Andresky S. 1968. *The African Predicament: A Study in the Pathology of Modernization.* London. Michael Joseph.

Andry R.G. 1960. *Delinquency and Parental Pathology: A Study in Forensic and Clinical Pathology.* London. Stevens and Son Limited.

Durkheim E. 1960. *Division of Labour.* Paris. P.U.F.

Grygier T., Chesley J., Tuters E.W. 1969. *Parental Deprivation: A Study of Delinquent Children.* British Journal of Criminology. 9:3, pp.209-253.

Kelvin C. 1955. *Tables for Statisticians.* London. Pearson.

Merton R.K. 1938. *Social Structure and Anomie.* American Sociological Review. 3, pp.672-682.

Odekunle F. 1986. *Corruption in Development: Definitional Methodological and Theoretical Issues.* In: Odekunle F. (Ed.). "Nigeria: Corruption in Development". Ibadan. Ibadan University Press. Part 1 Chapter 1.

Sellin T. 1938. *Culture Conflict and Crime.* New York. Social Science Council.

Sutherland E.H. 1960. *Principles of Criminology.* New York. Lippincott.

POLITIQUE CRIMINELLE AU CAMEROUN: ESSAI D'APPROCHE D'UN MODELE DE TRANSITION

Nathalie Grelet[*]

1. Introduction

Le concept de politique criminelle a une double origine: il est à la fois juridique et criminologique. C'est ainsi qu'il devient un instrument intéressant pour décrypter la réalité d'une société en mutation comme celle du Cameroun.

Au-delà de la dichotomie modernité-tradition, l'analyse par le biais de la politique criminelle tente de faire émerger des pratiques concrètes du droit, tant du côté de l'Etat que de celui de la Société civile.

Au travers de la construction théorique de modèles de politique criminelle, apparaissent deux grandes tendances, étatique et sociétale, recouvrant les réponses faites au phénomène criminel. Cet axe traverse la société camerounaise en une politique émanant du "haut" (l'Etat) et une politique émanant du "bas" (la Société civile), ceci pour mieux cerner "l'entre-deux", lieu où émergent de nouvelles dynamiques.

Des exemples concrets dans le domaine de la délinquance juvénile notamment rendent compte de pratiques originales; pourtant, l'Etat dans sa recherche hégémonique ne peut assurer sa prise sur le réel, tandis que les réponses sociétales restent isolées, sans véritable structuration.

Admettre l'existence d'une politique criminelle émiettée ne dispense pas de rechercher par son intermédiaire les relations, réseaux d'action, traduisant une réappropriation de leur Droit par les "acteurs" camerounais.

Aborder une société par le biais de sa politique criminelle permet une lecture de la réalité, d'essayer de comprendre les mécanismes, les articulations qui lui sont propres.

La politique criminelle n'est pas seulement un outil juridique au sens strict du terme. Elle est un reflet des outils idéologiques d'une société donnée dans sa logique de répression civile à un moment donné. Elle est donc une réflexion et une action.

Pour utiliser ce concept de politique criminelle, nous nous référerons tout d'abord à la construction théorique faite par Mireille Delmas-Marty (1983).

---

[*]   Doctorante en Droit, Université de Bordeaux, France.

Une politique criminelle correspond à "l'ensemble des procédés par lesquels le corps social organise les réponses au phénomène criminel".

Par procédé, il faut refuser de se limiter au système répressif, mais bien s'étendre aux notions de réparation, conciliations, médiations; de même, il ne faut pas se limiter à la réaction mais y inclure la prévention.

Les réponses considérées comme indicateurs de politique criminelle sont celles qui sont organisées et reconnues; l'initiative spontanée d'un membre du groupe par exemple n'est pas forcément une réponse sociétale.

Le terme de corps social est entendu dans son sens plein, tout comme celui de politique. Le corps social comprend deux axes: la tendance étatique et la tendance sociétale. Il s'agit des réponses élaborées par l'Etat d'une part, par la Société civile d'autre part, réponses faites à l'infraction et à la déviance. Cette distinction Etat-Société civile n'est pas toujours aussi nette dans la réalité et ne rend pas compte de schémas plus complexes. Nous l'utiliserons pourtant, mais avec réserve, pour une vision la plus claire possible.

La réponse étatique apparaît généralement comme la plus évidente. Max Weber (1971:57) définissait l'Etat "comme la structure ou le gouvernement politique qui revendique avec succès le monopole de la contrainte physique légitime". L'exemple type de réponse au phénomène criminel, celui qui vient immédiatement à l'esprit, c'est le droit pénal, promulgué par l'Etat. Mais trois remarques s'imposent:

- le droit pénal n'est pas la seule réponse possible produite par l'Etat;
- réponses étatiques ne signifient pas forcément réponses unifiées et cohérentes;
- une réponse étatique n'a pas obligatoirement son origine première dans l'Etat. Une réponse sociétale peut se voir étatisée et inversement.

Néanmoins, l'Etat apparaît fréquemment au détour de la politique criminelle comme lieu de légitimation: c'est le modèle étatique.

Le modèle sociétal est le fait de sociétés dites sans Etat, ou lorsque celui-ci ne remplit pas sa fonction.

Pour Mireille Delmas-Marty (1983) le passage d'un modèle étatique à un modèle sociétal ne peut se faire que par "saut-catastrophe", un bouleversement important. Or, en Afrique, il s'est produit souvent une sorte de superposition de ces deux modèles lors de la colonisation et lors de la décolonisation. Il en résulte des sociétés en mutation, où même les réponses à la déviance et la référence aux valeurs propres du groupe perdent de leur cohérence.

Nous ne pouvons donc, ni ne voulons, classer la société camerounaise dans un modèle fixe car la réalité est trop mouvante et il nous faut déjà ici admettre l'idée d'une politique criminelle éclatée, d'un modèle de transition.

De plus, les gouvernements africains se trouvent engagés sur la voie de la standardisation, à savoir modèle étatique et développement occidental. Cette notion de modèle étatique où l'état est source de politique criminelle et lieu de sa légitimité a été reprise par l'Etat camerounais et beaucoup d'Etats africains, et renforcée. Achille Mbembe (1988:141) fait remonter cette idée à la période des indépendances. Il écrit: "On pensait alors qu'il suffisait de conquérir le pouvoir politique et de le contrôler pour accélérer la transformation des sociétés, des économies et des cultures africaines. On pensait, comme aujourd'hui encore, que l'essentiel du pouvoir était de nature politique. Le politique lui-même était ramené - puis confondu - à sa matérialisation dans l'Etat". L'unique pouvoir imaginable en vint donc à consister en le pouvoir d'Etat. "Cette idéologie du tout politique permet de gonfler à l'excès les notions de subversion ou d'atteinte à la sécurité de l'Etat", condition nécessaire au regard du formalisme juridique propre aux régimes autoritaires.

C'est l'autorité et non la vérité qui fait le droit (Hesseling et Le Roy, 1990:4).

Les politiques pénales font donc partie des instruments utilisés par l'Etat dans sa recherche hégémonique. Elles sont un reflet de ses orientations et de ses projets. C'est ainsi que l'on peut concevoir que les hommes politiques africains fassent passer l'unité nationale avant la liberté d'expression comme ils ont préféré le développement à la défense des libertés (Masseron, 1966:45). Il s'agissait pour eux d'une construction étatique avec un but de développement économique, ce choix influant et légitimant les options prises par la suite. C'est dans cette optique que la politique pénale fut souvent conçue comme un instrument de développement et non plus seulement comme un moyen d'endiguer une criminalité plus ou moins galopante (Pie, 1990:65). Cette finalité permet, par exemple, d'utiliser le processus de pénalisation pour supprimer des comportements incompatibles avec le projet de développement formé par les jeunes gouvernements africains (incrimination du vagabondage, interdiction des scarifications ou autres marques tribales, suppression ou réglementation de la dot, ...). "Le rôle que le droit pénal est appelé à jouer dans la création d'un droit national est celui de l'instauration d'un ordre public, fondé sur une éthique de progrès social et économique" (Costa-Lascoux, 1975:96).

Le droit pénal n'est pas seulement le droit des criminels: il est éminemment politique, il agit par la contrainte de la force publique, il touche aux mentalités, il est instrument et reflet d'une volonté.

Ceci dit, et pour déplacer un peu notre angle d'observation, ces nouveaux Etats, dont le Cameroun, ont pour ambition d'organiser une justice moderne, répondant par sa structure et ses règles de fonctionnement aux exigences du modèle universel de l'Etat-nation, tout en essayant d'uniformiser la diversité culturelle sur laquelle ils reposent (Kamto, 1990:57). Mais si cette ambition est réelle, il faut savoir se dégager de l'illusionisme juridique et savoir saisir la réalité expressive et symbolique des institutions avant d'en admettre la portée instrumentale. "Ce n'est pas parce que l'on se trouve devant un texte à caractère juridique qu'il faut le traiter comme un véritable document juridique" (Medard, 1977:25). Il est impératif de considérer la prise réelle du droit sur la réalité. C'est pourquoi notre analyse doit comporter deux angles d'observation: à côté d'une vision "par le haut" des préoccupations étatiques, il est essentiel de se pencher "sur le bas", à savoir comment l'africain va gérer ce qui a été appelé "le mystère du droit" et se situer de part et d'autre d'une frontière entre loi et coutume (Hesseling et Le Roy, 1990:5). Ce terme de frontière apparaîtra d'ailleurs très vite comme bien rigide au regard d'une pratique juridique en réalité beaucoup plus complexe et métissée. Notre but est d'essayer d'appréhender les articulations existant entre une politique criminelle promue par l'Etat et sa réception par la société.

Nos exemples renverront surtout au domaine de la délinquance juvénile.

2. Politique criminelle par le haut

L'Etat camerounais est le lieu d'où émane la loi: le droit pénal est le support privilégié de la politique criminelle étatique. L'analyse commence donc par lui.

Le code pénal camerounais date de 1967. Le Cameroun a conservé un dualisme juridique en reconnaissant l'existence de tribunaux coutumiers, mais le droit pénal a toujours été l'apanage des juridictions "modernes". Après la promulgation du code pénal, le deuxième temps fort de la politique pénale fut les ordonnances prises en 1972. Elles sont une réaction face à la montée du banditisme urbain. Les unes portent une modification de certaines dispositions du code pénal (aggravation de certaines infractions et nouvelles incriminations), les autres portent simplification de la procédure pénale en matière de répression du banditisme. Elles ont permis d'élargir le domaine d'intervention de la loi pénale et de renforcer la répression.

Les infractions aggravées en 1972 sont le vagabondage dont le caractère économique est visible, le vol aggravé pour lequel le législateur a désormais exclu les circonstances atténuantes; la notion de récidive est élargie, la prostitution est incriminée, de même que l'homosexualité.

Ces dispositions sont intéressantes en ce sens qu'elles révèlent la position de l'Etat vis-à-vis de la jeunesse notamment, et par là même la position de la jeunesse vis-à-vis de l'Etat. Le pouvoir conçoit la politique à l'égard des jeunes en termes·de protection des mineurs et de lutte contre les fléaux sociaux, tels que la délinquance juvénile. En fait, la politique étatique a pour but de contrôler l'espace où évolue la jeunesse notamment, celui où pourrait se manifester toute contestation.

C'est face à la faiblesse des structures familiales et de l'autorité parentale que le sexe va être pensé par les jeunes (mais pas seulement par eux) en termes de rentabilité; il devient une véritable ressource (Mbembe, 1985:141). L'une des incriminations possibles liées au sexe est la prostitution. Au Cameroun, elle fait l'objet de l'article n° 343 depuis les ordonnances de 1972. Or, la prostitution n'est pas un concept universel. C'est une réalité répondant à des caractéristiques particulières suivant son contexte. "Si en Europe, les prostituées s'installent durablement dans le métier, il n'en est pas ainsi au Cameroun; la prostitution atteint surtout la jeunesse et elle est alors pour les jeunes filles ce que le vol est pour les garçons" (Melone, 1975:154), c'est à dire la majorité des infractions commises.

Le sexe est devenu, parce qu'il est une ressource économique et politique, un langage, un lieu de structuration du pouvoir, un moyen d'intégration dans la société, tout comme d'un mode d'affrontement du pouvoir (Mbembe, 1985:141). Cet affrontement peut être perçu lors d'une incrimination telle que celle pour propagation de maladie contagieuse, punie par un emprisonnement de trois mois à trois ans. Les plaisanteries courantes sur les maladies vénériennes traduisent leur utilisation comme moyen de contestation de l'ordre posé; les revendiquer permet de s'affirmer face à l'ordre public imposé. Cette réponse autoritaire de l'Etat vis-à-vis de la société conduit à faire de l'illégalité, un mode d'opposition, un moyen de saper l'autorité de l'Etat: plus on commet une infraction, plus on affirme son désengagement du modèle imposé. L'Etat, lui, veut contrôler une fraction la plus large possible de la société par le biais de l'incrimination pénale. En érigeant en infraction la prostitution, l'homosexualité, la propagation des maladies contagieuses, il affirme sa volonté de créer des normes morales mais aussi d'instrumentaliser les jeunes.

La jeunesse devrait être l'espoir, l'avenir, le bras de la nation. Mais en réalité, l'Etat la perçoit comme non productive, "débauchée", dangeureuse. C'est ce qui ressort des infractions créées ou aggravées par le pouvoir et qui sont aussi celles commises par les jeunes. "Or, la question des jeunes en Afrique ne peut pas se limiter aujourd'hui à une simple approche en termes de production, directe ou non" (Mbembe, 1985:98), tel la rêve l'Etat. Pour faire de sa jeunesse un élément docile, celui-ci crée une morale et sanctionne les comportements qu'il ne peut dominer.

3. Jeux des acteurs du système judiciaire

Après avoir vu comment l'Etat se voulait le seul lieu de pouvoir sur les normes sociales, le lieu de définition de la déviance et de l'infraction, il faut considérer le deuxième aspect nécessaire de toute politique criminelle, sa réception par la société. Mais s'il est pratique de distinguer d'un côté les options choisies par l'Etat et de l'autre les réactions de la société, la réalité ne reprend pas exactement cette dichotomie trop simple.

Le système pénal camerounais se réfère explicitement à l'école de la défense sociale nouvelle de Marc Ancel.* Mais la coexistence entre cette référence idéologique et les orientations répressives est peut-être un facteur d'anomie pour agents du système judiciaire en contact avec les jeunes.

Les magistrats et la police voient notamment leur action s'inscrire comme l'articulation reliant les deux aspects précités de lutte contre le banditisme et de prise en compte de la personalité. "Les juges font de la politique criminelle lorsque leurs décisions sont dictées par le danger qu'une catégorie d'infractions représente pour la société (Ndoko, 1985:136). Représentants du pouvoir, ils ont pour mission d'appliquer les options prises par l'Etat: mais ils sont aussi les premiers confrontés aux réactions sociales suscitées par cette politique, les premiers à la pratiquer et à en cerner les limites.

Une rapide approche de l'organisation judiciaire camerounaise permet de mieux saisir une certaine réalité aux travers de réformes successives.

Le système inspiré de l'organisation coloniale se révèla vite trop lourd, compliqué, et parfaitement inadapté aux réalités du pays. Les ordonnances de 1972 relatives à l'organisation judiciaire avaient pour but de remédier au manque de personnel compétent et de répondre à un souci de rapidité et d'efficacité. C'est ainsi que les personnels de la Sûreté et de la Gendarmerie purent, jusqu'en 1983, exercer les fonctions de Ministère public. L'ordonnance permet la confusion entre l'information judiciaire et la poursuite entre les mains du Parquet et, dans certains cas (ceux où la juridiction concernée n'aurait pas suffisamment de personnel du Parquet), a autorisé les présidents des tribunaux d'Instance à poursuivre et à informer pour ensuite siéger comme Président dans l'affaire qu'ils ont instruite (Nkouendjin, 1985:13-14). L'ordre social sera donc préféré à la protection des libertés individuelles et ce sont notamment les droits de la défense qui se trouvent marginalisés.

---

* Cité dans le "Rapport du Premier Colloque National sur l'Education en Milieu Ouvert et la Liberté Surveillée" (Ministère des Affaires Sociales, 1987:12).

En ce qui concerne plus précisément les mineurs, la loi n° 89-019 du 29 décembre 1989, dernière étape de l'évolution de l'organisation judiciaire, prévoit désormais que le tribunal de première instance est compétent en matière pénale pour juger les infractions qualifiées de délit ou de contravention, ainsi que les crimes commis par les mineurs sans co-auteur ou complice majeur.

Il n'existe pas un véritable droit des mineurs et ce qui existe est parfois soumis à des principes contradictoires. La volonté de protéger les droits des mineurs reste parfois trop au niveau des références idéologiques, comme l'Ecole de la défense sociale nouvelle, et ne tient pas suffisamment compte de la pratique judiciaire. Ainsi, l'ordonnance de 1972 a élargi à de nombreuses infractions la procédure du flagrant délit, celui-ci entendu en un sens très large. Ces infractions comme le vol, la prostitution, le vagabondage sont fréquemment liées aux mineurs. Mais les mineurs ne peuvent être soumis à la procédure du flagrant délit, ceci pour protéger leurs droits. Ils perdent le bénéfice d'une procédure rapide et connaissent fréquemment une détention préventive longue. En revanche, la confusion entre les mains d'un même magistrat des étapes d'instruction, poursuites et jugement rapproche la situation du juge camerounais de celle du juge pour enfants français. En l'absence de personnel spécialisé, ce sont les magistrats qui, par leur pratique, se forment aux problèmes posés par les mineurs.

Le policier camerounais bénéficie lui aussi de par son statut d'une marge de manoeuvre importante. Qu'il lui soit reconnu ou non par la loi des fonctions de poursuite et d'instruction, dans la pratique il est le premier à apprécier l'opportunité de la poursuite. Il va décider de déférer ou non le jeune délinquant devant le juge (le rôle de la victime mériterait une étude). Il possède un réel pouvoir de relâcher, d'admonester, de punir même (par l'emprisonnement dans une cellule du commissariat ou une correction à la "chicotte"). L'instauration de bureaux des affaires sociales au sein de certains commissariats ne paraît pas avoir donné de résultats, leur compétence se situant plutôt au niveau du conseil conjugal (Ministère des Affaires Sociales, 1987:45). Si le mineur est amené devant un magistrat, celui-ci appréciera à son tour l'opportunité de la poursuite: le mineur bénéficiera soit d'un classement sans suite, soit d'un placement, ou bien il sera renvoyé devant le juge après une détention préventive plus ou moins longue. La durée de la détention dépendra généralement de la présence de la famille lors du procès. Les magistrats répugnent à libérer un jeune sans garantie et ont tendance à renvoyer l'affaire si personne ne prend l'enfant en charge (la détention est prolongée d'autant). S'ils ne prononcent que peu de mesures de mise en liberté surveillée, c'est pour les mêmes raisons: l'absence de structure, de personnel répond à l'absence du cadre familial.

L'incapacité de l'Etat à concevoir une politique rationnelle en matière de délinquance juvénile oblige les magistrats à une pratique en contradiction avec les principes admis en la matière: primauté des mesures de liberté surveillée et d'éducation en milieu ouvert sur la détention, éviter la promiscuité entre délinquant et mineur, réduction des détentions préventives, restent des objectifs difficilement applicables.

Les institutions pour mineurs sont l'exemple même "des solutions bureaucratiques destinées à insérer les jeunes dans la société, mais imposées d'en haut par les appareils d'Etat" (Mbembe, 1985:97).

L'Institution camerounaise pour l'enfance (ICE) de Betamba était destinée à recevoir des mineurs délinquants, en ayant pour but la réadaptation de l'enfant dans la société: les enfants reçoivent une formation, les plus jeunes peuvent suivre les cours jusqu'au CM2, la durée de séjour est de trois ans. Les mineurs de ce centre sont soit des délinquants sortant de prisons, bénéficiant d'une mesure de placement, soit des enfants dits "en danger moral", placés au centre à la demande de la famille, ceci dans une optique de prévention. Or, depuis 1972, le nombre d'enfants en danger moral est largement supérieur à celui des enfants délinquants (ce phénomène se retrouve dans les autres établissements). Beaucoup de parents, face à un enfant difficile, cherchent à le placer dans un centre voulant ainsi dégager leurs responsabilités. Bien plus, on constate actuellement une importante proportion d'enfants abusivement étiquetés en danger moral; les parents qui le peuvent exercent des pressions sur les autorités habilitées à prononcer la décision de placement; la perspective d'une formation scolaire et professionnelle à bon compte motive les parents et l'ICE devient une sorte d'école d'apprentissage, perdant sa vocation de centre pour la réinsertion des jeunes délinquants. En fait, il faut tenir aussi compte du fait que les mineurs délinquants sélectionnés par le système pénal sont les plus âgés (16 ans et plus). Lorsque le juge prendra sa décision, il estimera souvent que le placement dans une centre ne sera pas profitable étant donné l'âge avancé. C'est ainsi que des institutions mal adaptées au départ sont "détournées" pour avoir enfin une fonction beaucoup plus pratique. Ce type d'institution prévue par l'Etat, peut-être pour une part par mimétisme, doit être vu sous un angle d'effectivité. Surtout, il faut savoir aller au-delà d'une ineffectivité apparente pour saisir la pratique.

Comment la société civile pratique-t-elle le droit et ses institutions plutôt que de s'attarder sur la constatation que le but premier n'est pas atteint.

4. Politique criminelle par le bas

La pratique du procès est, par exemple, révélatrice d'une réappropriation d'un système: beaucoup de gens assistent à ces audiences (ce qui permet de trouver un interprète dans la salle lorsqu'une des parties ne parle pas le français, ceci même à Yaoundé). Par contre, il est fréquent de renvoyer l'affaire car l'une des parties est absente. Les parties se présentent ensemble devant les magistrats, les avocats à leur côté. Le juge mène alors les débats: chacun peut s'exprimer, parfois très très longuement. C'est véritablement la parole qui est privilégiée. Plaignants et accusés ne sont pas face à face, mais côte à côte devant le juge. Il s'agit plus de dénouer une situation que de trancher un conflit. Les acteurs du procès, les magistrats comme les parties, puisent dans les principes coutumiers (palabres, affaires publiques ...) pour se réapproprier un système a priori étranger et le rendre intelligible.

L'effectivité et la pratique du droit vues par le bas sont difficiles à cerner car ces réponses ne sont pas vraiment structurées; l'observation permet de relever des pratiques, des distorsions, mais pas vraiment de réponses codées permettant de parler d'une véritable politique criminelle d'origine sociétale. Mais cette absence ne permet-elle pas de conserver une efficacité à ce qui existe?

C'est la pratique des acteurs eux-mêmes qui permet d'établir des liaisons qui compensent la rigidité des institutions. Le cas des juridictions de la ville de Foumban, capitale du pays Bamoun, en est un exemple. Le sultan est, entre autres fonctions, le magistrat suprême au niveau du tribunal coutumier mais dans l'enceinte de son palais existe une juridiction de notables où les bamouns peuvent se présenter pour régler leurs conflits; notamment ceux pour lesquels le tribunal coutumier officiel s'estime dépassé (affaires de sorcellerie). Inversement, les notables renverront devant le tribunal coutumier les affaires pour lesquelles ils ne peuvent, et ne veulent, être compétents. Ce type de relation entre des moyens de gestion des conflits officieux et officiels révèle l'existence d'une justice parallèle ni moderne ni coutumière mais pratique avant tout.

Un deuxième exemple de "passerelle" entre le système judiciaire et la société est celui des foyers recueillant les enfants délinquants. Généralement, à l'initiative d'un religieux, ces structures très souples comblent les énormes carences en ce domaine. Certains magistrats ont bien compris l'intérêt de ces foyers comme relais suppléant aux institutions défaillantes. Le personnel de ces foyers non seulement accueille les mineurs délinquants (parfois dès le commissariat) mais se charge aussi parfois d'un suivi en prison (essai de contacts avec les familles sachant que c'est là une condition de sortie). La coopération s'opère même avec l'administration pénitentiaire puisque à

Yaoundé, une fois par semaine, un groupe d'une quinzaine de détenus mineurs sort de la prison et passe une matinée dans l'enceinte du foyer.

Si dans les grandes villes, arsenaux policiers et répressifs se développent plus vite que les structures d'assistance sociale, il serait intéressant d'examiner le rôle social que peuvent être amenées à avoir ces institutions étatiques non prévues pour ce rôle précis.

Achille Mbembe estime que "la centralisation administrative hypothèque la créativité sociale". Or, les initiatives des foyers (Le Ministre Fofe du Foyer de l'Espérance. Cameroon Tribune, 14/2/1989) à Yaoundé et Douala jouent de façon informelle le rôle que les institutions prévues par l'Etat ne peuvent pas toujours assumer.

Les délinquants, jugés tels par leur famille, sont souvent envoyés au village. Les magistrats libèrent souvent l'enfant repris par sa famille. Les animateurs des foyers cherchent d'abord à faire reprendre contact à l'enfant avec sa famille. Ces logiques semblables peuvent exprimer une tendance sociétale.

Certes le pouvoir autoritaire ne permet pas aux relais possibles (associations, médias ...) la création d'un véritable consensus autour d'une politique criminelle. Ces initiatives sont tolérées tant qu'elles restent "individualisées", présentées comme des initiatives privées. Mais c'est peut-être là que réside une part de leur efficacité. Cette souplesse d'une structure qui n'est pas revendiquée dans le cadre d'une politique criminelle authentique assure l'effectivité de la démarche.

5. Une politique criminelle embryonnaire

Au travers de ces quelques exemples, nous voyons se poser le problème de la réception d'une politique criminelle par le pouvoir judiciaire et celui de sa compréhension ou non-compréhension par la conscience collective.

Les réflexions de Christine Lazerges (1984:37) sur la notion de politique criminelle éclatée ont permis de se dégager de la vision d'une politique criminelle cohérente, rigide et, somme toute, implacable. Des conflits, des contradictions existent au sein des politiques pénales. Cette situation n'est pas propre à l'Afrique, mais il faut ici considérer le contexte d'une société en mutation.

Ainsi, dans la société camerounaise, non seulement les normes légales, les normes morales sont souvent en contradiction, mais au sein même des normes morales existent des conflits. Ces différentes références morales (au sens large) émergeront les unes ou les autres suivant la situation, les circonstances, dicteront les conduites des individus et justifieront leurs actes. Ceci rend plus difficile l'appréciation exacte des valeurs sociales de cette société pluri-éthnique. Pour l'individu, il s'agit moins d'une perte de référents sociaux que d'une multiplication des valeurs. L'Etat veut imposer une nouvelle hiérarchie des valeurs, la société traditionnelle induit des réflexes toujours visibles, l'évolution de la société oblige à de nouvelles références. C'est ainsi qu'apparaissent des pratiques "métissées", repensées, bases d'une réappropriation du droit par ses acteurs.

Le fait de constater ces "difficultés" camerounaises à concevoir une politique criminelle en tant qu'action, tant du côté étatique que du côté sociétal, loin d'être un constat d'échec, met en relief l'aspect réflexion sur une société. Etudier la politique criminelle au Cameroun dans le seul but de tester son efficacité vis-à-vis de sa finalité, c'est seulement constater l'incapacité de l'Etat à avoir une prise réelle sur la réalité, et l'absence de réponses sociétales organisées.

C'est pourquoi les criminologues paraissent sceptiques quant à l'existence de politiques criminelles en Afrique sub-saharienne. "Il est évident qu'une distance énorme sépare le pays réel du pays légal dans l'Afrique Noire contemporaine. Il ne semble pas que l'on puisse parler, dans ces Etats, d'une politique criminelle ni dans le sens traditionnel ni dans le sens que nous avons adopté ici [...] Il y a peu d'espoir pour une criminologie ou pour une politique criminelle à brève échéance en Afrique Noire" (Szabo, 1986:100-101). S'en tenir à cette position, est-ce que ce n'est pas occulter toutes les interactions, les influences qui s'exercent au sein de la société et que cet instrument de réflexion qu'est la politique criminelle permet de faire apparaître. Nous espérons, au travers de ces quelques exemples avoir pu montrer que le Droit et ses pratiques sont des modes d'expression et d'utilisation à part entière: se pencher sur la politique criminelle d'une société, fut-elle embryonnaire, permet de saisir les mouvements, les dynamiques qui l'occupent horizontalement et transversalement et la font évoluer. Il s'agit plus aujourd'hui de savoir comment les camerounais vivent leur Droit que de constater l'absence ou non de toute politique criminelle organisée.

Références Bibliographiques

Costa-Lascoux J. 1975. *Le Droit Pénal, l'Unité Nationale et le Développement Economique.* Archives de Politique Criminelle. 1, pp.93-118.

Delmas-Marty M. 1983. *Modèles et Mouvements de Politique Criminelle.* Paris. Economica.

Hesseling G., Le Roy E. 1990. *Le Droit et ses Pratiques.* Politique Africaine. 40, pp.2-11.

Kamto M. 1990. *Une Justice entre Tradition et Modernité.* Afrique Contemporaine. 156, pp.57-64.

Lazerges C. 1984. *Les Conflits de Politique Criminelle.* Archives de Police Criminelle. 7, pp.37-48.

Masseron J.P. 1966. *Le Pouvoir et la Justice en Afrique Noire Francophone et à Madagascar.* Paris. Pedone.

Mbembe A. 1985. *Les Jeunes et l'Ordre Politique en Afrique Noire.* Paris. L'Harmattan.

---- . 1988. *Afriques Indociles.* Paris. Karthala.

Medard J.F. 1977. *L'Etat Sous Développé au Cameroun.* Paris. Année Africaine, Pedone. 1979, pp.13-84.

Melone S. 1975. *Les Grandes Orientations Actuelles de la Législation Pénale en Afrique: Le Cas du Cameroun.* Archives de Politique Criminelle. 1, pp.143-178.

Ministère des Affaires Sociales. 1987. *Rapport du Premier Colloque National sur l'Education en Milieu Ouvert et la Liberté Surveillée.* Yaoundé. 22-25 avril.

Ndoko N.C. 1985. *La Culpabilité en Droit Pénal Camerounais.* Paris. L.G.D.J.

Nkouendjin Y. 1985. *Soliloque sur Certains Problèmes Soulevés par l'Organisation Judiciaire de la République du Cameroun.* Penant. 751, pp. 5-34.

Pie F. 1990. *La Justice à la Recherche de son Effectivité: le Cas de la Justice Pénale.* Afrique Contemporaine. 156, pp.65-71.

Szabo D. 1986. *Science et Crime.* Paris. Vrin.

Weber M. 1971. Economie et Société. Paris. Plon.

DRUG TRAFFICKING AND DRUG ABUSE IN AFRICA

Tolani Asuni[*]

As in most other parts of the world, the drug trafficking and drug abuse situation continues to change in both type and in degree. These changes are due to different circumstances both local and external, and they may come about so rapidly that between the time of reporting and the circulation of the actual reports, the situation may well have changed.

One may present Nigeria as an example to illustrate the phenomenon of change. Prior to the Second World War, cannabis was practically unknown in Nigeria. The evidence for this statement can be found in the fact that there was no local name for it, and in the collection of useful plants of West Tropical Africa (Dalziel, 1936), prior to the War, cannabis was not included. It was with the return of Nigerian soldiers from the Middle East, the Far East and North Africa that cannabis became known in Nigeria. Foreign sailors calling in Lagos were also involved in the introduction and/or perpetration of the abuse of cannabis in this country.

Cannabis has remained the main drug of abuse in Nigeria and attention was first drawn to the problem by Asuni (1963 and 1964). Local conditions, such as the political upheaval in the country, tended to reinforce the abuse, when some political leaders gave their supporting thugs cannabis to give them courage to enable them to carry out their violent and aggressive behaviour.

At the United Nations Seminar on Narcotics Control for Enforcement Officers in Developing Countries in Africa, held in Lagos in 1965, cannabis was the principal drug mentioned. The other drug which was also mentioned was amphetamine. It is worth noting that the report also states:

> "In Africa today, the march of industrialization, the growth of big cities and the disruption of local communities had generated a variety of tensions and frustrations of different degrees of intensity. Such changes have been associated, in other lands, with the gradually increasing use of narcotic drugs by individuals and groups, providing a market for the activities of traffickers" (United Nations, 1966).

---

[*] Professor of Psychiatry, University of Lagos College of Medicine and Chairman of the Psychiatric Hospitals Management Board, Lagos, Nigeria and former Director of UNICRI.

117

The report gave a list of countries in which cannabis grew in the wild, and also those in which it did not exist. Some countries produced only supplies for local consumers, and at that time, gave no indication of being illegal exporters. Other countries produced cannabis largely for local consumption, but sometimes supplied an illicit market in neighbouring countries. Nigeria was one of the latter.

In the 1970s, while cannabis remained the major drug of abuse, other drugs began to emerge. Amphetamine was mentioned earlier. There was also Pethidine (Meperidine), Phenobarbitone, Morphine, Mandrax and Mogadon which came into prominence in the 1970s (Asuni, 1978; Anumonye, 1979; Anumonye et Al., 1980; Ebie and Pela, 1981; Odejide, 1980). These drugs originated mostly from developed countries (Europe and North America), and found their way to African countries where the control system is weak and defective due to a shortage of trained personnel and equipment. The trafficking then continues from one neighbouring country to another where the borders are porous from the point of view of customs surveillance.

The limited studies carried out, mostly by psychiatrists, who deal with the psychiatric consequences of these drugs, suggest some epidemiological characteristics of some of these drugs. For instance, amphetamine and its derivatives are commonly abused by students before and during academic examinations, and also by long distance drivers and labourers, not for the 'high' which is associated with some other drugs - but for its insomniac and energy-giving effects. Pethidine has been found to be abused mostly by those in the medical profession who have easy access to it, such as doctors, nurses and pharmacists. The non-medical individuals who abuse Pethidine have been inadvertently introduced to it by doctors, who have not been mindful of the dependence factor of this drug. Although there hasn't been trafficking in Pethidine. there has been cross-border trafficking in Amphetamines, Phenobarbitone and Mandrax.

There are, however, two African countries who have not followed the general pattern up until now. It is only in Mauritius that opium has been reported to be abused, and this comes from across the Indian Ocean from the Golden Crescent - Pakistan and neighbouring countries and the Golden Triangle. A large proportion of the population of Mauritius are of Asian origin and they still retain contact with their original countries and maintain their culture and customs.

The other special situation is the abuse of Khat which used to be limited to Ethiopia, Kenya, Madagascar and Somalia where it is grown. There has not been much trafficking in Khat, mainly because of its bulk and also because it has to be used fresh for it to have the most desirable effect. It has, however, recently been reported (Nencini and Ahmed, 1989) that while the

Khat habit is deeply rooted in Northern Somalia, Ethiopia and Djibouti, it has also spread to East Africa, particularly Southern Somalia and Kenya in the last two decades. There is also an indication that some of the Somali community in Rome have maintained the habit of using Khat, which probably reaches Rome directly from Kenya or via London.

It is pertinent to speculate on the spread of the growth and abuse of cannabis in Africa at this point. While nothing was reported about the existence of cannabis as far back as the 1930s, there were reports by Bouquet (1937) concerning North Africa and Watt and Breyer-Brandwijk (1936) concerning South Africa, which suggests that these two areas were plagued with the problem before it subsequently spread to other areas on the African Continent, most notably to West Africa, as previously stated (Asuni, 1964). This penetration was probably in terms of trafficking initially, but the West African countries soon learnt to grow their own, and this put a stop to trafficking within Africa, except in isolated cases like Togo, as reported by Johnson (1980). Trafficking, however, of cannabis to Europe and to a smaller extent to North America continued.

As we moved into the 1980s, another dimension of the drug developed. This involved the introduction of heroin, and to a smaller extent, cocaine. Africa was initially a transit area, but the local inhabitants of the transit countries soon started to abuse the drugs and also developed dependence upon them. This is in keeping with other observations in other parts of the world, that when a country is used as a transit station in the movement of illicit drugs, the country will, sooner or later, face the problem of dependence on the drug among the indigenous population.

The route for the trafficking of heroin starts mainly in India and Pakistan, and comes through East Africa (Ethiopia and Kenya) to West Africa, particularly Nigeria, and sometimes via another West African country, and from there it goes to Europe or North America. Many West African traffickers have been arrested in European and American airports, although they try all sorts of ways to beat the customs, including swallowing condoms containing the drug, usually heroin, or inserting the condoms in vaginal, in the case of women, or anal orifices in both sexes. Some of these carriers have died of an overdose as a result of burst containers in their innards. The 'fall out' phenomenon taking place in Nigeria has also been reported in Kenya.

It is believed that innocent passengers have also been used as carriers. Such passengers are asked to take parcels to be delivered to, or collected on the other side, by individuals who will, in turn, help them financially. This is, of course, an attractive proposition, especially these days when hard foreign currency is difficult to come by.

The general population only knows about drug trafficking when they read about the arrest and detention of a carrier, and this does not seem to affect them unless they know the carrier concerned. What is bringing the drug problem home to many people however, is the number of addicts that they are becoming acquainted with, hear about or see on the streets. What is even more disturbing is the fact that the children of the well-to-do and elite on whom a lot has been invested, appear to be over-represented among the addicts.

In Nigeria, for instance, the situation is becoming so frightening that the Government frequently reviews the legislation regarding trafficking and drug abuse. Initially, it would appear that the attitude of the people and the Government was tolerant, but now some sections of the population are asking for stiffer sentences.

Law enforcement is being increased in a number of African countries known to be involved in trafficking, and bilateral, and multilateral agreements being entered into with other relevant countries to strengthen the fight against the traffic and abuse of drugs.

International conferences, both at regional and interregional levels, are being organized to share experiences and exchange ideas in order to improve efforts to combat the problem.

Some of the issues that have emerged from African regional conferences are worthy of mention. It has often been stated that the approach to combatting the problem must be decided upon by the African countries, since developed countries have not been particularly successful in their efforts to solve this problem, and the only thing African countries have to learn is how not to do it. For instance, in some developed countries, drug abuse is indirectly glorified, for while eulogizing the achievements of artists, film stars, singers, athletes, etc., who are known drug users, their drug habit is also indirectly being promoted.

Some developed countries even allow the possession of a small amount for personal use. But how small is small? How does the abuser obtain that small amount? Of course, most of them get it through the black market. Is this not indirectly promoting trafficking? For fear of AIDS, some developed countries are giving out free syringes and needles to addicts. Is this not also encouraging the drug habit?

It is inconceivable for a poor African country to provide drug addicts with their drugs or drug-substitute, when they have not been able to provide free milk for young school children, or free prophylactic anti-malarial drug for children. It is understandable that the objective of the treatment of drug abusers is total abstinence. The method often used is sudden withdrawal (cold turkey) of the drug while, at the same time, treating the withdrawal

120

symptoms. Even if you want to adopt the gradual withdrawal method, the question arises as to who would pay for the illicit drug and from where would you get the drug - if you are not going to violate the law.

One of the difficulties in tackling this problem is the lack of knowledge of the extent of the problem. The only available index is the number of addicts who have been placed in psychiatric hospitals for treatment. This, of course, is less than the tip of the iceberg. It is an acknowledged fact that a number of drug abusers have been taken to private clinics and hospitals for treatment, and there is no means of knowing this, except all treatment facilities are requested, by law, to register all cases of drug abuse without prejudice to confidentiality; but this is rarely the case. A massive epidemiology survey is necessary to show the extent of the plight and to guide informed and rational planning to combat the problem.

It is generally agreed that the user should be distinguished from the trafficker, especially from the point of view of sanctions. The user should be treated, while the trafficker should go through the criminal justice process.

Another area which has been discussed is the issue of detoxification and rehabilitation. They should not be seen as discreet entities, but rather as a total composite package. While the whole process has to commence in a secure setting due to the tendency of addicts to escape to further indulge their craving, the latter stage of the process is the rehabilitation end of the continuum, and this should be in an open unit with gradual exposure to total freedom.

The issue as to whether the abuser is willing to give up his drug habit for treatment and rehabilitation to be successful, is not considered to be relevant. In the first place, it is like saying that a psychotic who has no insight and is consequently unwilling to receive treatment, will not improve if treated. Such is the nature of addiction, that the addict is so afraid of the pains of withdrawal, that he is not willing or ready to give up the habit.

Secondly, since possession and usage are criminal offences, the addict has only two options. He must either accept treatment as a condition of discharge from the court, or go through the criminal justice process which will assure him a prison sentence. Failure to co-operate in the treatment programme is failing to comply with the conditions of his discharge, and this, in turn, will lead to imprisonment. In other words, the criminal justice system can be called upon to ensure that drug abusers receive treatment by law.

The reasons why one would not recommend treatment and rehabilitation in prison, as is practiced in some developing countries, include the appalling conditions of prisons in most parts of Africa, and also the anti-therapeutic milieu of the prisons.

It has to be admitted, however, that there is an extreme paucity of treatment facilities in terms of trained personnel, equipment and physical structure. Most of the psychiatric facilities do not have the security necessary to hold abusers, especially of the highly addictive drugs.

Much attention and effort have been directed towards the reduction of the supply which, of course, involves law enforcement. It would appear that not enough attention is being given to the demand-reduction which involves the family, school, religious bodies, youth movements, such as the Boy Scouts and Girl Guides, etc. In most African countries where there is more emphasis on the group rather than the individual, the group, especially the primary one which is the family, can be used more effectively in the demand-reduction programme. It is recognized that in most cases of drug abuse, the family has partly contributed to the situation in terms of over-indulgence, lack of family cohesion, busy parents - so busy, that they have little or no time for their children - over strictness, etc. etc. Peer pressure is often quoted to be a contributory factor, but where there is family solidarity and cohesion, the effect of peer pressure can be minimized.

The extended family also provides a wider social network than the nuclear family, and this can be used again to minimize the effect of peer pressure and can provide a sort of armour against drug abuse. The negative attitude of the family and community at large to drug abuse should be maintained, without prejudice to appropriate drug education, treatment and rehabilitation.

The treatment of drug abusers should not be done in isolation away from the family if it is to succeed, especially since there is a dearth of social services. Even if there are enough social services, the principle of 'blood is thicker than water' should prevail. The social services should complement, and not replace the role of the family, except of course, where there is no identifiable family member.

The change in the drug profile has also led to a change in the reason for seeking help. The reason for seeking help for the abuse of cannabis was mainly because of the abnormal behaviour of the individual, ranging from amotivational syndrome to frank psychosis. It is usually the relatives of the drug abusers who bring them to the hospital, since they have usually lost the perception of their problem. When they enter for treatment, the risk of them escaping is less than for those who are hooked on Pethidine, heroin or cocaine.

They can therefore be treated in open units. There are two types of psychosis (Boroffka, 1966). One is acute psychosis starting 'de novo' in a person with a 'normal' pre-morbid personality following the abuse of cannabis. The other is the abuse of cannabis as a symptom of incipient psychosis which also accelerates and escalates the psychotic process.

The reason why help is sought for those dependent upon drugs like heroin and cocaine is usually anti-social and criminal behaviour, such as lying, stealing, burglary and absence from home. All this anti-social behaviour is either to get money to procure the drug or to hide the fact that they are dependent upon drugs, and it is usually within the immediate family, the extended family and friends. There is no evidence yet that the anti-social and criminal behaviour is extended to the ordinary person on the street - like street mugging. Receiving money under false pretences is practiced and this may involve a complete outsider. Unfortunately, parents do not think of their children as being responsible for the theft in the house and they often attribute it to domestic staff until it becomes so obvious that it cannot be denied.

Because their behaviour is not psychotic and because of the stigma of mental illness and psychiatric hospitals in general, the children of the elite, who are dependent upon drugs, are often placed in private general hospitals to allow for privacy, where the objective for the intervention is mainly detoxification. Of course, as to be expected, the relapse rate is practically one hundred percent. Psychiatric intervention is sought as a last resort, when admission to a psychiatric hospital is not so vehemently resisted and when the parents have reached the end of their tether.

The patients themselves tend to resist admission to psychiatric hospitals, insisting they are not mad. It is when they are confronted with the option of the criminal justice process that they agree to be to be admitted. Indeed, it is sometimes argued that psychiatry should not be so heavily involved, so that those who need help, may not be scared away. The fact of the matter is that psychiatry is the only discipline that has the comprehensive expertise to handle the problem in the context of a multidisciplinary team work approach. All the other members of the team, including psychiatrists, are in very short supply, with the exception of psychiatric nurses. In any case, in the African context, psychiatry has been in the forefront in the treatment and rehabilitation of those who are dependent upon drugs. This tradition was established when cannabis-induced psychosis and Amphetamine psychosis were the prevalent features of drug abuse.

It would appear that while the abuse of cannabis and consequent cannabis-induced psychosis have reached a plateau in the last decade, the abuse of cocaine and particularly heroin, has been increasing rapidly. This increase in abuse is also a reflection of the increase in trafficking, and it is a cause of great concern.

Another interesting observation is that the abuse of cannabis was initially prevalent among the marginal section of the community in West Africa, and only later did it spread to other sections including secondary school and university students. On the other hand, as pointed out earlier, the more well-to-do in the higher socio-economic bracket are over-represented among those abusing heroin and cocaine. This may well be a factor of the cost of heroin and cocaine which is far more expensive. While cannabis grows wild in a large part of Africa and can be easily cultivated, heroin and cocaine are not produced in Africa and are imported illegally. It can be logically predicted that those in the higher socio-economic bracket will continue to be over-represented among those dependent on heroin and cocaine, primarily because of the cost.

It has not been possible to monitor the situation regarding psychotropic drugs. It is known that since the banning of the importation of such drugs such as Amphetamine and Methaquolone in some countries like Nigeria, the problem of abuse of these drugs has been minimized, as the psychiatric sequalae of abuse of these drugs are now rarely seen.

In addition to heroin and cocaine, which are of international concern and which are relatively new to Africa, the issue of psychotropic drugs which are manufactured in developed countries and dumped in African countries, is of great interest to them. Even though the nationals of these African countries are also involved in the illicit importation, it is felt that not enough is being done by the international community to fight this problem. Indeed, the impression is given that the manufacturers are out to make a profit and they are free to do so; it is the responsibility of the recipient country to tighten its control system against the illicit importation of these drugs. This is seen as a double standard. When the problem touches developed countries, they plead with the countries of origin of the drugs (cocaine and heroin) to stop producing the drugs, but when it concerns developing countries, they are told to go and tighten their control mechanism. Great emphasis is placed on supply reduction in one case and not so great in another case.

It is, therefore, important to harmonize efforts to fight all drugs of abuse in a consistent manner irrespective of what countries are involved in the supply of the drugs.

References

Anumonye A. 1979. *Nigerian Drug Scene.* Rome. Stilgrat Litografia.

---- , **et Al. (Eds.).** 1980. *African Seminar on the Problem of Drug Dependence. Lagos, Nigeria, 26th-28th November 1980.* Proceedings. Lousanne. International Council on Alcohol and Addictions (ICAA).

Asuni T. 1963. *Drug Traffic in Nigeria with Special Reference to Indian Hemp.* In: Israel Drapkin (Ed.). "Twelfth International Course in Criminology held in Hebrew University of Jerusalem: 2-20 September 1962". Proceedings.

---- . 1964. *Socio-Psychiatric Problems of Cannabis in Nigeria.* Bulletin on Narcotics. XVI:2, pp.17-28.

---- . 1978. *The Drug Abuse Scene in Nigeria.* In: "International Challenge of Drug Abuse". NIDA Research Monograph 19. DHEW Publication, pp.78-654.

Boroffka A. 1966. *Mental Illness and Indian Hemp in Lagos.* East African Medical Journal. 43, p.377.

Bouquet J. 1937. *L'Etude de la Cannabis.* Archivest. 26. Institut Pasteur de Tunis.

Dalziel J.M. 1936.*The Useful Plants of West Tropical Africa.* London. Crown Agents for Overseas Government and Administration.

Ebie J.C., Pela O.A. 1981. *Some Socio-cultural Aspects of the Problem of Drug Abuse in Nigeria.* Drug and Alcohol Dependency. 8.

Johnson R.M. 1980. *Overview of the Situation of Drug Dependence in Togo.* In: Anumonye A. et Al. (Eds.). op. cit.,. pp.39-115.

Nencini P., Ahmed A.M. 1989. *Khat Consumption: A Pharmacological Review.* Drug and Alcohol Dependence. 23.

Odejide A.O. 1980. *Problems of Drug Abuse in Nigeria. A Review of the Existing Literature and Suggestions on Preventive Measures.* Nigerian Medical Journal. 10:1-2.

United Nations. 1966. *Report of the United Nations Seminar on Narcotics Control for Enforcement Officers.* New York. ST/TAO/Ser. c/84.

Watt J.M., Breyer-Brandwijk M.G. 1936. *The Forensic and Sociological Aspects of the Dagga Problems in South Africa.* South African Medical Journal. 10, p.573.

RITUAL HOMICIDE IN SIERRA LEONE

Muctaru Kabba*

1. Background

While this paper concentrates on ritual homicide in Sierra Leone, West Africa** it should be noted that, historically, as well as in more recent times, the phenomenon is global in scope. Ringgren (1962:7) provides us with two historical cases in connection with "The Mexican Aztec who kills a young man and offers his heart to the sun-god in order to secure the vital forces of the sun for his land", and "The Moabite King Mesha who offers his son to his national god in order to win victory over the attacking Israel".

In more recent times cases of ritual homicide have been reported in England and India. In England, as recently as in September 1990, it was reported that in Rochdale a child recounted stories of rituals involving the killing and burial of babies, and the stories were taken seriously enough to warrant the placing of a number of children under council protection and custody (BBC, News About Britain, 14 September 1990, 16.09 hours). In India, according to a report carried in the October 10, 1975 issue of the Sierra Leone newspaper "The Daily Mail", India's Supreme Court refused to allow an appeal from a man and his two sisters against their conviction on the charge of killing a child as a sacrifice to an evil spirit and then cooking and eating its flesh.

It is appropriate at this juncture to comment on the sources of the data for this paper. For the pre-colonial and colonial periods, the study depended on newspaper reports, official (colonial) documents and a number of books written on the subject of human leopards. For the post-independence period, however, the author has had to depend almost exclusively on newspaper reports of cases of ritual homicide or, as it is popularly referred to in Sierra Leone, ritual murder.

In what follows, we first develop a classificatory scheme for discussing/analysing the phenomenon of ritual homicide. We then proceed to analyse the available data on ritual homicide in Sierra Leone in relation to the scheme. This will be followed by a comparative consideration of

* Lecturer and Head of the Department of Sociology, Fourah Bay College, University of Sierra Leone, Freetown, Sierra Leone.
** See Map

traditional and modern legal principles applied to ritual homicide, investigative practices and legal evidential procedures as well as the nature and efficacy of the sanctions utilised against offenders. The paper will conclude with some observations regarding the need for an imaginative integration of traditional and modern legal principles and practices.

2. Ritual Homicide - a classification

For purposes of analysis, it is useful to classify ritual homicide into three major categories as follows:
- *Communal Ritual Homicide*: ritual homicide as an act of the whole community;
- *Group Ritual Homicide*: ritual homicide as an act of a more or less organised group of persons within a community, often taking the form of a secret society;
- *Individual Ritual Homicide*: ritual homicide as an act of one or more individuals within a community.

2.1 Communal Ritual Homicide

This type of ritual homicide is characterised by community-wide acceptance of the necessity of making a sacrifice of a human being, either regularly or when considered necessary, with a view to establishing relations with a deity, spirits, force, etc, as a way of expressing thanks, fulfilling a vow, propitiating the anger of a deity or spirit, warding off evil or misfortune, etc. (Awolalu, 1979:143-161). In other words, the ritual homicide is intended to serve the interests not of a group or of an individual but of all members of the community.

This type of ritual homicide is exemplified by pre-19th century Yoruba traditions. According to Awolalu: "Human beings were sacrificed, not because of a sadistic desire for wanton destruction of life or a lack of respect for human life, but mainly because the people's philosophy of life with regard to sacrifice held that it was better to sacrifice one life for the good of the community than for all to perish. A human victim was seen as an ambassador: believed to be going to represent the people before, and carry their petitions to the higher power" (1979:167-168).

In Sierra Leone, there is no clear-cut evidence of this type of ritual homicide, although an account by Lindskog carries an implication to that effect. Thus he notes that: "When Governor Bendoo landed in Sierra Leone in 1852, he came across the porro grove where human beings are sacrificed. This was probably a matter of official communal sacrifice since porro was a tribal organisation which took part in maintaining the established order of things" (1954:55). Porro was a community-wide organisation whose laws and activities where officially sanctioned and since every adult male person was a member of the Porro, the sacrifices referred to may be said to come under the category of community ritual homicide.

For the purposes of this paper, the rarity of communal ritual homicide, even in historical times, coupled with its abolition in virtually every society, does not justify further consideration of it either in general terms or in relation to Sierra Leone.

3. Ritual Homicide in Sierra Leone

In considering the two other forms or ritual homicide in relation to Sierra Leone, we shall be concerned with the following aspects, where relevant and subject to the availability of empirical data:
- origins, spread and intensity, organisational issues, criteria of membership, initiation rites, medicines, etc;
- motives or objectives of ritual homicide;
- how the victims are obtained;
- characteristics of the victims with regard to gender, age, relationship to participants in the ritual homicide and whether the victim is resident in the community in which he was murdered or an outsider;
- what is done to the body of the victim; which parts are removed, what they are used for and what is done to the remaining parts of the body;
- the status of the participants and the nature of the relationship between organisations engaged in ritual homicide and the community or society at large.

3.1 Group Ritual Homicide

It has been observed that group ritual homicide occurs in the context of a more or less organised group which takes the form of a secret society. In Sierra Leone, a number of these societies have historically emerged which, in order of notoriety and predominance, are the Human Leopard Society, the Alligator Society and the Human Baboon Society. However, the frequency or intensity of their activities varies from one period of time to another. Also, other secret societies engaged in ritual homicide have emerged, while there is an apparently increased tendency for practitioners of ritual homicide to use community-wide and societally recognized and accepted secret societies for their operations.

In what follows, we shall first consider the three secret societies already mentioned, followed by cases of ritual homicide involving other secret societies, especially in the post-independence period, i.e. 1960-1990.

3.1.1 The Human Leopard Society

This is the best known and most documented secret society and, during the pre-colonial and colonial periods, the one most predominantly engaged in ritual homicide (Alldridge, 1901; 1910; Beatty, 1915; Berry, 1912; Crooks, 1903; Fama, 1939; Fitzgerald 1912; Ingham, 1894; Little, 1951; Lindskog, 1954). There is continuing controversy as to whether it originated in Sherbroland and then spread to Mendeland or vice versa, but there can be no doubt that the phenomenon was concentrated in areas inhabited by the Sherbro and the Mende with sporadic occurrences in the Northern districts.

There has been much debate as to whether or not human leopardism is an organised phenomenon. Thus the "Early Dawn", a newspaper based in Sherbroland and which carried frequent reports of cases of human leopardism, portrays the leopard man as a person who pursues a private hobby (May 15, 1888); and Fenton (Command 267/419:12/12/1950) talks of leopard men as being employed by private persons who make use of their services. There are also indications of variations in the degree of organisation. Thus, Lindskog (1954:43) observes that while the South had stable organisations, in the North individual appearances were said to be the practice.

Membership may be voluntary or involuntary. In the latter case, a person may be tricked into becoming a member. After having unknowingly partaken of a meal prepared with human flesh, or having drunk palm wine mixed with human blood, he is made to understand that he is now a member of the society by virtue of having consumed "leopard food", i.e. human flesh or blood. This is followed by an initiation rite which includes the use of the society medicine, "borfima", a red box in which the "borfima" is placed, and a leopard knife. Holding the knife with his right hand and knocking on the box with it, an oath is made by the aspirant who has to repeat the following words: "As I come now to get this medicine from these people, afterwards if I reveal them, if I walk on the road, big snake must bite me, if I walk on the sea, I must drown, if I walk on the road again, lightning must kill me" (Lindskog, 1954:16).

In addition to oath-taking, members carry a mark on their buttocks - although the mark cannot be used as conclusive evidence of membership. Members are also said to be able to recognize each other by the "movement of the second finger across the palm and a peculiar rolling of the eyes" (Beatty, 1913:4-8).

The available evidence indicates that membership is not an attractive proposition, because there is an obligation for each member to provide a victim. There is some argument in the literature concerning when a member is to provide a victim, but the overwhelming weight of the evidence indicates that every member is obliged to provide a victim at one time or another.

Mention has been made of the society's "medicines", the most essential of which is known as "borfima", of which three aspects need to be mentioned. Firstly, there was and still is a widespread belief in its powers. It is a highly prized fetish and is believed to be a panacea against all evil and to produce all good. Secondly, its preparation requires the use of parts of the human body obtained from a person who has been specifically killed for that purpose and including: "the skin from the palm of the human hand, the sole of the foot and the forehead. There are also parts of certain organs - such as the genitals and the liver as well as a cloth taken from a menstruating woman" (Little, 1951:233). Thirdly, the maintenance of the energy, power, and efficacy of the borfima requires its regular "blooding" or "feeding", involving the use of human fat. In other words, both the preparation of borfima and the maintenance of its power and efficacy necessitated the sacrifice of a human being. In the colonial period, borfima was believed to grant immunity from detection and success in the society's often nefarious activities (Lindskog, 1954:61).

One of the objectives of the acts of ritual homicide committed by the society has already been hinted at in connection with the preparation of borfima and the maintenance of its power. It is the requirements for the maintenance of its power, namely human blood and fat, which necessitate continual acts of ritual homicide. It would appear that when borfima has operated to bring about the elevation of a member to the position of paramount chief, section chief or village or town headman, for instance, its powers become attenuated and it becomes hungry. It therefore needs to be "blooded", "propitiated" or "satisfied" in order to ensure its continued efficacy. The ritual of blooding, feeding or propitiating calls for the mixing of the blood and fat of a murdered victim and the smearing of the mixture on the medicine.

We noted earlier on that ritual homicide may be cannibalistic or non-cannibalistic. The overwhelming weight of the available evidence as regards group ritual homicide is that in virtually all cases, consumption of parts of the victim's flesh is involved. In the specific case of the Human Leopard Society, "the existence of cannibalism in the society has been considered as proven by the discovery of kettles or cooking pots and human leftovers" (Lindskog, 1954:27).

There appears to be no consensus regarding explanations of the phenomenon of cannibalistic ritual homicide. The satisfaction of the craving which some savages have for human flesh - pure cannibalism - has been proposed as a possible explanation (Merewhether, 1913:2). It has also been suggested that it constitutes only a part of the ritual process, perhaps a loyalty rite which bound all participants together in the leopard cult (Burrows, 1912). Beatty says that: "The reason given by ex-members of the society for eating human flesh is that it is supposed to have the effect of increasing the mental and physical powers of the consumer and incidentally enable him to acquire power and wealth" (1913:20-21). And in the colonial period one explanation that is said to have been offered by members is that "The eating of human flesh would give power over the white man. For, say they, the white men have more power than black men; but in cannibalism you get some power so that when you do wrong, you will not be found out by the white man" (Berry, 1912:5).

Victims are procured or obtained by either force, abduction from their homes or ambush. In a number of cases, they are lured to the place of murder. Force may be used even in cases when there is a familial relationship between the victim and a member or members of the society. The most risky of these methods is abduction since it may alert non-members who may be able to recognize and later identify the perpetrators, even though in all cases, the operations take place at night.

It is appropriate at this juncture to consider the characteristics of the victims. Table 1 provides empirical data on the characteristics of victims of the Human Leopard Society drawn mainly from cases brought before a Court specifically set up to try cases of human leopardism, the Special Commission Court of 1912-1913. The characteristics considered are gender, age, relationship of victim to a member or members, whether the victim resides in the community in which the murder is committed or outside of it. Not all of the data is available for every case but it is clear that the available data substantiate Lindskog's observations (1954:45) to the effect that no clear-cut patterns or categories are discernible.

The Table makes clear the concentration of Human Leopard Society operations in the Southern Sherbro District which comprises what today are the Bonthe and Moyamba Districts. The murders are neither age nor gender specific. In three of the cases, the victims are relatives of the members involved in the ritual homicide. In all cases for which data is available, the victims were residents of the communities in which the murders were committed, and in all five cases, some of the persons involved were highly placed individuals in their communities.

We have chosen to include a post-colonial case of human leopardism in the Table in order to demonstrate that while it may be on the decline, it is still not extinct, although it now appears to be confined to the Bonthe District.

The killing of the victim may take place either at the society's usual place of meeting or in the community itself, with the body being conveyed to the society bush. The equipment used to carry out the murders is indicated by the description of the murderers as "men in leopard skins with iron claws and sharp knifes in their hands" (Cole, 1886:82). All the equipment mentioned is of course necessary in the case of an ambush or abduction, while in those cases in which the victim is lured to the place of killing, only a sharp knife is necessary.

After the victim has been killed, the parts required for feeding or blooding the borfima are removed and the other parts of the body are divided up among the members, with what are considered to be the choice parts going to the "big" men. The meat is either eaten raw on the spot or taken away and cooked. According to Beatty, a witness in the aforementioned Kale case remarked as follows: "Some like it raw, some roast and some prefer it boiled with rice" (1913:47).

The mention of "big" men raises the issue of the status of the membership of the participants. According to Beatty (1913:25) in the pre-protectorate period, it was the lesser men in the chiefdom who took part in these murders and societies, and the chiefs took part in trying to suppress the society; but things changed - the societies became too strong for the chiefs and many have been drawn into, and have become leaders of them.

Table 1 makes clear the degree of involvement or participation of highly-placed individuals in the Human Leopard Society even in the post-colonial period - paramount chiefs, chiefdom and village speakers, village headmen, chiefdom councillors. In fact, one of the reasons for the setting-up of the Special Commission Court was because a great number of these chiefs were implicated and had been arrested in the protectorate. Earlier, a Circuit Court which included paramount chiefs as assessors had presided over cases of ritual homicide. The Special Commission Court has no chiefly representation.

The fact that highly-placed persons participated or were involved in the activities and operations of the secret societies and in ritual homicide, is one of the reasons for its continuation, and accounts for part of the difficulty involved in apprehending perpetrators and bringing them to justice.

3.1.2 The Human Alligator Society

Even before the British declared a Protectorate over the hinterland of Sierra Leone in 1896, the Human Alligator Society was already in existence. There were frequent reports about its activities in the newspapers, particularly the "Early Dawn" and the "Sierra Leone Times", between 1886 and 1895.

According to Beatty, the Human Alligator Society: "Appears to have been an offshoot of the Human Leopard Society, and the usual meeting place of this society was in the vicinity of rivers where crocodiles, or as they are locally called, alligators abound" (1913:13). Reports on the activities of the society, which were concentrated in the riverain Sherbro Northern District, were so frequent that in 1901: "There was found sufficient cause to complement the leopard ordinances with provisions against alligator men" (Lindskog, 1954:183). It was made a felony for any person without lawful authority or excuse to have in his possession, custody or under his control, an alligator knife and an alligator skin shaped or made to make a man wearing the same resemble an alligator (Beatty, 1913:13).

According to Lindskog (1954:182), the alligator men of Sierra Leone are described as having characteristics similar to those of the leopard men. In addition, they were organised as a secret society. The members of the society were also reputed to devote themselves to cannibalism.

The ordinance of 1901 did not take into account an essential instrument in the operations of the society, namely the "Kunkube", a canoe made to resemble an alligator. "In this canoe is concealed the alligator man with iron gloves made like claws with which he seizes the victim and drags him into the canoe" ("The Independent", Freetown, 9/12/1875). The Kunkube is described as a mystic canoe which glides unseen around the river, seeking its victim. The September 30, 1891 issue of the "Early Dawn" talks about cannibals "travelling by some mysterious proceed below the water in canoes shaped in the form of alligators" who "seized upon their prey whilst performing ablution in the river or from small canoes in which they may have been plying". The impression given is that the kunkube operates like, or is in fact submarine, and this is still the popular belief in present day Sierra Leone.

In consequence of the frequent reference to the kunkube as an essential element in the operations of the Human Alligators Society, the colonial government passed an amended ordinance in 1909 making it a crime to "possess an alligator canoe or konkobai shaped or made so to resemble an alligator, or made in a manner differing from that ordinarily in use among the people".

The "Early Dawn" carried the most frequent reports on the activities of the society. Thus, in an article which appeared on September 15, 1886, it was reported that a young man had been "seized by the leg and drawn under the water while a woman and a little boy witnessed the incident. It was quite clear on investigation that the man had been taken by a human alligator as the track of the canoe could be seen on the mud; and as the investigators were crossing the creek, they felt something under their feet which upon being brought to the surface turned out to be the body of the young man whose head had been severed by a sharp instrument. One arm had also been cut off plus some flesh from one leg. The blood was still flowing from the wounds as if it had been done quite recently".

The report of Chalmers (1899) who in 1898 was appointed to investigate the circumstances leading to the widespread disturbances following the declaration of the Protectorate, implies that the society had become virtually extinct by 1896 as a result of the apprehension, prosecution and execution of many of its members. This is however contradicted by the passing of the 1901 and 1909 ordinances referred to earlier. While information on the society is hard to come by after 1913, its continued existence in the ensuing decades may be assumed, for the contemporary evidence is very much to the effect that it is still existent and active in the Bonthe (Sherbro) and Moyamba (Mende and Sherbro) Districts. Thus, as recently as in 1975, the frequent reports of persons disappearing in these districts as a result of the operations of the kunkube, as well as allegations that its activities were spear-headed by the paramount chief of the Nongowa Bullom Chiefdom, Bonthe District, led the government to set up a commission of inquiry into these and other allegations against the chief, resulting in his deposition ("Daily Mail", March 16, 1975).

3.1.3 The Human Baboon Society

According to historical and contemporary records and reports, this is the least active of the three secret societies; in any case, there is less documentary evidence of its activities and operations. It is to be found in all three provinces, although the available evidence indicates that it is today more prevalent in the Southern Province.

While there were few reports about the society in the colonial period, its existence was recognized as demonstrated by a 1912 amendment to the Human Leopard and Alligator Societies Ordinance of 1909 which declared it as one of the unlawful societies.

The following account relating to the killing of a small girl in May 1913 in a village called Bokamp in the Northern Karene District provides some information on the membership and mode of operation of the society. In the case under consideration (Beatty, 1913:147), the society consisted of 21 members made up of eleven men and ten women; seven victims, all of whom were children, had been provided at various times for the society. As a general practice, one of the members dresses himself in a baboon skin and attacks the victim with his teeth. The spirit of all the members of the society is believed to become centred in the person who is for the occasion wearing the baboon skin which, when not in use, is kept in a small forest where it is guarded by evil spirits. The "baboon" bites pieces out of the victim which the other members of the society devour.

That the society continues to exist, is indicated by the results of the author's canvassing of national newspapers in the post-colonial period (1960-1990) which produced four cases of Human Baboons in operation as is shown by Table 2.

3.1.4 Other Secret Societies - The post-colonial period

The author's coverage of national newspaper reports for the period 1960-1990 produced thirty-two cases of definite or apparent ritual homicide.

Of these, thirteen were in connection with group ritual homicide and thirteen in connection with individual ritual homicide, while the insufficiency of data does not permit any definite conclusions regarding the categories to which the other six cases belong. Of the thirteen cases of group ritual homicide, one was connected with the Human Alligator Society, four with the Human Baboon Society and the rest (eight) with other secret societies.

Table 3 provides some data on these other secret societies. The Table indicates the continuation of the practice of group ritual homicide into the post-colonial period. It also indicates a continuity in some patterns. Thus, group ritual homicide is still predominantly a southern province phenomenon, concentrated mainly in the Bonthe and Moyamba Districts, although the Eastern Province and the Western Area are also represented. Most of the victims are residents in the communities in which the murders were committed. There is however, scanty information with regard to the relationship between victims and participants in ritual homicide, although in one case the victim was a grandson of one of the accused persons. There is no clear-cut pattern of gender or age selectivity where the victims are concerned - they may be male or female and they may be young persons or adults.

In two of the cases for which information is available on which parts of the body are removed and what is done to them, we again find a pattern similar to that for the Human Leopard Society; some parts, particularly private parts, are used in the ritual preparation of "medicines"; the blood is used to feed or blood the God of the Hengor Society (case 3); some parts - the heart, liver and lungs - are cooked and eaten (cases 4 and 8). The evidence is inconclusive regarding whether all the cases also involved cannibalism.

There is a particularly interesting development regarding the sale of some parts. Thus, in the case of the Hengor Society, the fat was reported as having been sold in Liberia, which borders the Kailahun District and which is, itself, a hotbed of ritual homicidal practices (Butt-Thompson, 1929; Sibley and Westermann, 1929). In the Fornakukuna Society case, the victim's blood is sold at Le20.00 (at the time roughly £10) a tablespoonful. These examples indicate the influence of the spread of the money economy on the practice of ritual homicide.

Another noticeably novel development is the participation of women in secret societies engaged in ritual homicide. Of course, women cannot possibly be involved in cases having to do with the Porro society, so we can safely conclude that those societies in which women are involved are necessarily non-Porro secret societies. It is significant that women are involved in all the three non-Porro secret societies.

The status of the participants or members is not different from that of those in the colonial period - they continue to include paramount chiefs, speakers, village or town heads, chiefdom police constables, etc., although it should be mentioned that some of those charged are subsequently acquitted and discharged.

The objectives of ritual homicide also display the same pattern as in the colonial period - to make or "feed medicines" to which certain powers are ascribed, and for ritual cannibalistic purposes. There are what may be viewed as secondary motives, such as the sale of blood and fat; the performance of ritual ceremonies intended to bring about a desired end (to ensure more fish catches); and, lastly, simply the desire to maintain a tradition.

3.2   Individual Ritual Homicide

In the analytical framework, this type of ritual homicide was conceptualised as being carried out in the interests, not of an organised group, but of one or more individuals. Individual ritual homicide may be carried out with or without the participation in the killing of victims by the individual who stands to benefit, and sometimes even without the knowledge of the intended beneficiary. Table 4 provides some data on cases of individual ritual homicide reported in the newspapers for the period 1960-1990. The data enable us to draw the following conclusions:

- Individual ritual homicide is a nation-wide phenomenon. All the provinces in the country - Eastern, Northern, Southern and Western Area - have witnessed cases of it. However, it is more prevalent in the Eastern and Southern Provinces.
- The gender of victims is more often female than male - 8 out of 13 cases. Apparently, the attainment of the objectives of this type of homicide often requires the procurement of certain parts of the female anatomy, particularly breasts and private parts.
- The age of the victims ranges from 2 to 53 years of age. However, there is some indication of a preference for children and adolescents, particularly the former. Of the 13 reported cases, 8 of the victims were between 2 and 15 years old.
- In all cases the victims resided in the community in which the killing was carried out.
- Related to point 4 above is the fact that there is a pattern of a close relationship, familial or otherwise, between the victim and the beneficiaries of, or participants in the ritual homicide, who may be grandfathers, aunts, uncles, husbands, guardians, etc. of the victims. In those cases where a familial relationship does not exist between the direct or immediate beneficiary and the victim, the latter is obtained through the payment of a sum of money by the beneficiary to relations of the victim, who may or may not themselves take part in the killing. Instances of payment indicate a nexus between pecuniary motives and ritual homicide.
- The killing of the victim is carried out in secrecy and usually at night. It invariably involves the participation of at least two persons. In most cases, the direct beneficiary takes part in the killing of the victim and is often the person who removes the required parts. In a few cases, the beneficiary may hire others to do the killing and remove the required parts. In one of the reported cases (case 11) where the ritual homicide was committed with a view to ensuring the reinstatement of the beneficiary to a position of power, the beneficiary had no knowledge of the ritual homicide.
- All the cases reported are conceived of as sacrifices which invariably involved the removal of parts of the body. Apparently, the general idea of sacrifice has to be complemented by the removal of parts of the body with which to make charms in order to ensure the attainment of the beneficiary's objectives. In virtually all cases, the parts are removed after

138

the victim has been killed. In one rare case (10), the parts - breasts and vagina - were cut off while the victim was still alive.

- The motives or objectives of the ritual homicide relate to the following:
  a) to ensure success in a competition for power and status. Three definite cases - 4, 9 and 11 - and three apparent or presumed cases - 1, 7 and 12 - are reported in this connection;
  b) to ensure the maintenance of individuals in positions of power and status - case 2;
  c) to ensure the reinstatement of individuals to positions of power and status - case 11;
  d) to ensure an increase in wealth. Two definite cases - 8 and 10 - are reported in relation to an expected increase in wealth through increased diamond discoveries. It is noticeable that the two cases occur in the diamondiferous Kenema District, Eastern Province. Since case 3 occurs in the same area, it is reasonable to assume that it was similarly motivated.

- Alphamen, sorcerers and herbalists play an essential role in cases of individual ritual homicide as the Table clearly indicates. They are persons who are recognized in their communities as specialists in the knowledge and use of the occult, non-material forces. It is on the basis of their recommendations that individuals undertake the killings. It is they who recommend the human sacrifices; it is they who specify the parts required; and it is they who mix the parts removed with "nessi" or herbs and other ingredients. The resultant mixture, when used according to instructions given by the alphaman, sorcerer or herbalist, is believed to ensure the attainment of the individual's objectives, whatever these may be. For the performance of these services, they are paid in cash and/or goods. Thus, in case 5, the herbalist demanded payment as follows: Le40.00, a fowl, and a bushel of clean rice. The influence of the money economy is evidenced by the demand for a cash payment. With the mention of "alphamen", persons who use their Islamic knowledge to make charms, it is appropriate to comment at this juncture on the relationship between Islam and the phenomenon of ritual homicide. It is quite clear that Islam, as such, does not condone or encourage ritual homicide. On the contrary, in the colonial period, the "Sierra Leone Gazette" (7/12/1912:694) noted that the position of the Legislative Council is that it is futile to search for Leopard Societies in areas where Muslims are numerous since, as a rule, they were opposed to the things for which the Human Leopard and Alligator Societies existed. This position applied as much to the colonial period as it is does to the present, and the use of charms, in so far as it involves the use of any part of the human body, is to be considered as a deviation from, and a perversion of, the tenets of the Islamic religion.

- None of the cases reported involved the consumption of human flesh.
- A significant pattern that emerges is that the large majority of the beneficiary are:
  a) persons who were or are highly placed and who seek to regain, maintain or increase their power and status;
  b) persons who aspire to positions of power and status in a highly competitive context;
  c) persons who wish to increase their wealth.

The fact that the motives for individual ritual homicide are dominantly influenced by a desire to acquire, maintain, regain and increase an individual's quota of the three most valued things in life - namely, wealth, power and status - in the context of a belief system based on the notion that these things can be attained with the aid of non-material forces, indicates that the practice of individual ritual homicide will continue for a long time to come.

4. Ritual Homicide in Sierra Leone - Traditional and modern legal principles and practices

In this section, we examine traditional and modern legal principles and practices in relation to the phenomenon of ritual homicide.

Traditional will here refer simply to the principles and practices prevailing in the pre-colonial period, while modern refers to principles and practices in relation to the colonial and post-colonial periods.

We shall first set out modern legal principles and practices and, by way of comparison, consider these in relation to traditional legal principles and practices. This will be followed by a consideration of their relative efficacy in dealing with the problems and the opportunities available for forging an integration between the principles and practices of the two systems.

The modern system operates on the basis of Western legal principles which involve the following major elements:
a) What is considered as unlawful is clearly defined, formulated as laws or ordinances, proclamations, etc., and set out in writing. These may be operative for a specific period of time or, as in the case of a proclamation, in a specific part of a territory and are all subject to modification over time in the light of evolving circumstances and conditions. There is thus an in-built dynamism in the laws, ordinances, etc.

b) The process of establishing whether or not an unlawful act has been committed involves a careful consideration of the laws/ordinances etc., in the context of a definite, clearly defined structure in the form of *specialised roles* (police, judges, assessors, lawyers, etc.), *clearly defined procedures*, and a *set of technical rules relating to what constitutes admissible adequate or satisfactory evidence.*

c) The sanctions to be imposed, in the event that it is established that an unlawful act has been committed, are clearly defined and their severity is related to the nature/enormity of the offence.

d) A convicted person has a right of appeal to a higher legal authority up to the Supreme Court against a decision made by a lower legal authority.

Now, so far as traditional legal principles in relationship to ritual homicide are concerned, there is a close relationship between the belief system and legal principles and practices. In Africa generally, and in Sierra Leone in particular, there is a belief in the ability of individuals to change themselves into all kinds of beasts or animals. This belief is also found in the North, especially among the Temne ethnic groups who believe that this capacity is associated with witchcraft.

From the point of view of traditional legal principles and practice, the capacity of anyone to transform himself into an animal is not at issue. In Northern Sierra Leone, the act of transforming oneself into an animal was considered as much a crime as any homicidal act committed while in an animal form, and was punishable to the same extent, namely, by burning. "The Methodist Herald" (25/5/1893) reports that general native practice with regard to leopard men homicides was to impose the death penalty. In addition, the possessions of the convicted person were seized by the investigating court.

In contrast, Western legal principles do not involve a belief that death, resulting from an attack by a wild beast, is or could be the work of a human who has metamorphosed himself into a beast or animal. Rather, a number of other possibilities are considered, including the following that:

a) the death may be the result of an attack by a real animal;

b) the death may be an ordinary murder blamed falsely on an animal;

c) that the death may be the result of an attack by a man disguised as an animal.

The phenomenon with which we are concerned relates to the third possibility. However, it took a long time before the colonial regime recognized the reality of murders committed in the context of this possibility. Thereafter, ordinances were passed to handle the existence and address the murders committed by what became known as the Human Leopard, Alligator and Baboon Societies.

These ordinances, the first of which was passed in 1895, were usually limited in their operation to one year, and saw many and frequent revisions and modifications involving the progressive extension of the powers of colonial officials on the spot, with a view to ensuring a more effective assault on the phenomenon of group ritual homicide.

The observations made above are related to some important differences between traditional and modern legal principles and practices. Firstly, modern legal principles and practices recognize that, in view of the nature of the secret society and the obligation imposed on its members, membership of it may be involuntary; traditional law and practice does not. Secondly, while in traditional law and practice any indication of involvement in the affairs of the secret society was punishable by death, modern legal practice takes into consideration the extent of an individual's involvement in determining the severity of the punishment.

According to modern legal principles, whether or not an individual is found guilty depends on the availability of evidence against him, and the severity of the punishment or sanctions is a function of the degree or extent and even the nature of his involvement. In all cases, the establishment of the guilt of an accused person involves a definite procedure in a court of law, and requires the adducing of tangible, conclusive, adequate and satisfactory evidence. The onus of the proof of guilt is on the prosecution and the accused is allowed to defend himself and/or to be defended by a legal expert. In fact, in contemporary times, it is a requirement that persons accused of homicide be defended by legal counsel.

Traditional or "native" practices related to the detection, investigation and establishment of guilt were radically different.

An accused person was not given an opportunity to defend himself or be defended. His fate depended solely on the findings of specialists in crime investigation and detection known as Tongo Players, and on the decision (or whim) of the chiefs who hired their services. There was no appeal against the findings of the Tongo Players, the finality of their findings being based on the idea that their revelations made no mistake (Lindskog, 1954:97).

The methods and procedures used by the Tongo Players were deplored by colonial officials and newspapers, who described them as finding out crime by primitive ordeals and fetish; as "the ascription of guilt regardless of by what means the convictions had been pressed forth". The Colonial Office considered the form of punishment used as "a crime against humanity and civilization", and the Secretary of State for the Colonies suggested that the Colonial Government put pressure on those chiefs who were outside British jurisdiction, "to execute their cannibals in a more humane manner". Not surprisingly, in May 1895, the Colonial Government issued a proclamation

142

against Tongo Play, declaring it illegal and making participation in it subject to a penalty.

In spite of the negative view which the Colonial Government and the press held about Tongo Play, and although a proclamation was issued against it, both government and press demonstrated a degree of ambivalence in their reactions to it. This ambivalence was apparently related to the fact that, despite statements to the effect that Tongo Play had no noticeable impact on the practice of ritual homicide, the viewpoint that it had the impact of reducing the incidence of ritual murders was more dominant.

In contrast to the efficacy of Tongo Play, a strict adherence to modern legal principles and practices rendered the Colonial Government incapable of dealing effectively with the problem. As the "Sierra Leone Times" declared (October 1, 1892), ritual murder and cannibalism had not always been dealt with sternly by English courts in the colony and this, according to the paper, accounted for the fact that the people themselves called on the Tongo Players.

The crux of the problem with English legal principles and practices was the requirement that a conviction could be secured only on the basis of tangible, satisfactory, adequate and conclusive evidence. The legal procedure and technical rules of evidence were such that the possibility of obtaining such evidence was very remote considering the following factors: the murders were conducted with considerable secrecy, the maintenance of which was ensured by the oaths of secrecy sworn to by members, and the fear of reprisals on the part of non-members; and the fact that leading members of the community, including chiefs, were members of the societies. In this connection, the "Sierra Leone Times" (May 4, 1895) observed that the attitude of the leopard people towards the authorities was to keep everything secret since they knew that Western legal practices required evidence. It noted further that it had been in order to pierce the secrecy of their activities that the native authorities had found themselves forced to rely on the Tongo Men.

The Colonial Government sought to come to terms with this problem by making modifications in the ordinances calculated to facilitate the obtaining of evidence. These modifications were also made with a view to ensuring that where conclusive evidence was not available against accused persons, especially highly-placed ones, it would still be possible to impose some form of punishment. In virtually all such cases, the sanction was deportation to another colony or to some other part of the colony.

The end result of the modifications was that in a good many cases, the provisions ran counter to what some legal minds considered to be English legal principles and practices. Stridently critical voices were raised in connection with, among other matters, the extension of police powers of search, arrest and detention, with the procedures involved in establishing membership of an unlawful society which was said to be indicated by a peculiar mark on the buttocks, and the power of the Governor to deport for life, persons who had been acquitted by the courts if the judge so recommended.

In answer to these criticisms and objections, Governor Merewhether, during the debates on the 1912 ordinance observed that "We are dealing with an absolutely exceptional state of affairs", and that the things could not be made to stagnate because the district commissioners who had been vested with what were considered to be exceptional powers "have failed to observe some legal technicalities" (Sierra Leone, "Royal Gazette", 23/11/1912:696). Other government spokesmen responded by saying that legislation in Africa was something different from legislation in England.

In our view, an effective assault against the phenomenon called for a policy not of outright rejection of traditional popular beliefs, legal principles and practices, but for an imaginative blending or integration of the principles and practices of the two systems. To be efficacious, and do not operate in a socio-cultural vacuum, laws, legal procedures and practices have to take account of, and be related to, the socio-cultural realities of the people concerned. It was the recognition of this fact that led to the frequent revisions and modifications of the ordinances against group ritual homicide. However, these modifications did not take into account traditional legal procedures and practices and this, in our view, accounted for the marginal impact of English legal principles and practices on the phenomenon of group ritual homicide.

The inability or unwillingness to see any use or virtue in traditional legal principles, procedures and practices was based on the assumed moral superiority of everything Western to anything that could be found in the colonised societies. Besides, the assertion and maintenance of power of the coloniser required a rejection of the policy of integrating the principles and practices of the two systems.

It is true that, initially, the colonial regime involved the traditional rulers - the chiefs - in their attempts to tackle the problem of group ritual homicide through the inclusion of some of them as assessors in the circuit court, and that they were eventually excluded from participation in these courts when it came to light that they constituted part of the problem the court was supposed to address. However, it was also clear that not all of them were involved, and that their inclusion was half-hearted and somewhat in the nature of tokenism. If the colonial regime had had any respect or regard for traditional legal principles and practices, it would have pursued an explicit policy geared to an integration of the principles and practices of the two systems.

Such a policy would have operated along the lines suggested by one of the most vocal newspapers of the time, the "Sierra Leone Weekly News". In its edition of 10 August 1895, the paper suggested that persons with local experience and knowledge of local conditions, i.e., indigenous persons working in conjunction with colonial officials, should be given the responsibility of devising means of putting an end to group ritual homicide. In our opinion, this is the kind of approach which, if followed, would have led to the imaginative integration of the principles and practices of the two systems.

In our view, if the colonial authorities had accorded attention to traditional popular beliefs, legal principles and practices, it should have been possible to establish areas in which these principles and practices, appropriately modified, could have been utilized with the effect that the processes of investigation, detection and obtaining evidence could have been more efficient and effective.

That this is possible, is indicated by events related to one of the cases of ritual murder in recent times. In the Bureh Town Ritual case (Table 3, case 7), the body of the victim of the ritual homicide was found by the Ariogbo Society after a long and fruitless search by the police and the members of the Bureh Town Community. The Ariogbo Society specialises, among other things, in identifying persons engaged in witchcraft activities. After the body had been found, the Ariogbo "devil" proceeded to point out two members of the community as being involved in the murder of the 4-year old victim. These two members were handed over to the police who, obtained from them very useful information about the secret society that had carried out the ritual homicide, and its membership; 17 members of the secret society eventually being charged for various offences.

The example indicates that while in the post-colonial period, modern (Western) legal principles and practices play a dominant role in handling and solving cases of ritual homicide, there are points at which traditional principles and practices can be helpful in providing or facilitating the provision of information that throws plenty of light on the circumstances surrounding cases of ritual homicide, whether of the group or individual type.

The issue of the integration of traditional with modern principles, methods and practices is not restricted to the field of ritual homicide. Other areas that spring to mind are the integration of traditional and modern family laws, as well as traditional and modern medicine. The integrational possibilities can be appreciated and realised only to the extent that there is an acceptance of the idea that whatever their shortcomings, traditional systems have their own relevance and virtues even in modern times.

Map and Tables

Sierra Leone - Administrative Division

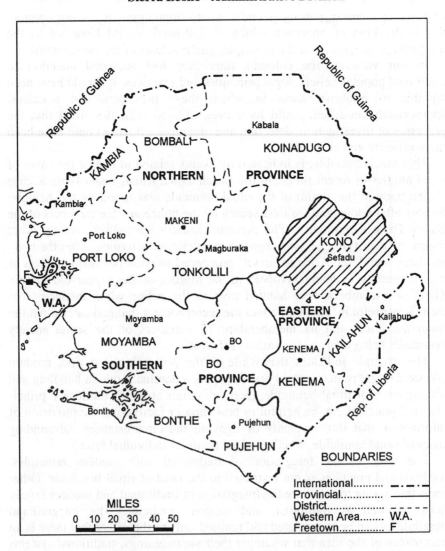

Table 1: Some data on Victims and Members of the Human Leopard Society

Title of case	Chiefdom	District	Characteristics of victims				Residential status		Membership of highly placed members of community
			Age of victim	Gender of victim	Victim's relationship to member(s) of society		Within community	Outside community	
Imperri Case 1913	Imperri	Northern Sherbro	20	Male	One member was sociological father and another biological uncle of victim		yes		Of 14 persons charged, 3 were village headmen and 2 village speakers
Kale Case 1913	Jong	Northern Sherbro	14	Male	Victim son of a member		yes		All 3 persons charged were village headmen
Kahati Case 1913	Jong	Northern Sherbro		Female described as full grown with 2 children			yes		3 persons finally charged. 2 highly placed - one a paramount chief and the other village head
1912	Symira	Koinadugu	3 victims aged 7, 12 and 12-13	All female	Information not available		yes		Witnesses deposed that murders were committed at instance of aspirants for paramount chieftaincy who must have been highly placed
1973	Imperri A police raid on a bush in which members met found human remains	Bonthe			Information not available		Information not available		Of 10 persons arrested, 3 were chiefdom councillors

Table 2: The Human Baboon Society in operation in post-colonial period

Newspaper Title and Date	District in which event took place	Province	Gender of Victim	Age of victim	Detail of events
Daily Mail 13 February 1975	Moyamba	Southern	Male	10	Boy attacked by Human Baboon. Was badly hurt. No indication as to whether he was captured or escaped.
Daily Mail 26 February 1985	Bo	Southern	Male	Adult	Human Baboons reported to be on the rampage, attacking people in different parts of the District. Two attacked a bailiff between Dodo and Gbaima Chiefdoms on his way to executing his duty of revising chiefdom voters list. Baboons seemed to recognize victim and one of them remarked: "He is our workmate; let him go". Victim admitted in Bo Government Hospital for treatment.
We Yone 27 February 1985	Bo	Southern	Male	Adult	Victim was bailiff on his way to execute a search warrant after an accused person failed to appear in Chiefdom Court. Was attacked by a group of Human Baboons, put up a fierce struggle during which he unmasked some of the men. Victim escaped with severe back and hand injuries inflicted by claws. 8 persons arrested and held in custody.
Daily Mail 19 January 1990	Bonthe	Southern	?	3 and a half months	Mother of baby was at her farm when Human Baboon attacked. She fought exhaustively with "Baboon" who made gashes on her back and attempted to grab the baby. During the struggle, woman was able to unmask the "Baboon" and recognized him: a one-eyed man from a nearby village. Baboon then took of. Woman and child admitted in hospital. Baboon inflicted deep cuts on baby's skull. One-eyed man and other villagers arrested and held in custody.

Table 3: Some data on the Secret Societies

	Case 1 Daily mail 3.9.1963	Case 2 Daily Mail 11.8.1964	Case 3 Daily Mail 11.8.1964	Case 4 Daily Mail 7.12.1964	Case 5 Daily Mail 30.5.1968	Case 6 Daily Mail 3.4.1969	Case 7 Daily Mail 5.4.1972	Case 8 We Yone January 1981
Name of society	Porro society	Hengor society	Hengor society	Name not provided but mention of Borfima indicates secret society	Name not provided but mention of Borfima indicates secret society	Name not provided but mention of native medicine indicates secret society	Fornakukuna Society. Inner circle of the Porro society	Porro
1) District 2) Chiefdom 3) Village	Moyamba Bagruwa Sembehun	Kailahun Kissy Teng Yendeh	Kailahun Kissy Teng Yendeh	Moyamba Makonde	Moyamba	Bonthe Kpanda - Kemoh Jahun	Waterloo judicial district Bureh Town village	Moyamba Bumpe
Province	Southern	Eastern	Eastern	Southern	Southern	Southern	Western area	Southern
Character of the victims — Gender	female	1 male 1 female	male	female	female	female	male	male
Age	adult	adult 1 year	adult	adult	12	adult	4	11
Resided in the community	yes	yes	yes	yes	yes	yes	yes	yes
Residential Status — Resided outside community		yes (foreigner)						
Victim's relationship to society members	no information available	N/A	N/A	N/A	N/A	N/A	One of accused grandfather of victim	N/A
Highly placed persons in community implicated	Paramount chief, section chief, speaker, pcs orderly, chiefdom police constables	Woman-town chief, court member & tribal authorit.	Woman-town chief, court member & tribal authorities.	N/A	N/A	N/A	Some village elders	N/A
Motives/ objectives of secret society	No information available (N/A)	N/A	Blooding the medicine of the God of Hengor Secret Society at Annual Festival	Parts used to make Borfima	Parts used to make Borfima	Parts used to make native medicine	Ritual homicide was part of annual custom of villagers. 4 previous victims. Ritual homicide also to enable all fishermen to catch more fish. Prayers offered before killing victim. Boy sacrificed to porro devil and ancestors of society	Apparently to make society medicine
Parts of body removed	N/A	N/A	Blood collected in red bowl. Heart, liver and some fat removed	Several internal organs removed	Several internal organs removed	Internal organs removed	Victim decapitated. Blood collected. Left hand, scrotum, penis lungs, trachea, heart, liver, spleen and intestines removed.	Boy found with several parts missing
How victim obtained	N/A	N/A	Victim went hunting and was attacked by one of the members; gun snatched, victim shot dead. Head cut off, abdomen split open.	N/A	N/A	Of accused, a woman prepared a medicine which she put in victim's mouth rendering him dumb and helpless. Victim then taken to a coffee plantation and killed	Apparently lured to the porro bush by grandfather. Each member required to bring a human being for annual sacrifice.	N/A
What was done to parts removed	N/A	N/A	Town chief cooked heart and liver. All ate. Fat sold in Liberia	Parts used to make medicine Borfima	Parts used to make medicine Borfima	Parts used to make native medicine found near body	Private parts used to make society medicine blood sold at Le 20.00 a tablespoonful. Blood of previous victims sold Le 720. All other parts cooked with mackerel in soup; all ate with rice Skull would have been used by society elders as drinking cup on festive occasions.	Apparently used to make medicine. Some parts perhaps consumed.
Other details	16 arrested. 2 for nolle prosequi, 1 died, 1 (PC) discharged, 12 sentenced to 10 years hard labour	14 arrested	18 arrested. Appeared before Magistrate and special session of Supreme Court with puisne judge assisted by 2 assessors	No indication of arrest	No indication of arrest	4 persons arrested including one woman	19 charged. By June 1973, 9 had died before passing of judgment	9 arrested. 4 freed after Magistrate Court. 5 for High Court. All 9 members of Porro Society

Table 4: Data on cases of individual ritual homicide

	Case 1	Case 2	Case 3	Case 4	Case 5	Case 6
Newspaper title & Date of first report	Daily mail 31.10.1963	Daily Mail 31.10.1963	Daily Mail 13.02.1975	We Yone 13.02.1981	We Yone 16.01.1984	Daily Mail 7-13.1.1990 We Yone 03.02.1990
1) District 2) Chiefdom 3) Village	Koinadugu Korofime	Port Loko Sanda Magbolonto Magbeli-Kadelay	Konoma Kanjatu	Kailahun, Jaluahun	Bonthe Nongowa Bullom Mogbanda	Moyamba Kagboro Katta
Province	Northern	Northern	Eastern	Eastern	Southern	Southern
Character of the victims: Gender	Male	Female (pregnant) Male	Female	Female	Male	Female
Age	5	Adult 2	11-12	5	2	13-14
Residential Status: Resided in the community / Resided outside community	yes	yes	yes	yes	yes	yes
Victim's relationship to beneficiaries or participants	Information not available. 4 accused.	1 of accused husband of woman and father of boy. 2 of accused brothers of woman and uncles of boy 4 accused.	One of 10 accused father of girl.	Two of 7 detainees, husband & wife were guardians of victim.	Victim grandson & grand nephew of 2 accused.	Accused who sold girl was her aunt.
Status of beneficiaries or participants or persons implicated	One of accused was section chief of Kabala	A minister of government, a paramount chief, a regent chief.	N/A	Chiefdom speaker (CS) Tribal Authority, (TA)	N/A	N/A
Motives/objects, purposes of ritual homicide	N/A	Minister wanted a young and developed woman with robust breasts and a fair complexion to be offered as sacrifice to win hearts of his constituents. Regent chief was assured by Minister he would convince President to make him substantive paramount chief. Prosecution concluded ritual homicide was for maintenance of power.	N/A	Confessional statement of one accused was that CS engaged services of jujuman/alphaman to help him in his bid to become PC. TA was promised of CS if CS became PC.	Grandfather confessed that herbalist has asked for human flesh to mix with other things to make juju in order to cure him of hernia.	To enable an aspirant to the position of Town Chief to attain it. Alphaman has indicated need for human flesh to mix with other ingredients.
How victim obtained	Boy was procured by one of 2 persons who actually carried out murder. Stuffed victim's mouth with something which made him helpless.	The two brothers, in collusion with husband, sold sister. Two brothers apparently sold nephew. Husband said he was not involved in transaction for sale of son.	N/A	Sold to main beneficiary by guardians.	Boy was taken to stream by two accused and portions of his flesh removed.	By sale of victim to beneficiary.
Parts of body removed	One of victim's hands, bowels. The two murderers washed themselves with the blood.	From the woman: both feet, both breasts, private parts, 3 teeth, heart, lungs. From the boy: heart, brains and blood	Body found lying in stream with private parts removed.	Throat cut. Skull, thumbs, last fingers, skin and nails of both hands and feet, private parts removed.	N/A	Parts removed to make a ritual mixture/charm for use by aspirant.
What parts were used for	N/A	To carry out a sacrifice apparently prescribed by an "alphaman".	N/A	To make charms to enable CS and TA to obtain more power	N/A	N/A
Other relevant details	The procurer of victim hit boy on neck, stepped on his back, and cut his throat with a matchet. He later committed suicide. Boy's body was discovered by police. 4 accused. 13 prosecution witnesses gave evidence at Magistrate Court. Case went on to Supreme Court. Section chief had nolle prosequi entered	Long trial. Charge of murder and dealing in person. Jury returned unanimous verdict of guilty against 4 accused of murder of woman. 3 guilty of dealing in person sentenced to death. Separate charges for murder of boy.	Girl left with 5 year old brother to fetch water at stream. Brother returned but not girl.	After a fruitless search for victim, sorcerer helped find her body in company of PC. CS and policemen. Sorcerer also helped to identify accused.	N/A	9 suspects were detained, 3 were women. Aunt did not receive promised payment of Le 6,000. Quarrel ensued leading to disclosure of murder.

Table 4 (continued)

	Case 7 New Shaft 07-13.1.1990	Case 8 Daily Mail 11.04.1990	Case 9 New Citizen 02.06.1990	Case 10 We Yone 23.06.1990	Case 11 Daily Mail 29.07.1976	Case 12 Daily Mail 12.01.1984	Case 13 Daily Mail 29.05.1987
Newspaper title & Date of first report							
1) District 2) Chiefdom 3) Village	Moyamba Bagruwa Mosangor	Konoma Lower Bambara Lowuna	Pujohun Sorogbema	Kenema Lower Bambara Kobowama	Moyamba Kori	Kailahun Yawai Bendu	Freetown (Kissy)
Province	Southern	Eastern	Southern	Eastern	Southern	Eastern	Western area
Character of the vict. — Gender	Female	Male	Female	Female	Female	Male	Male
Age	Adult	Adult	53	27	Adult	15	5
Residential Status — Resided in the community	yes	yes	yes	yes	yes	yes	yes
Resided outside community							
Victim's relationship to beneficiaries or participants	Information not available	Town Chief, one of 8 persons arrested, boss of intended victim.	One of 13 arrested husband of victim.	1st accused, who was main beneficiary, was uncle of victim. Wife of first accused, who was a suckling mother and one of accused, was step-aunt.	N/A	N/A	N/A
Status of beneficiaries or participants or persons implicated	N/A	Town Chief & prominent diamond miner	Prominent herbalist /Alphaman, aspirant to position of PC.	Well-known diamond miner in Kenema District. He was also an Alhaji, having gone on a pilgrimage to Mecca.	N/A	N/A	N/A
Motives/objects, purposes of ritual homicide	Mention of sorcerer indicates involvement of aspirant/s for some position.	Apparently to offer victim as sacrifice for more diamond finds. Victim had been forced by boss to carry food to miners in late evening, even though he had reported earlier in the day.	Aspirants for the position of PC had approached herbalist for help. Two of those who did not died mysteriously. Herbalist asked them to produce blood for use in the making of charms	Main beneficiary, well-known diamond miner. He was arranged with alphaman for the latter work charms for him so his pit would yield more diamonds. Alphaman said that human sacrifice was necessary. Alhaji agreed to provide victim.	To attain power and reinstatement to position of power. Alphaman told one of accused, an aspirant to the position of PC of Kori chiefdom, to provide human flesh with which to make charms. Also to ensure reinstatement of a relation to ministerial position.	Victim was presumably sacrificed to ensure attainment of power or wealth.	Presumably to enable some individual to achieve a personal objective.
How victim obtained	N/A	Victim was to have been captured on his way to deliver food to diamond diggers at night.	Was waylaid by husband and others, captured and murdered.	Victim lured to a farm owned by uncle who asked her to go there and assist his wives prepare meals for workers. Uncle followed after she left.	N/A	N/A	N/A
Parts of body removed	N/A	N/A	Two hands and private parts removed.	Hair, breast, vagina, blood.	Private parts, blood.	N/A	Private parts, some flesh from right arm.
What parts were used for	N/A	Parts would have been used to make ritual mixture/charm.	Parts used to make charm.	Victim killed as a sacrifice and parts removed to be used in making charms.	Private parts & blood used to make charms.	N/A	Presumably to make a charm.
Other relevant details	There is an allegation of political interference in this case, leading to the release of 5 of the detained persons. Sorcerer was a key prosecution witness.	Victim was set upon by diamond miners and others known to him. Was thrown to the ground, his hands and feet bound, and mouth gagged with cloth after some drugs had been forced into his mouth. Then tied to a tree. Rescued by passers-by.	Victim waylaid, captured, slaughtered like a sheep, private parts and blood obtained, and body concealed under a growth 50 yards off main road.	Uncle grabbed victim and presented her to alphaman who told him to do the killing himself. Alphaman handed him sharp double-edged knife and, after reading "Alfatiya", proceeded to slaughter her. Victim held down by 3 others. Since murder was carried out at night, step-aunt held up lamp to provide light.	9 persons arrested and charged.	Of 16 accused, 3 died in prison during preliminary investigation. One of the three confessed in his death bed that he had cut the throat of the victim after he had been paid Le 300.00 for doing so.-	Victim stayed with uncle, who reported disappearance to police. CID dismembered body being found in cesspit with mentioned parts cut off. 10 persons, all tenants in same house as boy, arrested.

References

Alldridge T. 1901. *A Transformed Colony - Sierra Leone*. London.
——. 1910. *The Sherbro and its Hinterland*. London.
Awolalu J.O. 1979. *Yoruba Beliefs and Sacrificial Rites*. London. Longman.
Beatty K.J. 1913. *An Account of the Trial of Persons on Charges Connected with Ritual Cannibalism before the Special Commission Court of Sierra Leone and Other Matters: The Human Leopard and Other Secret Societies*. Available in: Freetown, Sierra Leone Archives Repository, Fourah Bay College, University of Sierra Leone.
——. 1915. *Human Leopards*. London. H. Rees.
Berry R. 1912. *The Sierra Leone Cannibals*. Dublin. Proceedings of the Royal Irish Academy. 30C.
Burrows D. 1912. *The Human Leopard Society of Sierra Leone*. Journal of the African Society. 13.
Butt-Thompson F. 1929. *West African Secret Societies*. London.
Chalmers D. 1899. *Report of Her Majesty's Commissioner and Correspondence on the Subject of the Insurrection in the Sierra Leone Protectorate, 1898*, London. H.M.S.O.
Cole J. 1886. *A Revelation of the Secret Orders of West Africa*. Columbus (OH). Ohio State University Press.
Command (CO). 1950. *Despatches from Colonial Officials to the Governor and the Colonial Secretary; Despatches from the Governor to the Secretary of State for the Colonies, Colonial Office*. London. Available in: Freetown, Sierra Leone Archives Repository. Fourah Bay College, University of Sierra Leone.
Crooks J. 1903. *A History of the Colony of Sierra Leone*. Dublin.
Fama M. 1939. *The Human Leopard Society*. Sierra Leone Studies.
Fitzgerald M.H. 1912. *The Secret Societies of West Africa*. Journal of the African Institute. 29.
Ingham E. 1894. *Sierra Leone after a Hundred Years*. London. Seeley & Co. Ltd.
Johnson J. 1899. *Yoruba Heathenism*. Exeter.
Lindskog B. 1954. *African Leopard Men*. Uppsala. Almqvist & Wiksells Boktryckeri Ab.
Little K. 1951. *The Mendes of Sierra Leone*. London. Routledge & Keegan Paul.
Merewhether E.M. 1913. *Measures Adopted to Deal with Unlawful Societies in the Protectorate*. Available in: Freetown, Sierra Leone Archives Repository, Fourah Bay College, University of Sierra Leone.
Ringgren H. 1962. *Sacrifice in the Bible*. London. Lutteworth Press.
Sibley J., Westermann B. 1929. *Liberia Old and New*. London.
The Sierra Leone Royal Gazette. 1912. Issues available in: Freetown, Sierra Leone Archives Repository, Fourah Bay College, University of Sierra Leone.

THE CONTRIBUTION OF THE LABELLING THEORY TO THE UNDERSTANDING OF OPPRESSION, CONFLICT AND VIOLENCE IN SOUTH AFRICA

Apollo Rwomire[*]

1. Labelling Theory

The labelling theory is one of the most popular sociological theories of deviance today. In a nutshell, the theory claims that deviance may result from an individual being defined and labelled as deviant, and subsequently, behaving accordingly. In other words, the individual accepts society's label and acts as society expects him to act.

The labelling theory, also known as the interactionist perspective, is one of those processual theories which focuses on the social psychology of deviance. The principal contributors to the theory include Edwin Lemert (1951 and 1972), Herbert Blumer (1969), Alfred Schutz (1967), Howard Becker (1973), Erving Goffman (1963), Thomas Scheff (1984), Kai Erikson (1962), John Kitsuse (1962), Edwin Schur (1971), Ken Plummer (1979) and others.

According to labelling theorists, the carrying-out of the so-called deviant or criminal act is not as important as the official labelling of it. The theorists are not interested in explaining the characteristics of deviants but rather, how such definitions or labels as 'thief', 'homosexual', 'mental patient' or 'drug addict' are applied to individuals and what the consequences are for the individual's future behaviour. Thus, special attention is paid to the "consequences of interaction between the deviant and conventional society, particularly with representatives of society such as official agents of social control" (Clinard and Meier, 1989:93).

Becker (1973:9) contends that the deviant is someone to whom the label of deviant has been effectively applied, implying that labels are not uniformly applied to all individuals and groups. Many people engage in deviant or criminal behaviour, but since they are not discovered and labelled

---

* Senior Lecturer in Sociology, Department of Sociology, University of Swaziland, Kwaluseni, Swaziland.

as criminals, they do not regard themselves as criminals and are not regarded as such by society. To reinforce this point, Erikson notes: "some men who drink heavily are called alcoholics and others are not, some men who behave oddly are committed to hospitals and others are not ... and the difference between those who go their own way in peace is largely determined by the way in which the community filters out and codes the many details of behaviour which come to its attention" (1962:308).

More often than not, certain acts are defined as deviant or criminal simply because they are closely associated with the lower classes. For example, the smoking of marijuana is very often associated with the disadvantaged and therefore tends to be regarded as a crime, whereas the smoking of cigarettes, which also has harmful effects, is not seen as a crime, simply because it is associated with the middle-and upper-classes. Thus, the labelling process involves differing interests and values as far as both the labellers and the labelled are concerned.

The process of labelling is a political one and is of particular importance when we consider South Africa's racial structure. The people who label are those who have the power to do so, the power to make the labels stick and to institute sanctions when the need arises. More often than not, those who label are those who benefit from this practice. They are, for example, politicians, civil servants, judges, lawyers and the police force. As a political exercise, labelling is also an act of dominance.

Deviance becomes what it is because of the subjective definition of the dominant class. This means that the norms of conformity and non-conformity are the values of the powerful labellers of society. According to Karl Marx, this dominant class of labeller, who possess the means to produce are in a minority, that is, the capitalists or bourgeoisie. Their values are the values of an affluent society and are reflected in the economic, cultural and political super-structure, which nourishes and consolidates their ideology.

According to scholars of Karl Marx, the prevailing ideas in any society serve the ruling or dominant class. They argue that, "laws are not an expression of value consensus but a reflection of ruling class ideology. They serve to legitimize the use of ruling class power. Thus, a general commitment to laws by members of society as a whole, is an aspect of false class consciousness since, in practice, laws benefit only a ruling minority" (Haralambos and Heald, 1981:442). This assertion is very much applicable to South Africa, a class-ridden society, in which social stratification has been established by racial and ethnic differences. The numerous labels used by the apartheid state are fundamentally designed to further the socio-economic interests of the dominant class, composed largely of whites.

One of the major consequences of labelling is to transform a simple action of "primary" deviance, through an "amplifying" process into an action of "secondary" deviance. To illustrate this point, a hungry boy who attempts to steal, if caught, may be called a thief or crook, resulting in his rejection by peers, neighbours and members of his family. He may then be taken to court, prosecuted and sent to a juvenile prison, thus being officially labelled a delinquent or criminal and upon his release, may be refused a place in his school. As a result, he may resort to stealing again, including burglary and armed robbery. He may then eventually join a sub-cultural group of thieves, with whom he shares a similar label and who provide him with understanding, a sense of belonging and much-needed support. According to Becker, those who have been labelled "deviant" have one characteristic in common: " ... they share the label and experience of being labelled outsiders" (Rubington and Weinberg, 1971:188).

By labelling people, we declare them to be outsiders, and as such, a process of stigmatization is set in motion. The fact that the labelled are termed and treated as outsiders and outcasts is illustrated by the presence of prisons, mental hospitals, remand centres, and reformatories. When passing a maximum security prison in any country, it is easy for a passer-by to see the barbed wire fence and high walls, and imagine with horror "the other world," which this symbolizes. Many who languish behind those prison walls, do so not because of a morally outrageous act against the nation as a whole, but for some deed which threatened the political and economic interests of a minority and propertied class.

The relevance of labelling in explaining deviance, crime and other social problems, such as racism, lies in the several advantages that it has over other theories. By treating these problems as the products of society, rather than the labelled individuals, as in the case of many theories, labelling theorists instead, draw our attention to those who label, why they label and the conditions under which they do so, and the eventual consequences. By ignoring the hereditary, biological, individualistic, and even culturalistic attributes of deviants, and emphasising instead the societal determinants of deviance, the theorists focus on the social structure and the concomitant conditions which provoke labels. Hence, as ways of resolving conflict and deviance, as will be noted later, they recommend a change in the definition and eliminating labelling profits.

2. The origins and nature of Labelling in South Africa

In identifying who labels who in South Africa, it is necessary to outline the history and character of the country's racial structure upon which conflict and violence have been based. Needless to say, the country in question has for decades been divided along the lines of the colour of the skin; racism has become a way of life. According to Beteille, "of all contemporary multi-racial societies, South Africa is the most complex and rigidly stratified on the basis of race ... and the one which is most ridden with conflict and internal contradictions" (1969:32). Although South Africa is a modern society, it still embraces a caste system based upon a long catalogue of discriminatory laws, which separate five million whites from thirty million blacks, ensuring that the former own most of the land, run the government and control the economy. But how did this situation come about?

In 1652, Jan Van Riebeeck and a group of Dutch settlers arrived at the Cape of Good Hope. Their first African contacts were with the Khoikhoi and the San (the "Hottentots" and "Bushmen') of the Cape Peninsula, who were dispossessed of their land and livestock through the superior arms of the invaders. They were either killed, forced into farm labour or driven away, and years later, slaves were brought from West Africa and East India.

Through invasion and territorial expansion, the Boers penetrated at the cost of much bloodshed as the Africans defended their property. In 1806, the British seized the Cape from the Dutch and an escalation of terror, violence and brutality between blacks and whites continued until the beginning of the twentieth century. This violence was characterized by a campaign of terror launched by a well-equipped white minority group of people against the poorly-armed black majority, a situation that continues until today.

In the latter half of the nineteenth century, vast mineral deposits, such as gold, diamonds and iron ore, were discovered. Apart from use on white-owned farms, vast sums of money and vast labour forces became necessary for mining. Like land, the newly-discovered mineral wealth came to be owned exclusively by the colonialists and settlers, who, through slavery, forced labour and a variety of policies and actions effectively controlled black labour.

By 1906, what is now known as South Africa, comprised four territories: Natal and the Cape under the British and the Orange Free State and the Transvaal under the Voortrekkers. Following the Anglo-Boer War (1899-1902), British rule was established in all four territories until 1910, when the Union of South Africa was established. The Constitution of the Union established the status quo as far as white superiority and black inferiority was concerned. Africans were moved into reserves after the enactment of the 1913 Land Act. The year 1948 ushered in the Nationalist Party which gave the institutional and legal articulation to racism through its policy of "apartheid" (separatedness), resulting in the pervasive domination and exploitation of the black people. Blacks were thus effectively seen as outsiders and outcasts. "The white sees a member of that race (the black race) not as an individual personality like himself, but as a representative of an alien race, whose most striking characteristics are an inferiority in intelligence and knowledge, inferiority in standard of living and occupation, a tendency towards violent and criminal practices, a behaviour which is childish and often ridiculous, in short, the opposite of all those qualities which form the image which the white has in mind when he thinks of his own race" (MacCrone, 1978:78).

Based upon this ethnocentric and paranoid conception of the black man, South Africa's rulers have subjected the blacks to all kinds of oppression and indignities, including degrading labels.

The 1950 Population Registration Act classified the South African population into three racial and colour groups: white, coloured and black. Later, a separate classification of 'Asian' was added. Although the whites constitute less than 20% of the population, they control 87% of the land, while the blacks, who comprise roughly 80% of the population, are squeezed into the remaining 13% Thus, the whites have a monopoly over both wealth and power in the Republic of South Africa. In such a situation, it is easy to realize that it is the whites who do the labelling. They are, therefore, the members of the dominant class who impose moral standards through a political and economically exploitative process. Apartheid is the consequence of the inferiority associated with the black man from the day he was conquered by the white man and his land and property seized. It grew out of violence and is, until today, maintained by violence. The labelling theory is useful because in looking at those who label, we also discover the history of racism and discrimination and the social relationships between the labeller and the labellees.

3. The rationale and conditions of Labelling

In analysing the answers he received from twenty-five students, male and female, who were asked to describe and give reasons for their attitude towards the black community, MacCrone (1978) came up with several factors which condition white attitudes towards blacks.

Firstly, he identifies historical factors such as those mentioned previously in this paper. They include stories of past contacts between blacks and whites as they have been transmitted from generation to generation. The interpretation of these contacts in the textbooks and through popular tradition stresses massacres by blood-thirsty blacks of innocent white men, women and children.

Secondly, MacCrone notes that the present South African economic, political and social structure invariably tends to place the stigma of inferiority on the black man. From early childhood, the white man is used to treating his black compatriot as such; the black man is no more than a servant of the white man, all menial and irksome tasks are reserved for him The government, parliament, police, judiciary and the army convince him and encourage him to treat the black man thus.

Thirdly, MacCrone argues that the black man is always the villain of the peace in real life, in the cinema or on the stage. To the white child, he is the wicked man who haunts his imagination for ever.

Fourthly, is a "pseudo-scientific" factor, which regards the native as still a child in mentality, intellectually backward and lacking a sense of responsibility.

Fifthly, there are factors which build barriers around each racial group, prohibiting intimate social intercourse and understanding between blacks and whites. A good example of these are the racial laws which regulate every aspect of black-white relationships.

Apart from these, he also identified those factors which he said reflected themselves unconsciously and spontaneously in white attitudes towards blacks. He observed that the colour black in every race is associated with ill-luck, danger, witchcraft, evil and sin. Moreover, popular tradition equates the black man with a savage, who is free of the restrictions and inhibitions which are found in the life of the civilized white. Of the black man's savage qualities, the most important are an amazing sexual attraction and excessive lust.

The black man's attempt to mimic, emulate or copy the white man's lifestyle provides justification and credibility for white-imposed labels to be placed on him. It is common among Africans, for instance, to put on three-piece suits, regardless of weather conditions, speak the white man's language with a non-distorted accent, even to those who do not understand it. Such people are sometimes referred to as 'mimic-people' or 'white-blackmen'.

MacCrone's study is very useful in portraying the typical circumstances under which labelling takes place in South Africa, and hence, why whites label blacks. Nonetheless, it does not account for the economic determinants of labelling, or the benefits that the white man derives from labelling the black man.

With respect to South Africa, it is clear that the need to label and restrict the freedom of the black man has always been necessitated by the need to exploit him and force him into the mines, the white-run farms and the Reserves. To accept the black man as an equal, and therefore, to 'de-label' him, would require an equitable distribution of resources.

3.1   The consequences of Labelling

As noted earlier, the labelling perspective maintains that labelling leads to secondary and increased deviance and crime. This is particularly true in the case of South Africa. This country is unique in the world today, in that it is the only one with institutionalized racism and accepted oppression, blessed and supported by political, religious, judicial, military and cultural institutions. It is interesting to note, therefore, in view of the labelling explanation, that South Africa also has the highest crime rate in the world.

According to a survey conducted by the Institute of Criminology at the University of Durban in 1982, two million offences were reported annually, the prison population was twice that of the United States and six times more than the United Kingdom.

It is common knowledge that the criminal population in the Republic of South Africa is dominated almost exclusively by black prisoners. The acceptance by whites that blacks are the criminals is reflected in attitudes and actions at both the private/domestic level and the public/state level, where security precautions are directed totally towards blacks. According to MacCrone, "If we wish to protect our houses against burglary, it is against the black man that our precautions are almost invariably taken ... though we see black recruits being marched through the streets the white convicts (of whom there must be some) are conspicuous by their absence. The white individual never sees a white convict" (1978:77).

The fact that most of the so-called criminals are blacks is mainly explained by the economic condition of the latter. In a situation of excessive poverty and plenty, such as exists in South Africa, a basic contradiction emerges which generates conflict between the rich and the poor. In their legitimate struggle to get their fair share of the cake, the poor are labelled "terrorists", "savages" and "Kaffirs". Another explanation is that the whole political machinery discriminates against blacks. Hence, blacks are arrested for the slightest offence, whilst whites have, for instance, been left un-prosecuted after committing the murder of blacks on the grounds of self-defence.

3.2   The policy question

At least two approaches could be adopted to resolve racial conflict and violence in South Africa. The first approach, according to the labelling theorists, would be to change the negative definitions. This implies either getting rid of the labels completely or substituting them with more acceptable ones. It also means becoming more tolerant of other people's traditions, values and actions.

To a considerable extent, apartheid is built on definitions and labels. The Population Registration Act imposed the racial labels, the Group Areas Act imposed the residential labels, the Reservation of Separate Amenities Act defined racial boundaries in the use of public facilities, the Prohibition of Mixed Marriages Act limited sexual relations across racial boundaries, and the labelling theorists are therefore realistic in their advocacy of a change in definitions as a way of minimizing the adverse consequences of labelling. In the case of South Africa, this would mean changing all those definitions which portray blacks as "inferior", "barbaric", "stupid", "criminal", "communists" and so on. Such an approach is advocated by those who are presently opposed to apartheid and committed to the creation of a united and peaceful South Africa.

The second approach revolves around the elimination of the labelling profits. Removing the profits made out of labelling means eliminating the gains which make it necessary to create and apply negative labels. The elimination of labelling profits means not only scrapping the oppressive laws and erasing racial labels from the statutes, but also ensuring that whites forego the economic, political and security benefits they currently enjoy. This requires that blacks, coloureds and Asians must have their fair share of resources, facilities and services. This is what the oppressed masses of South Africa are fighting for, and this is exactly what the apartheid system and related labels deny them. In the past two years, the South African Government has scrapped most of the apartheid laws. Nevertheless, legislative reform has not been followed by any meaningful efforts to restructure political and economic power.

4. Labelling Theory: an evaluation

The labelling theory has greatly contributed to our understanding of how deviance, including crime, can be socially generated and the extent to which labelling may affect the labellee's self-concept and future behaviour. The theory is most relevant in understanding the nature and consequences of racism in South Africa. Thanks to the labelling theorists, we are able to examine the history of the present social structure, and the circumstances under which it developed and we can clearly see who labels who and why in the apartheid state. A persistent theme throughout the paper concerns the conflict and violence that characterizes the past and present existence of

South Africa. Instead of seeking explanations of this violence in genetic and cultural terms, our attention is focused on the social structure as well as the economic and political forces in which it breeds. Notwithstanding the strengths of the labelling theory, it has certain shortcomings, as noted below.

Although the theory sheds considerable light on the process through which primary deviation degenerates into secondary deviation, it is silent on why certain people commit deviant or criminal acts, at least initially. Thus, "labelling theorists focus on the way that the rules are socially constructed and on the meaning given to behaviour that breaks those rules, rather than on background characteristics or social arrangements that are conducive to rule-breaking behaviour" (Conklin, 1984:115). In other words, the theory does not pay sufficient attention to the social structure which generates social inequality, stratification and conflict.

Secondly, according to the labelling theorists, labelling is ultimately a political process; but why do people label others at all? Politics is a process of deciding who gets what, when, how and where. As a resource allocation process, politics are an economic necessity. Hence, labelling in the final analysis is also an economic process. This South African case study proves this. The labelling theory does not go this far, and hence its economic implications had to be stretched further in order to suit the South African case.

Thirdly, the labelling theorists believe that the problems of labelling could be alleviated by changing the definitions and eliminating the labelling profits. But they do not indicate who should do this - the labellers, through reformed "class suicide" or the labelled through violent revolution. We see here, therefore, the moderate and conservative nature of the "labellists". The labelling theory would appear to contrast with Marxist explanations of domination and economic exploitation and the recommended proletarian revolution that is supposed to end it.

Fourthly, the labelling theory does not cater adequately for undisclosed and unlabelled deviance. There are two categories of unlabelled deviants; those who commit crimes, but are not labelled (for example, whites who murder blacks) and those who commit crimes but are not discovered (for example, a black or white thief who successfully disappears with his loot).

Finally, by treating deviance and crime exclusively in terms of acts that violate established rules or laws, the theory in question seems to ignore those acts which may not be a violation of any such rule of law, but are nevertheless, morally outrageous and criminal. For instance, apartheid or institutionalized racism is widely seen by virtually all modern societies as abhorrent and criminal, with the exception of South Africa. From the labelling perspective, we can only treat as criminal, those acts which violate apartheid laws. The oppression and bloody massacres perpetrated by the South African State against blacks, such as the atrocities of Sharpeville (1960), Soweto (1976) and Boipatong (1992) are not viewed as crimes because they do not constitute a violation of any rule or law of the State.

References

Becker H.S. 1973. *Outsiders: Studies in the Sociology of Deviance.* New York. Free Press.

Beteille A. 1969. *Social Inequality.* London. Penguin Books Limited.

Blumer H. 1969. *Symbolic Interactionism.* Englewood Cliffs (NY). Prentice-Hall.

Clinard M.B., Meier R.F. 1989. *Sociology of Deviant Behaviour.* New York. Holt, Rinehart and Winston Inc.

Conklin J. 1984. *Sociology: An Introduction.* New York. Macmillan and Company.

Erikson K.T. 1962. *Notes on the Sociology of Deviance.* Social Problems. 9, pp.307-314.

Garfinkel H. 1967. *Studies in Ethnomethodology.* Englewood Cliffs (NY). Prentice-Hall.

Goffman E. 1963. *Asylums.* New York. Doubleday/Anchor.

Haralambos M., Heald R. 1981. *Sociology: Themes and Perspectives.* London. University Tutorial Press.

International Defence and Aid for South Africa in Co-operation with the United Nations Centre Against Apartheid. 1983. *Apartheid: The Facts.*

Kitsuse J.I. 1962. *Societal Reaction to Deviant Behaviour: Problems of Theory and Method.* Social Problems. 9, pp.247-256.

Lemert E.M. 1951. *Social Psychology.* New York. McGraw-Hill.

---- . 1972. *Human Deviance, Social Problems and Social Control.* Englewood Cliffs (NY). Prentice-Hall.

Levy S.C. 1981. *Labelling: The Social Worker's Responsibility.* Social Casework. 62: 6.

McCaghy C.H. 1976. *Deviant Behaviour.* New York. Macmillan and Company.

MacCrone I.D. 1978. *Psychological Factors Affecting the Attitude of White to Black in South Africa.* In: Lever H. "Readings in South African Society". Cape Town. Jonathan Ball.

Magubane B. 1979. *The Political Economy of Race and Class in South Africa.* New York. Monthly Review Press.

Plummer K. 1979. *Misunderstanding Labelling Perspectives.* In: Downes D., Rock P. (Eds.). "Deviant Interpretations". Oxford. Martin Robertson, pp.85-121.

Quinney R. 1979. *Criminology: Analysis and Critique of Crime in America.* Boston. Little Brown.

Reid T.S. 1979. *Crime and Criminology.* New York. Holt, Rinehart and Winston.

Rubington E., Weiberg. 1971. *Deviance: The Interactionist Perspective.* New York. Macmillan.

Scheff T.J. 1984. *Being Mentally Ill.* Chicago. Aldine.

Schur E.M. 1971. *Labelling Deviant Behaviour.* New York. Harper and Row.

Schutz A. 1967. *The Phenomenology of the Social World.* Evanston (IL). Northwestern University Press.

CHANGEMENTS SOCIOCULTURELS ET MARGINALISATION DES ENFANTS ET DES JEUNES EN AFRIQUE SUBSAHARIENNE

Manga Bekombo*

1. Introduction

Le phénomène du changement socioculturel, pris comme objet spécifique de la réflexion sociologique, diffère du processus "normal" de l'évolution de la société en ce sens que le premier implique une discontinuité particulièrement sensible du cours de l'histoire, alors que le second n'est que l'expression de l'adaptation progressive des idées et des pratiques aux innovations diverses, sans que, pour autant, les valeurs, et les normes fondatrices de la civilisation considérée soient nécessairement et fondamentalement remises en question. Dans le premier cas, le problème de la perpétuation des groupes se pose de deux manières, théoriquement contradictoires, puisqu'il est question, tout à la fois, de sauvegarder leur identité et leur capacité d'agir, et de céder à une réelle dépersonnalisation se donnant comme préalable à leur nécessaire métamorphose. Ces processus de transformation s'inscrivent dans l'histoire; ils requièrent ainsi des durées extrêmement longues au cours desquelles les sociétés concernées sont appelées à surmonter des conflits et des crises de nature et d'intensité fort variables, selon les secteurs et les niveaux de la personnalité individuelle, de la vie sociale et des systèmes idéologiques et institutionnels qui sous-tendent celle-ci. Les phénomènes d'acculturation et de reconstruction sociale revêtent ainsi un caractère éminemment global et nécessitent une approche pluridisciplinaire.

On observe, par ailleurs, que l'époque contemporaine, fortement marquée par la culture technologique, est largement dominée et gérée par les sociétés industrialisées, hautement développées, lesquelles lui assignent un ordre qui est le leur et qui s'impose alors avec plus ou moins de violence à l'ensemble des autres sociétés; celles-ci apparaissant ainsi comme de grands groupes de consommateurs avides des produits de cette culture technologique. En d'autres termes, ces sociétés en cours de mutation culturelle se trouvent, de

---

* Chargé de recherches au CNRS, Laboratoire d'Ethonologie et de Sociologie comparative, Université de Paris X, Nanterre, France.

surcroît, dans l'impossibilité matérielle d'élaborer, par elles-mêmes, leur propre projet de civilisation. L'un des effets majeurs de cette situation est la soudaine vacuité de l'héritage culturel local constitué par les Anciens et la caducité aussi rapide du savoir détenu par les aînés: nous assistons bien, dans un tel contexte, à un véritable phénomène d'anémie sociale, la transmission intergénérationnelle des savoirs et des connaissances n'étant plus assurée, comme il paraît naturel, de la génération des parents vers celle des enfants. Davantage encore, on observe une sorte de distorsion entre la génération fondée sur l'âge et ce que nous appellerions la "génération socio-historique": si la première, à fondement biologique, reste immuable, la seconde, en revanche, doit être repensée et redéfinie; en effet, dans ces sociétés soumises aux transformations, le flux des innovations est si abondant et si rapide que parents et enfants deviennent les témoins des mêmes évènements et doivent, les uns comme les autres, satisfaire les mêmes besoins d'adaptation. Dans de telles circonstances, les jeunes qui sont davantage disponibles et plus fortement sollicités, se révèlent également plus aptes à capter et à assimiler les innovations: d'où le phénomène, en apparence paradoxal, qui consisterait à faire de ces jeunes les "éducateurs" de leurs parents.

C'est dans le cadre de cette conjonction de données que les sociétés africaines se sont trouvées intégrées dans le mouvement de "modernisation" qui suppose de manière impérative leur restructuration à partir de critères relativement nouveaux, ainsi que la conversion des mentalités que cela implique et un réexamen, voire une redéfinition, des objectifs sous-jacents aux initiatives de tous genres prises tant au niveau individuel qu'au plan collectif. A cet égard, l'ensemble des sociétés africaines se donne aujourd'hui comme un vaste domaine d'observation sociologique qui permettrait d'appréhender avec plus d'aisance autant les mécanismes de transformations économiques et politiques (qui retiennent plus généralement l'attention) que ceux donnant lieu à de nouveaux types de différenciation sociale et à d'autres modes de répartition des rôles et des statuts sociaux. Ces transformations sont évidemment davantage perceptibles dans les milieux urbains que dans les zones à caractère rural bien que ces dernières représentent encore, en moyenne, 75% de l'espace territorial et 80% du volume des activités de production.

Les catégories sociales qui préoccupent le plus sont, d'une part, celle des vieillards (personnes âgées de plus de 60 ans) dont le nombre croît de manière sensible et, d'autre part, celle des enfants et des jeunes (0 à 15 et 15 à 20 ans), laquelle est constitutive de près de 40% de la population totale dans différents pays de la région subsaharienne. La réduction du taux de mortalité infantile et l'augmentation de l'espérance de vie ainsi constatées sont dues, principalement, à la mise en oeuvre généralisée des mesures d'hygiène et à l'expansion des techniques médicales modernes. Or cette heureuse évolution ne va pas sans poser de graves problèmes socio-économiques auxquels les pays africains vont être confrontés au fil des décennies à venir, d'une part, du fait même du développement de ces deux catégories de consommateurs, et d'autre part, compte tenu de la stabilité du taux de productivité plutôt relativement faible, assurée par une population active qui ne représente environ que 20% de la population totale (Shuman, 1984; Amos et Harrel, 1981:XIII-XXI).[1] Il convient cependant de regarder ces estimations avec prudence; en effet, si les enfants de moins de 15 ans comptent pour près de 30% de la population globale dans différents pays (Charmes, 1985), on observe, en même temps que nombre d'entre-eux ont, depuis longtemps, abandonné l'école pour entrer dans le monde du travail.[2]

La proportion de ces "jeunes au travail" est mal définie: elle est toutefois estimée à 50% des membres de cette tranche d'âge, composée d'enfants qui n'ont jamais été scolarisés et de ceux ayant précocément interrompu leur scolarité pour des raisons essentiellement économiques, aux deux niveaux du primaire et du secondaire (Bekombo et Al., 1978).

C'est de ces enfants-là qu'il va être question ici. Ils se trouvent, pour la plupart, concentrés dans les grandes villes, à Kinshasa et à Dakar, à Abidjan et à Brazzaville, à Accra et à Lagos, à Douala, à Yaounde, à Libreville et à Naïrobi. Evoluant dès lors entre la maison familiale et les portes de l'école, ils se retrouvent dans cet espace nu, ouvert à tous les publics, que l'on appelle la rue, y rejoignant alors, comme par le fait d'un recrutement spontané, des aînés déjà chomeurs ou en quête d'un quelconque moyen de subsistance. D'ores et déjà, ces enfants portent une identité: on les appelle *les enfants de la rue*; ils sont également porteurs d'un statut, celui "d'encombrements humains"; communément perçus comme des délinquants en herbe, leur destin social semble déjà bien défini autant par les autorités publiques que par la communauté sociale dans son ensemble. De fait, ils constituent l'une des principales cibles des agents de l'ordre, parce qu'ils expriment, par ailleurs, l'un des défis les plus manifestes opposé aux politiques sociales des différents Etats africains.[3]

2. Caractéristiques et fonctions de la ville africaine

Du point de vue historique, la ville africaine actuelle est une création du colonisateur. Elle a constitué son espace de vie et elle s'offre encore aujourd'hui comme lieu de concentration, de reproduction ou d'adaptation des projets et des techniques en général issus des pays développés et comme centre de diffusion des idées nouvelles et des comportements qui leur sont associés. L'acquisition de ces multiples objets est le signe indiscutable de la volonté de modernisation. D'un point de vue purement fonctionnel, la ville est aussi donnée comme lieu du confort et de l'abondance, ce qui lui confère une force d'attraction à laquelle ne résiste aucune catégorie d'âge et face à laquelle cèdent d'autant plus facilement les enfants et les jeunes ayant vécu jusque-là en milieu rural.

Par ailleurs, la ville africaine concentre, en son sein, l'ensemble des institutions du pouvoir. Elle est, en effet, le siège de l'autorité publique suprême et de l'administration centrale, en cela, elle est le centre des décisions qui déterminent le destin social, collectif et individuel: il faut résider à la ville pour être perçu, éventuellement apprécié en raison de ses capacités et, finalement, pour être introduit dans un quelconque circuit donnant accès aux cadres de la société intégrée. Dans cette perspective, la ville africaine assure le contrôle de deux principales filières dont le parcours permet inéluctablement l'accession à la modernité. L'un des lieux de passage proposés aux jeunes migrants est alors l'école, laquelle est conçue pour procurer différents niveaux de connaissance et permettre de formuler des aspirations à des emplois: cette fonction essentielle de la ville explique assez largement l'importance de la proportion d'enfants et de jeunes constitutive de sa population globale (Franqueville, 1985).[4]

En dépit de ses attributs et de l'importance des fonctions qu'elle assure, cette ville africaine (nous visons ici les capitales économiques ou politiques) affiche davantage les caractéristiques d'un espace urbanisé qu'elle n'assure véritablement la fonction de complément économique de la campagne. Certes, elle connaît un taux de croissance relativement élevé (3 à 5%) et accueille en général plus du tiers de la population totale des pays considérés. Or, au sein de cette population, figure une importante proportion d'habitants de fraîche date, venus résider tout naturellement à proximité de leurs "frères de village". Si bien que la ville se présente moins comme une cité capable de produire et d'inspirer une mentalité unitaire typique que comme un ensemble d'îlots résidentiels, où domine une activité à caractère commercial ou artisanal, dispersés dans un espace en extension régulière et encore sensiblement marqués par le mode de vie rural. A cet égard, on remarquera que la plupart des nouveaux quartiers dont elle se compose sont généralement désignés par le nom de l'ethnie numériquement dominante. A la périphérie de ces îlots abritant des groupes homogènes constitués principalement sur une base ethnique, s'installent d'autres groupes, ethniquement hétérogènes ceux-là, composés de migrants récemment arrivés ou dont les revenus ne permettent pas une installation à l'intérieur même de la ville. Ces groupes ne cessent de grossir, recrutant continuellement de nouveaux membres parmi ceux - notamment les enfants et les jeunes - qui quittent quotidiennement le village. Cette zone, dite suburbaine est caractéristique des capitales africaines: elle constitue, en effet, la première étape en vue de l'intégration, le lieu "d'atterrissage" de ceux qui viennent de l'intérieur du pays (les ports maritimes et aériens étant réservés aux étrangers qui débarquent). Cependant cette zone abrite, en même temps, des groupes d'autochtones économiquement faibles et exclus des échanges s'opérant dans le cadre de la cité moderne, en raison du manque d'éducation scolaire ou de leur inadaptation au genre et au rythme de la vie moderne. Elle est, en même temps, le lieu d'apprentissage des stratégies conduisant à concilier efficacement l'expérience ancestrale acquise auprès de la génération des ascendants et le savoir-faire désormais nécessaire, permettant de satisfaire les contraintes inhérentes à la vie citadine. C'est là où s'effectue la recomposition des rapports sociaux interindividuels et intergénérationnels; c'est là aussi que sont redéfinis les rôles associés aux catégories d'âge et de sexe, lesquels ont pour finalités principales la survie des groupes familiaux, l'intégration progressive de ceux-ci dans la société urbaine et la promotion sociale des individus qui les composent.

L'extrême diversité de cette population se manifeste, en effet, du point de vue de l'origine ethnique; mais le facteur distinctif pertinent des groupes reste la condition socio-économique dont l'évolution conditionne la mobilité sociale des individus. La structure sociale globale revêt ainsi une extrême complexité dans la mesure même où les catégories en présence se constituent en fonction de critères et de normes inspirés tout à la fois par la modernité et la tradition locale. Or, la possibilité ainsi donnée aux individus et aux groupes placés dans des situations identiques de recourir à l'un ou à l'autre de ces deux cadres de référence incite à des comportements différenciés en fonction de l'efficacité, c'est-à-dire à la satisfaction du besoin ressenti. En sorte que l'enjeu n'est plus guère la conformité aux règles - condition première de l'ordre social - mais, plutôt la réalisation du gain par tous moyens. Dans cette société urbaine à double niveau de référence culturelle, les statuts conférés à un même individu peuvent être contradictoires - cette contradiction n'étant autre que l'expression d'un antagonisme plus global affectant les rapports entre l'univers des valeurs traditionnelles et l'ensemble des valeurs véhiculées par le processus de modernisation.[5]

Ce contexte social n'est sans doute pas particulier à l'Afrique: il est évoqué à propos de la plupart des "pays en développement" et, notamment, ceux de l'Amérique latine; cependant il fait l'objet d'analyses multiples, leur variété étant naturellement liée à la spécificité historique des aires culturelles considérées. Concernant les sociétés africaines, la problématique la plus pertinente qui se donne dans ce contexte comme objet de réflexion est sans doute le processus d'émergence de la singularité du sujet, c'est-à-dire, l'avènement de *l'individu* là où l'appartenance lignagère s'imposait jusque-là comme principal enjeu et comme unique mode de production et d'affirmation de l'identité de chacun et de tous. La dynamique socioculturelle à l'oeuvre ici est génératrice, avant tout, de nombreux déséquilibres qui se manifestent par des phénomènes secondaires de marginalisation dont les premières victimes se recrutent en majorité dans les classes d'enfants et de jeunes.

3. Le phénomène de la rue

La rue est un des éléments de l'espace urbain dont la fonction évolue parallèlement à celle de la ville; son importance croît donc proportionnellement au développement du centre urbain. En Afrique comme ailleurs, elle ne se définit pas seulement comme élément d'un réseau de circulation des personnes et des véhicules; l'histoire sociale des sociétés européennes nous apprend qu'elle est aussi un lieu d'expression collective. Et même si la rue continue à se donner principalement comme un espace "libre" qui fait la jonction entre un point de départ et un lieu de destination, elle se définit de plus en plus aujourd'hui comme "l'espace de liberté" qui échappe donc à l'appropriation individuelle et qui, du moins en principe, réduit les inégalités statutaires entre les individus-usagers. La rue doit être appréhendée, non pas uniquement comme un lieu de passage où les personnes se croisent, une *voie* qui, par exemple, mène de la maison familiale au lieu de travail ou à l'école: elle compte parmi les autres espaces spécifiques de vie (espace familial, par exemple), et l'un des traits de sa spécificité est qu'elle fait l'objet de lois et règlements particuliers, qui sont, soit décrétés par les pouvoirs publics, comme ils peuvent être générés par sa dynamique propre. De ce point de vue, on peut d'ailleurs observer qu'elle est, elle aussi, le lieu d'une contradiction fondamentale en tant qu'elle est, d'une part, conçue comme "espace libre" et "espace de liberté", et d'autre part, soumise à des ensembles de prescriptions et d'interdictions. Cette contradiction revêt par moments un caractère de conflit, du fait même que la rue est par excellence, l'espace voué à la foule[6], le lieu où l'on peut tout dire et tout faire, parce qu'elle réunit constamment, en son sein, une multitude dont les éléments n'ont aucun lien fondé entre eux et ne se sentent nullement obligés, les uns envers les autres. Comme nous l'avons déjà souligné, c'est le lieu où les hiérarchies sociales s'estompent, pour laisser place à un ordre essentiellement fondé sur les aptitudes et les capacités individuelles, lesquelles s'exercent alors dans les domaines les plus variés, aussi bien par des actions conformes à la norme et à la règle que par des actes de transgression susceptibles de menacer l'ordre social. En cela, la rue constitue, en soi, un risque important - un pari, pourrait-on dire: on peut y gagner le savoir-faire, mais, aussi, on peut y perdre toute notion de mesure. Et ce risque auquel se trouvent confrontés de manière particulièrement violente les enfants et les jeunes, engendre l'angoisse chez les parents et les autres adultes qui, par impuissance, par indifférence, par égoïsme ou en raison de leur propre désorientation, se "protègent" en les marginalisant.

Ces enfants sont ainsi intégrés dans les grandes catégories "d'inadaptés sociaux", de "déviants" et de "délinquants" que traitent médecins et psychologues, sociologues et criminologues. Pour ces spécialistes, le problème semble se situer principalement au niveau de la personnalité des individus; ils omettent alors de considérer la marginalisation comme une interaction dans laquelle on est, tour à tour, agent et sujet et de prendre en compte la partie jouée par l'environnement social. Si les phénomènes d'inadaptation, de déviance et de délinquance renvoient, chacun, à la notion de "marge" (celle-ci conçue comme indicatrice de la position occupée par l'individu dans un contexte défini), la rigueur méthodologique oblige, partant de cette notion, à préciser chaque fois le phénomène auquel elle est rapportée. Or les enquêtes, conduites au sein de ces groupes d'enfants, ne permettent pas de conclure à une véritable pathologie comportementale: ils interpellent les membres adultes de la société de laquelle ils participent, et cela, dans un langage qui embarrasse, déroute, culpabilise, et que l'on évite de percevoir.

4. Une catégorie sociale propre

Cette marginalisation s'opère au double niveau de la famille et de la société globale, dès le moment où, notamment avec l'abandon de l'école, l'enfant cesse d'être le sujet des investissements pour devenir uniquement une charge. On estime qu'elle atteint plus des deux-tiers de la population d'enfants et de jeunes, celle-ci comptant environ pour le tiers de la population totale des villes-capitales (cf. note No. 2).

Cette population d'enfants et de jeunes se répartit en différentes catégories: ceux issus de familles "d'immigrés" (provenant d'autres régions ou d'autres contrées de l'Afrique) représentent la plus grosse proportion par rapport à leurs camarades de l'ethnie autochtone; ils appartiennent, tous, à deux principales tranches d'âge (8-12 ans et 13-17 ans), ce qui explique que certains sont encore théoriquement en cours de scolarité, tandis que certains autres ont définitivement abandonné l'école. La plupart des jeunes "immigrés" conserve des liens avec le milieu familial situé au village où ils retournent parfois de leur propre gré ou lorsqu'ils se sentent menacés de placement autoritaire ou d'emprisonnement. Les familles établies dans la ville reçoivent plus souvent la visite de leurs enfants sans qu'elles exercent sur eux une quelconque autorité.

Une enquête menée à Douala (Cameroun) sur 162 enfants âgés de 9 à 17 ans (Bekombo, 1968) montre que ces derniers abandonnent le milieu familial pour cause d'insatisfaction générale; les raisons invoquées sont, en premier lieu, le caractère archaïque du milieu rural et la pauvreté des parents; ils évoquent, ensuite, le sentiment d'insécurité qu'ils éprouvent dans un milieu envahi par les forces de la sorcellerie et l'autoritarisme des aînés, aggravé par leur incapacité d'apporter aux enfants l'aide dont ils ont besoin pour leur épanouissement personnel. Enfin, l'exode rural est motivé par la recherche d'établissements scolaires jouissant d'une bonne réputation, ou d'un emploi rémunéré grâce auquel on peut acquérir quelques objets de prestige. Tous ces enfants ont été scolarisés jusqu'au niveau du primaire, et la plupart d'entre eux ont abandonné l'école pour des raisons économiques car, dans la majorité des cas, ils vivaient avec un seul des deux parents (ou chez un oncle ou une tante). On note le même type de relation entre la destructuration de la famille et l'accomplissement des actes délictueux qui les ont conduits au "centre d'hébergement ou de redressement" ou à la prison. Ils ont tous rêvé d'exercer un métier - plus souvent, un travail manuel (menuisier, mécanicien); quelquefois, un travail social ou religieux (infirmier, prêtre).[7]

On s'aperçoit alors que l'étude de l'évolution des structures familiales s'insère totalement dans les recherches portant sur les changements socioculturels en Afrique, et que c'est par une approche globale des transformations sociales en cours de développement qu'il devient possible de cerner, de manière compréhensive, le phénomène aberrant des "enfants de la rue".

L'indifférence affichée des parents est due, la plupart du temps, à leur incapacité d'entretenir matériellement des enfants réputés sans avenir, c'est-à-dire sans bagage scolaire suffisant leur permettant d'entrer normalement dans le marché du travail; il s'agit aussi d'un profond sentiment de déroute qu'ils éprouvent du fait même qu'ils se voient désaisis de leur rôle d'éducateurs, car, pour beaucoup d'entre-eux, ils ne détiennent plus et ne peuvent donc pas transmettre à leurs enfants le savoir qui leur est requis à l'âge de leur entrée dans la vie active. Peut-être pourrait-on encore traduire l'attitude de ces adultes en termes de contestation non explicitée du modèle de société en émergence, marqué, entre autres phénomènes, par l'idéologie individualiste et une acception fort étroite de la notion de solidarité. En effet, ils se souviennent encore des dispositifs socioéducatifs qui, dans le contexte de la société traditionnelle relativement peu exigeante, rendaient les enfants et les jeunes de 10 à 15 ans capables de parer aux difficultés de la vie courante. De nos jours, livrés à l'école dès leur jeune âge, ils en sortent, quelques dix ans après, avec l'unique et inopérant avantage de savoir lire.

En commun, ces enfants ont des conditions de vie marquées essentiellement par le dénuement et l'absence quasi-totale d'encadrement. Ils se trouvent ainsi dans la nécessité de subvenir, par eux-mêmes, à l'ensemble de leurs besoins. D'où leur disponibilité pour toute sollicitation et leur disposition à tout entreprendre. Parfois, ils inspirent la pitié mélée d'une indignation à l'encontre de la famille ou des gestionnaires de la chose publique. Plus souvent, ils attirent la sympathie en raison même de l'intelligence et de l'aisance qu'ils manifestent, de la maturité dont ils font preuve et de leur savoir-faire. Contraints qu'ils sont de mettre en oeuvre simultanément diverses aptitudes, ils ne peuvent vivre et tirer leurs moyens de survie dans un cadre fonctionnellement défini et clos, qu'il s'agisse de la famille ou d'un "centre d'hébergement" (où le bas niveau des apprentissages proposés ne laisse espérer aucun débouché). Dans ces conditions, il ne leur reste que la rue (qu'ils occupent de jour et de nuit) - celle-ci étant donnée comme un espace chargé de tous les objets en circulation dans les réseaux sociaux et dans l'imaginaire de chacun, et comme une scène sur laquelle se joue la quasi-totalité des actes de survie.

En quittant la famille, ces enfants découvrent sans médiation initiatique aucune, la liberté dont ils ont pu rêver; ils accèdent d'emblée aux lieux les plus divers et se livrent à des activités qui, d'une manière ou d'une autre, leur auraient été interdites en raison de leur âge et de leur condition sociale; et là s'opère une auto-éducation dont la visée manifeste se limite à la préservation de l'existence et à son mantien au sein de ces groupes de pairs dotés d'une éthique et d'un fonctionnement qui échappent au contrôle des adultes (Bekombo, 1968; 1968a; 1969).

En définitive, ces enfants ne constituent, nullement, un rebut de la société mais une véritable catégorie sociale. A l'intérieur des groupes qu'ils organisent, les différences d'appartenance ethnique s'estompent, car, s'ils se repèrent les uns les autres par leur nom ou le surnom qu'ils s'attribuent, ils ne se soucient guère de connaître l'origine ethnique ou familiale des uns et des autres. Ils se connaissent, se regroupent ou se séparent au gré des circonstances, uniquement en fonction de leurs projets ou des actions qu'ils accomplissent ensemble. De même, les différences liées au degré d'instruction scolaire s'effacent, car, dans leur ensemble, les niveaux atteints ne permettent aucune mobilité sociale. On est ainsi en présence d'une entité sociologiquement homogène, abusivement désignée sous l'appellation "d'enfants de la rue", mais qui mériterait le nom "d'enfants du défi".

A l'intérieur de ces groupes règnent les deux règles complémentaires de la compétition et de la solidarité - ce qui assure le maintien de leur cohésion.

Ainsi, comparé à l'éthique sociale traditionnelle ou moderne, le mode de vie qu'inaugurent ces enfants est inconnu des aînés, réprouvé et rejeté par les autorités publiques, lesquelles ne peuvent guère jouir de la collaboration des familles pour exercer efficacement leur contrôle sur eux.

Cette catégorie sociale est encore mal circonscrite et mal définie. Du point de vue des échanges sociaux, elle reste utilisable à l'occasion, mais conserve son autonomie, ne se soumettant jamais à une complète maîtrise extérieure. Son mode de recrutement aussi bien que sa variation démographique échappent aux statistiques. Il est en effet intéressant de noter la mobilité de ces groupes d'enfants: atteignant la tranche d'âge de 20-25 ans, certains d'entre-eux quittent la rue et y sont remplacés par des plus jeunes. Ceux qui en sortent, ainsi, intègrent d'autres milieux: les garçons cessent alors de pratiquer les petits vols et les filles se stabilisent dans une vie familiale, soit en se mariant, soit en allant s'occuper de leurs propres enfants confiés jusque-là à leurs parents (Zumbach, 1964).

De même, les modes de production qu'ils mettent en oeuvre et les sommes d'argent dont ils disposent pour eux-mêmes ou qu'ils font circuler échappent à la comptabilité économique. En effet, leur domaine d'activité est extrêmement diversifié, allant du portage au gardiennage, du rôle d'informateur à celui de messager, de la quête à la revente. Dans le même souci de réunir un peu d'argent et d'affirmer leur présence dans les multiples circuits typiques des villes africaines, ils pratiquent régulièrement le vol de menus objets et la prostitution précoce, mais sans se livrer à la violence.

Enfin, ces enfants peuvent être complaisants et conciliants, amers ou revendicateurs vis-à-vis des adultes en général et, plus particulièrement à l'égard des pouvoirs publics représentés par la police: dans une certaine mesure, ils défient les uns et les autres, se situant, par naïveté et par ruse, à l'écart de la loi moderne et de la norme traditionnelle. Leur défi consiste aussi à donner à la rue son plein statut d'espace non attribué, défini par eux comme simple espace de vie disponible et globalement exploitable. Or, bien qu'elle soit fondée et initialement justifiée par la quête de moyens de subsistance, cette interprétation du statut de la rue traduit aussi une certaine remise en question de la légitimité du droit que les pouvoirs publics entendent exercer sur cet espace. Et cette attitude constitue sans doute l'une des données qui suscitent autant d'intérêt pour ces groupes d'enfants qui interpellent ainsi constamment, par leur présence et leur moindre agressivité, de même que par leurs actions aussi ingénieuses que révoltantes (Collignon, 1984:573).

5. Quelle approche et quel traitement?

Ces groupes "d'enfants de la rue" ont fait l'objet de nombreux travaux scientifiques, en criminologie (Houchon, 1982). Ils sont alors appréhendés, la plupart du temps comme des groupes de jeunes délinquants et, comme nous l'avons déjà souligné, cette perspective conduit à situer le phénomène à l'étude dans le champ plus large et mal défini de la *déviance sociale*. Ces approches comportent le défaut de ne pas rendre suffisamment compte de la spécificité de ces groupes qu'il conviendrait d'envisager plus globalement comme un phénomène social total généré par la conjonction d'un certain nombre de déterminants dont l'analyse requiert sa mise en relation constante avec d'autres phénomènes caractéristiques des sociétés en mutation rapide. Ce phénomène de marginalisation des enfants participe de la dynamique sociale d'ensemble et se donne comme révélateur des discontinuités et des distorsions ou des inadéquations multiples qu'il convient d'analyser. En d'autres termes, il contribue à la mise en lumière des déséquilibres structuraux, des incohérences idéologiques et des dysfonctionnements. La démarche scientifique ne peut ici se contenter de considérer uniquement le sort des individus que la société dirige vers le juge ou l'assistant social. Et les processus de marginalisation à l'oeuvre dans ce contexte ne peuvent être réduits à des mécanismes de discrimination ou d'exclusion; ils résultent de multiples interactions inscrites dans le mouvement général de restructuration sociale conduisant à considérer les nouveaux rapports de pouvoir et d'autorité, les règles qui, en Afrique, régissent désormais les rapports de l'individu et de la société, ainsi que les modalités nouvelles des échanges au sein de l'espace familial et au niveau plus large de l'ensemble de la société.

Notes

1 Selon les projections réalisées par les Nations Unies pour la période 1980-2025, la région Afrique devrait connaître l'*un des accroissements en nombre, de personnes de 60 ans et plus, les plus importants parmi toutes les régions du monde*. Sa population âgée devrait, d'après les estimations, faire un bond représenté par un facteur de 4,4 pour passer de 22,9 millions en 1980 à 101,9 millions en 2025 - accroissement supérieur à celui qui est prévu pour l'ensemble de la population du continent" *in* Tarek Shuman T. (1984:3).

2   Dans un autre article paru dans le même ouvrage (1985a:297), J. Charmes rappelle les indications suivantes concernant quelques pays:

Pays	Classe d'âge 4-19 ans	%	Pop. totale
Sénégal (1976)	1743	34,8	4998
Mali (1976)	2223	35,6	6395
Côte d'Ivoire (1975)	2025	35,1	6710
Bénin (1975)	1034	35,2	3112
Cameroun (1975)	2567	35,9	7131

3   Le phénomène des "enfants de la rue" n'est ni nouveau ni spécifique aux sociétés africaines; on le rencontre en Europe et dans les Amériques, où il est en quelque sorte célébré à travers la littérature romanesque ou théatrale. Est-il constitutif de la vie sociale - ce qui reviendrait à insinuer qu'il est permanent et inhérent à un type donné d'organisation de la société? Etait-il alors moins manifeste dans les sociétés traditionnelles africaines constituées sur la base de l'ethnie ou du lignage, c'est à dire, entre autres caractéristiques, de petite taille et où les procédés du banissement et d'expatriation pouvaient avoir pour effet la dissimulation des situations de marginalisation des individus? Il est intéressant d'observer que, dans tous les cas, ce phénomène ne devient objet de préoccupation que dans une situation de crise générale de la société, lorsque celle-ci traverse une période d'anomie accentuée par le sous-développement économique.

4   Dans son enquête réalisée à Yaoundé, au Cameroun (cf. *Cah. ORSTOM*, XXI), André Franqueville observe avec perspicacité:
"Ecoliers, élèves et étudiants forment à Yaoundé 43% de la population totale, contre 28% à Douala, et 40% contre 32%, si l'on ne tient compte que de la population de plus de 4 ans. Mais on observe encore qu'à Douala les deux-tiers (66%) de la population scolarisée sont des élèves du primaire, tandis qu'à Yaoundé ils ne sont que 55%, laissant ainsi une place nettement plus importante aux élèves du secondaire et du technique (29% au lieu de 24%) et aux étudiants (5% au lieu de 0,3%).

5   On observe souvent une sorte de distorsion dans les modes de classement, selon qu'ils procèdent du système de référence traditionnel ou moderne. Ainsi, des secteurs résidentiels les moins urbanisés, donc inappropriés à l'accueil d'un moderniste "évolué" (un haut-fonctionnaire, par exemple), sont en même temps des secteurs refuges jouissant d'une valeur d'authenticité et régis par un ordre tout autre qui s'impose avec la même autorité à ce même haut-fonctionnaire. Dans ces conditions, la position sociale octroyée dans le système moderne (en fonction du niveau d'instruction, de la profession exercée et du niveau d'enrichissement) peut être en contradiction avec le statut social d'origine d'un individu, souvent déterminé coutumièrement, par la condition de naissance. En fait on observe ici le type d'opposition susceptible de se manifester entre le principe et la pratique, à l'occasion d'une restructuration sociale consécutive à des actions de type révolutionnaire: les valeurs fondatrices de la société restent des valeurs de référence, quand bien même elles sont idéologiquement dénoncées et rejetées. Ainsi par exemple, l'instauration de la démocratie qui se fonde sur l'idée de l'égalité des hommes et des citoyens n'exclut-elle pas la reconnaissance du statut de noble institué par l'Ancien Régime en Europe?

6   En effet, les lois et règlements afférents à l'utilisation de la rue relèvent du droit moderne emprunté par l'Afrique aux pays européens; dans son ensemble, ce droit considère en priorité l'individu et sa mise en application suppose la conscience partagée de la responsabilité individuelle. Dans ce cas, la foule est perçue comme un phénomène "anormal" qui représente un obstacle à l'application de la loi: d'un point de vue théorique, elle est antinomique à l'ordre social, et la rue est la scène sur laquelle se manifeste cette aberration.

7   Cette enquête a été conduite en 1968 auprès d'enfants et de jeunes repérés comme des délinquants, emprisonnés pour délit ou placés dans un "centre d'hébergement". Des interviews très longues nous ont permis d'explorer leur cadre de vie familiale, de sonder leurs aspirations, de déterminer les circonstances dans lesquelles ils ont été "pris" et de recueillir leurs opinions sur l'environnement social dans lequel ils évoluaient. Outre la question du pouvoir économique qui est au centre de leurs préoccupations, la déchirure du tissu familial apparaît comme l'un des principaux facteurs déterminants de leur comportement: sur les 22 enfants interviewés au centre d'hébergement (Bekombo M., 1968, p. 34 et s.), 2 seulement se sont déclarés sans domicile, 3 habitaient chez leurs parents réunis et les 17 autres vivaient soit chez l'un des parents, soit chez la soeur ou le frère mariés, soit chez un oncle ou une tante, soit chez un "parent de village". La quasi-totalité (68%) a été arrêtée pour vol d'argent et, sans exclusion, tous aspirent à un métier, si modeste soit-il.

Références bibliographiques

Amos P.T., Harrel S. 1981. *Other Ways of Growing Old.* Anthropological Perspectives. Stanford. Stanford University Press.

Andriamirado S. 1981. *Abidjan, l'Envers du Décor.* Jeune Afrique. 1074.

Bekombo M. 1968. *Vie Familiale et Délinquance Juvénile en Afrique Noire.* Paris. Fédération Internationale des Ecoles de Parents et d'Educateurs.

---- . 1968a. *Aspects Sociologiques des Causes de l'Inadaptation des Jeunes en Afrique Noire Urbaine.* Les Carnets de l'Enfance. 7, pp.94-101.

---- . 1969. *Autorité Parentale et Délinquance Juvénile en Afrique.* Psychopatologie Africaine. IV:1, pp.101-121.

---- , **Houseman M., De Sales A.** 1978. *L'Ecole et la Famille en Afrique.* Etude Ethno-Sociologique. Paris. Unesco - Département de l'Education.

Bonzon S. 1967. *Modernisation et Conflits Tribaux en Afrique Noire.* Revue Française de Sciences Politiques. XVII, pp.862-888.

Castells M., Godard E. 1974. *Monopolville: l'Entreprise, l'Etat, l'Urbain.* Paris. Mouton.

Centre International de l'Enfance. 1966. *Les Conditions de Vie de l'Enfant Africain Vivant en Milieu Urbain [Lagos, 1959; Dakar, 1964].* Paris. Centre International de l'Enfance.

Charmes J. 1985. *Présentation.* Cahiers ORSTOM. XXI:2-3, p.175.

---- . 1985a. *La Jeunesse et le Secteur non Structuré.* Cahiers ORSTOM. XXI:2-3, pp.295-304.

CNRS. 1972. *La Croissance Urbaine en Afrique Noire et à Madagascar.* Paris. Colloques du CNRS. No.539.

Collignon R. 1984. *La Lutte des Pouvoirs Publics Contre les "Encombrements Humains" à Dakar.* Revue Canadienne des Etudes Africaines. XVIII:3, pp. 573-582.

Franqueville A. 1985. *Etre Elève à Yaoundé.* Cahiers ORSTOM. XXII:2-3, pp.347-353.

Gugler J., Planacan W.G. 1978. *Urbanization and Social Change in West Africa.* London. Cambridge University Press.

Harris P. 1961. *Family and Social Change in an African City: A Study of Rehousing in Lagos.* London. Routledge and Kegan Paul.

Houchon G. 1982. *Théorie de la Marginalité Urbaine dans le Tiers-Monde. Etude Différentielle du Squarting et de l'Economie Informelle dans leurs Aspects Criminologiques.* Psychopatologie Africaine. XVIII: 2, pp.161-228.

Hugot S. 1969. *Le Problème de la Délinquance Juvénile à Dakar.* Psychopathologie Africaine. V:1, pp.75-99.

Le Guérinel N., et Als. 1969. *La Conception de l'Autorité et de son Evolution dans les Relations Parents-Enfants à Dakar.* Psychopathologie Africaine. V:1, pp.11-73.

Marie A. 1981. *Marginalité et Conditions Sociales du Prolétariat Urbain en Afrique.* Cahiers d'Etudes Africaines. XX, pp.346-373.

Osmont A. 1980. *Modèles Culturels et Habitat, Etude de Cas à Dakar.* Anthropologie et Société. IV:1, pp.97-114.

Park R. 1975. *Changement Social et Organisation Sociale.* In: Birnhbaum P., Chazel F. (Eds.). "Théorie Sociologique". Paris. PUF.

Peattie L.R. 1980. *Anthropological Perspectives on the Concept of Dualism. The Informal Sector and Marginality in Developing Urban Economics.* International Regional Science Review. V:1, pp.1-31.

Shuman T. 1984. *Le Vieillissement en Afrique.* Gérontologie Africaine. 1, pp.3-10.

Thomas L.V. 1974. *Acculturation et Nouveaux Milieux Socio-Culturels en Afrique Noire.* Bulletin IFAN. XXXVI:B1, pp.164-215.

Vernière M. 1978. *A Propos de la Marginalité: Réflexions Illustrées par Quelques Enquêtes en Milieu Urbain et Suburbain en Afrique.* Cahiers d'Etudes Africaines. XIII:49/52, pp.582-605.

Zumbach P. 1964. *La Délinquance Juvénile au Cameroun.* Rapport pour l'ONU. Genève. Union Internationale de Protection de l'Enfance.

RURAL-URBAN MIGRATION AND THE PROBLEMS OF CRIME AND DELINQUENCY

Andargatchew Tesfaye[*]

Rural-urban migration is a world-wide phenomenon. Due to the harsh social contrast exhibited by the differences between rural and urban life, people flocked to the cities. In the industrialized countries of Europe and North America, rural people migrated to urban areas in stages as agriculture became more and more mechanized and commercialized and required fewer farm hands and the cities became increasingly industrialized and needed more labour. Rural people first moved to the nearest towns and then to larger cities. However, the situation in developing countries, and particularly in the African continent, has been notably different.

In Africa, during the last century, the number of Africans living in cities with a population of 100,000 or more inhabitants, grew from less than one-third of a million to eleven million people and twice as many lived in towns of over 20,000 inhabitants. Thus, one African in twenty lived in a town or city by the middle of the twentieth century. But in spite of this rapid rate of urbanization, Africa had the lowest ratio of city dwellers to rural residents compared to other continents. Africans were no longer completely bound to the 'traditional village-centered agrarian way of life.' The rate of rural-urban migration in Africa is now so high, that compared to other continents, urbanization shows a 41 fold growth compared to 9 in Asia and twice in Europe (Caldwell, 1969:5).

Dramatic changes in the life patterns of people in Africa have been observed during this century. Though the majority of Africans still live in rural areas, the past fifty to one-hundred years have witnessed great population movements from rural to urban areas. In 1975, in Sub-Saharan Africa, about 21 percent of the population lived in urban centres, but by the year 2000 it is anticipated that it will reach 38 percent. This means that during this period, i.e. from 1975 to the year 2000, the population will grow from roughly 66 million to 252 million. By then, 59 percent of all Africans will be living in urban centres and the growth rate of the urban population will be two-and-half times more than the growth rate of the rural population. (Donohue, 1982:27)

---

[*] Director, Institute of Development Research, Addis Ababa University, Ethiopia.

What are some of the major reasons for such an exodus of the rural population? A large scale flow of the population from rural areas where people have been dependent upon agriculture to the industrialized and rapidly expanding urban centres of Sub-Saharan Africa, has become an accepted fact. This population movement began primarily during the colonial period and has continued ever since. Various attempts have been made to explain why such movements have taken place. Some of the explanations are more controversial than others, but it would be of little value at present to enter into these controversies (Amin, 1974:84-98). Therefore, only the most salient and accepted explanations of rural-urban migration will be briefly presented here.

The colonization of Africa and the growth of agricultural plantations, the exploitation of minerals and the expansion of industries accelerated the rural-urban exodus. Rural inhabitants were in constant need of money to pay colonial taxes, buy highly valued industrial goods and other necessities of life and such money was only available in urban areas where there was a constant demand for labour. Therefore, rural residents moved in large numbers in search of employment, with the influence of labour-recruiting agents whetting the appetites of prospective migrants, and the profits which could be gained in developing agricultural, mineral and industrial enterprises near or proximate to urban centres. Two good examples of such population movements in search of employment are the Gezira Cotton Plantation Scheme in the Sudan and the mineral enterprises in South Africa (United Nations, 1957).

On the other hand, the demands by the population on the remaining available arable land which was left for cultivation, led to under-employment or unemployment and, consequently, a poor standard of living. People, young and old, were left with no alternative but to migrate to the nearest large towns with the hope of securing possible employment. That the problem of rural-urban migration is a continuing phenomenon has been documented by the ILO as follows:

"Large-scale periodic migration between subsistence agriculture and industrial employment is a chronic condition of the employment market in African countries South of the Sahara. It is not certainly a transient phase in development, for in South Africa it has been continuing for nearly three-quarters of a century and its volume is on the increase" (Caldwell, 1969:10).

Many young Africans visited towns and cities for one reason or another. Some go to the cities for marketing purposes while others follow family members who have already moved there. In the process, they were attracted to the way of life and the many real or imagined opportunities for personal advancement. Such imagined possibilities for improved material welfare and independence tempted many to break away from the monotony and rather strict tribal control at home and remain. Some, however, felt the shock from the exposure to urban life early enough to have the courage to return to the security of their villages, but the majority stayed and continued to struggle to survive. The important question is, however, will they survive?

Kenneth Little had this to say about the vital attraction urban areas had on rural people:

" ... closely coupled with these rural practical considerations is the idea of the town being a centre of civilization. Its modern amenities like electric lighting, large stores and shops, cinemas, bars and dance halls have a particularly strong appeal for individuals whose mental horizon has hitherto been bounded by the bush enclosing their village" (Caldwell, 1969:10).

The desire for education creates the tendency for rural-urban migration on two counts. On the one hand, young people who do not have the opportunities for an education in their villages decide to move to the nearest town in the hope of being able to satisfy this desire. On the other hand, young rural people with little education and unable to satisfy their thirst for further education in their own villages, move to towns in search of opportunities to fulfil their dreams. The findings of a survey of young boys who lived on the streets of three towns in Ethiopia in 1964, vividly illustrate the reasons why young people migrate. Out of the total of the boys examined, 61 percent migrated to the cities from their villages, and out of these young migrants, 46 percent went to the cities in search of possible employment, while 15 percent migrated to satisfy their educational needs.

Thus, contacts with western cultures created various needs and aspirations among Africans which could not be fulfilled in the countryside. This caused the flight of people from the land and, with the opening up of more and more means of transport, stimulated massive population shifts. The periodic movement of young people seeking work in urban centres became a permanent feature in most African countries. As a result, most African cities housed a relatively higher proportion of young adult males in relation to the age-sex distribution of the urban population, and it was this group that was most likely to become involved in deviant behaviour (Milner, 1969).

These newcomers to the cities were uprooted from the closed, static patterns of rural life and were thrust into the uncertain turbulence of the city where everyone was a stranger. They were forced to learn to survive in an environment that was completely alien to them and did not know how to regain the sense of community that they had lost in the transitional process. In this connection, writing about the situation in Ghana, Kingsley Davis and Helda Hertz Golden reported:

" ... the flow of migrants from countryside to city in Africa corresponds to a rapid transition telescoping several millenia into a short span. The social disorganization to which it gives rise is probably greater than that ever before experienced by urban populations. The native coming to the city cannot immediately divest himself of his tribal customs and allegiances, his superstitions and taboos; yet these are fantastically inappropriate to a modern urban milieu. Nor can he acquire suddenly the knowledge and habitudes necessary to make city life easy and workable. The result is a weird and chaotic mixture which gives to the average African city an unreal, tense, jangling quality. Yet urbanization is probably going ahead faster in this region than anywhere else in the world" (Caldwell, 1969:8).

The problems newcomers to cities face are limitless. There is the lack of employment coupled with a lack of marketable skills. There is also a physical problem, such as housing and the loneliness people feel in the middle of a huge crowd, together with the dilemma of the breakdown of the family, of new situations, stresses and strains. All these pressures may eventually boil up into various social ills including the problem of alcoholism, crime, delinquency and prostitution. Young people, prematurely thrown into the free competition of the labour market, eventually end up either on the streets or in unsuitable types of work because of insufficient training. The situation is aggravated by a too rapidly acquired independence which is often a stepping stone towards the development of a street culture.

The undesirable effects of rapid social change were described very well by A.M. Khalifa:

"In fact, excessively rapid change, does not afford to all individuals the opportunity to achieve an easy transition to the new culture. It causes many to be hesitant and irresolute in the face of contradictory values, a state of mind which not only affects their behaviour but also their inner life. They become prone to law-breaking or to various psychic and behavioural disturbances" (1962).

The fact that most rural-urban migrants in Africa live in slum areas is evident from the figures in Table 1. As the figures in the Table indicate, out of the population of some of the major African cities 30 to 79 percent of the people were identified, by a United Nations study, to be squatters and slum dwellers. Leading examples are Addis Ababa with 79 percent and Casablanca with 70 percent of their inhabitants living on the streets and in slums.

The fact that rural-urban migration is continuing and people are still living in slum areas in the 1980s was again revealed by the United Nations study. The figures in Table 2 indicate the rate at which the urban population has grown since the 1950s. This growth will continue into the year 2000 at an alarming rate. Cities like Nairobi, Cairo and Addis Ababa were already accommodating 57.3 percent, 38.6 percent and 36.6 percent of the total urban population respectively by 1980, and they are expected to grow further in the immediate future. From these figures we learn not only the fact that the population is expected to increase in urban Africa, but also the fact that life in African cities is likely to deteriorate further because of the population growth. It is this deterioration in the way of life in urban areas that leads to the increase in crime and delinquency in the African continent. Alan Milner aptly summarises the condition as follows:

"The impact of development is thus being felt in the creation of new social patterns in the cities and towns of Africa. The anomic newcomer, the unassimilated village-oriented African transposed into a different context, is one aspect of the problem; the destitute children, looking to the big city for thrills and finding only markets to sleep in, and pilfering and prostitution to keep them fed, are another; the second generation town-dweller, caught up in a status-conscious, acquisitive culture, with ends in view but no means to reach them, is another. These are the personnel of most of the known crime in Africa to day" (1969:3).

Various studies throughout the world are replete with the findings that in areas that are undergoing social change, such as slum areas in towns and cities, informal social control mechanisms, both familial and tribal, are greatly weakened. Hence, it has been reported on many occasions to be an important and decisive factor in the emergence of crime and juvenile delinquency. There is a strong belief that slums produce violent gangs because social control mechanisms, particularly parental control, are completely lacking in slum areas. This is why Clinard pointed out that "...increased urbanization and urbanism have been generally accompanied by increased rates of juvenile delinquency, crime, mental disorder, alcoholism and many other forms of deviant behaviour in almost all countries" (1970:115-116). Examples from the experiences of many countries can be cited to show that South Africa is no exception to this.

J.C. De Rider speaking of Alexandra Township, the worst slum area in South Africa, described it as a place where one can find everything one finds in other African slums "except that one must always expect a more liberal supply: crime, cruelty, sporting achievement, business, delinquency, sexual laxity, the lot" (Clinard, 1970:58).

A survey conducted in Kampala, Uganda, revealed that offenders, as compared to non-offenders, were mainly migrants from villages. As the figures in Table 3 below indicate, out of 136 offenders, 70.6 percent were migrants from villages, whereas among the non-offenders, only 48.6 percent were village residents before moving to Kampala. This further indicates the strong relationship between rural urban migration and criminality" (Clinard and Abbott, 1973:122-123).

A study of the problem of juvenile delinquency in Ghana by D.N.A. Nortey of the University of Ghana in Legon sustains earlier statements to the effect that rural-urban migration is a large contributing factor to delinquency and crime.

" ... the problem of juvenile delinquency is confined largely to the urban centres - Accra-Tema, Kumasi, Sekondi-Takoradi - and the industrial areas - Obuasi and Tarkwa. A certain amount of delinquent juveniles are also found at the smaller commercial areas, such as Koforidua, Cape Coast, Nsawam, Ho and Tamale, but in these areas, it is believed that conditions are due rather to destitution than to serious delinquency ... Most of the migrants in the urban and industrial centres, especially a majority of the unskilled labour, come from the North. They are lured to the Southern towns as a result of stories spread by relatives who have been to the south ... A fairly large number of juveniles attach themselves to the adult migrants travelling south. In the urban areas, both juveniles and adults usually sleep in parks and verandas of commercial houses ... " (Nortey;6).

Until the mid-1960s, the urban population in Ethiopia was no more than 5 to 6 percent of the total population. But suddenly, the rate of urbanization was accelerated due to various reasons. This increase in rural-urban migration led to the increase of hitherto unheeded problems of juvenile delinquency. Steven Lowenstein, a man who is closely associated with the Ethiopian penal system, described the problem as follows:

> " ... The rapid migration to urban areas, especially Addis Ababa, with the consequent dissociation from family and often church, together with the introduction of western educational and economic values, is likely to have caused the considerable confusion of standards to which adolescents are particularly prone. This has led to a break-down of the traditional authority structure and patterns of social stratification which has increased the possibilities of juvenile crime. The family has been profoundly affected by these changes, and in Ethiopia, where divorce and illegitimacy are widespread, crime by young persons may well have deep psychological significance. Poverty, unemployment and limited educational opportunities may also be substantial causes of juvenile crime, particularly with respect to the high incidence of theft" (1969:48).

The findings of a comparative study concerning four different youth groups (school boys, boys committed to a training centre and remand home, street boys, and needy boys accommodated in hostels) in Addis Ababa, do not only strongly substantiate what Lowenstein has maintained, but also support the idea that migrants continued to contribute a great deal to the problem of delinquency and deviance. As indicated in Table 4, with the exception of the school boys, the majority of the youths were born outside of Addis Ababa where they were residing at the time of the study. As the figures in the Table indicate, only 29 percent of the school boys and 35 percent of the delinquents committed to the training centre and remand home were from outside of Addis Ababa. On the other hand, 59 percent of the potential delinquents living on the streets and 79 percent of those being accommodated in hostels were from outside of Addis Ababa (Blake and Holland, 1972).

Annual police reports for Ethiopia indicate that out of the crimes reported to the police, the majority were committed in urban areas, and most of the crimes were committed by people who had migrated to the cities and by unemployed youth. For instance, in 1987 some 44,117 cases of crime were reported and out of the total, 51.5 percent of the crimes were committed in urban areas and 48.5 percent in rural areas. Similarly, out of 44,339 cases of crime reported to the police in 1988, roughly 56 percent were reported from urban areas and 44 percent were from rural areas. This means that the urban population which was about 11 percent of the total national population in 1988, contributed 56 percent of all the crimes reported to the police, whereas 88 percent of the population residing in rural areas contributed only 44 percent. This means that in 1988, there was one crime reported to the police for every 203 people in urban areas, while in rural areas, it was one for every 2,164 persons. It was also established, that in 1988, the urban population was growing by about 7 percent, that is 2.9 percent through natural growth and 4.1 percent through migration. Therefore, the majority of urban dwellers in Ethiopia were migrants from rural areas*.

Similar conditions were found to hold true for Nigeria and Kenya according to a recent study by Basil O. Owomero. According to him, in Nigeria, urbanization is an important factor in explaining property and personal crime, while for Kenya, the question of employment helps to explain more clearly the rates of both property and personal crime (Owomero, 1987). The findings by Owomero, strengthen the findings of Erasto Muga, made in an earlier study, that in Kenya, urbanization contributes significantly to the problem of crime and delinquency. In 1970, out of the total arrests that were made, 42.75 percent were in urban areas and the remaining 57.25 percent were in rural areas. Yet, the urban population was only 10 percent of the total national population. Thus, 10 percent of the population contributed almost 43 percent of the crime, while 90 percent of the population contributed 57 percent. Knowing that urbanization in Africa is being accelerated more by migration rather than by natural increase, we can safely conclude that rural-urban migration in Kenya is an important factor in the explanation of the causes of crime and delinquency, as is the case in other African countries.

In the foregoing pages an attempt has been made to show the enormous extent of rural-urban migration in Africa and its consequences. Effective social control, which largely depends on the effectiveness of the tribe and the family has been eroded since the role of the tribe and the family has been weakened by the impersonal way of life and the newly-found freedom and independence gained far too soon by the migrants in urban areas. Social

---

* Unpublished Annual Police Report for Ethiopia for 1987 and 1988, p. 21 and 19 respectively. See also The Central Statistical Authority, Census Suppliment 1, Addis Ababa, December 1985, Table 1.5.

control, therefore, is left to the formal sanctions of the law, which emphasizes the corrective rather than the preventive aspects of social control. Formal social control is more imperceptible in the day-to-day life of the people in the over-crowded cities, particularly in slum areas. It becomes visible only after the individual has gone beyond the limits of the law and has almost reached the point of no return.

On the other hand, the new migrant villager faces many problems in his new environment. He will not have the security he would have enjoyed in the village, the extended family will not come to his rescue in times of need. Yet in his new environment, there are scores of things he needs, such as food, shelter and security, to say the very least. These necessities are beyond his means since he is without skills to earn a living. It is to meet these daily essentials, therefore, that he becomes involved in crime, which is the only option left open to him under the circumstances. The pressures exerted on him to get these apparently plentiful stocks of goods in urban areas are not matched by legitimate ways or opportunities to acquire them. Therefore, he resorts to illegal means which eventually lead him to fall victim to his own behaviour.

The high rate of urbanization in Africa is likely to continue, since the population movement from rural to urban areas, as shown earlier, cannot be halted. On the other hand, the likelihood of authorities in urban areas being able to cope with the various problems that follow urbanization, in terms of providing the necessary socio-economic amenities, is very limited. Therefore, the problem of crime and delinquency and other related problems such as alcoholism, prostitution, begging, etc are going to continue as the major coping mechanisms of the marginalized urban population in African urban areas.

Tables

Table 1: Proportion of Squatters and Slum Dwellers in Selected Cities

Cities	Year	City Population (in thousands)	Slum, dwellers, squatters (in thousands)	% of Slum dwellers, squatters in city population
Addis Ababa	1981	1,200	948	79
Casablanca	1971	1,506	1,054	70
Kinshasa	1969	1,288	733	60
Nairobi	1970	535	177	33
Dakar	1969	500	150	30

Source: Donohue, 1982:36.

Table 2: African Urban Agglomerations Expected to have Populations of over 5 million in the Year 2000

Cities	Population (in millions)			City's population in 1980 as a percentage	
	1950	1980	2000	National population	Total urban population
Cairo (Egypt)	2.5	7.4	12.9	17.6	38.6
Addis Ababa (Ethiopia)	0.2	1.7	5.8	5.2	36.6
Nairobi (Kenya)	0.1	1.3	5.3	7.9	57.3
Jos (Nigeria)	0.4	2.7	7.7	3.5	17.0
Lagos (Nigeria)	--	1.2	5.0	1.6	7.9
Kinshasa (Zaire)	0.2	3.1	8.0	11.0	28.0

Source: JDonohue, 1982:40.

Table 3: Previous Residence Before Migration to Kampala: Offenders Versus Non-offenders

Previous residence	Offender		Non Offender	
	No.	%	No.	%
1. Village	96	70.6	90	48.6
2. Town	23	16.9	54	29.2
3. City	17	12.5	41	22.2
Total	136	100.0	185	100.0

Source: Clinard and Abbott, 1973:123.

Table 4: Place of Origin of Four Different Groups of Youth in Addis Ababa

Place of birth	School		Remand home		Street boys		Hostel residents		Total	
	No	%	No	%	No	%	No	%	No	%
Born in Addis Ababa	40	71	21	53	205	41	16	21	282	42
Born outside of Addis Ababa	16	29	14	35	295	59	59	79	384	52.7
No response	--	--	5	12	--	--	--	--	5	0.8
Total	56	100	40	100	500	100	75	100	671	100

Source: Blake and Holland, 1972:p.26.

References

Amin S. (Ed.). 1974. *Modern Migrations in Western Africa.* Oxford. Oxford University Press.

Blake J., Holland E. 1972. *The Juveniles: An Interview Study of Four Groups of Youth in Addis Ababa.* In: Beckstrom J. H. (Project Director) "Juvenile Delinquency in Addis Ababa : The Police, the Courts and the Juveniles". Unpublished. Addis Ababa. Part. III, pp.1-91.

Caldwell J.C. (Ed.). 1969. *African Rural-Urban Migration: The Movement to Ghana's Towns.* London. C. Hurst and Company.

Central Statistical Authority. 1985. *Census Supplement.* Addis Ababa. N.1. December.

Clinard M.B. 1970. *Slums and Community Development: Experiments in Self-Help.* New York. The Free Press.

---- , Abbott D.J. 1973. *Crime in Developing Countries: A Comparative Perspective.* New York. John Wiley and Sons.

Donohue J.J. 1982. *Some Facts and Figures on Urbanization in the Developing World.* Assignment Children. 57/ 58.

Khalifa H. 1962. *Problems of Behaviour in the Course of Economic Development and Urbanization.* Paper delivered at the United Nations Conference on the Application of Science and Technology for the Benefit of the Less Developed Areas. (Conf. 39/G/15, 1962).

Lowenstein S. 1969. *Ethiopia.* In: Milner A. (Ed.). "African Penal Systems". London. Routledge and Kegan Paul.

Milner, A. (Ed.). 1969. *African Penal Systems.* London. Routledge and Kegan Paul.

Nortey D.N.A. *The Treatment of Juvenile Delinquency in Ghana.* Legon. Unpublished and undated. University of Ghana, Department of Sociology.

Owomero. B.O. 1987. *Crime Rates and Development in Africa: Empirical Analysis of Data From Nigeria, Kenya and Tanzania.* Indian Journal of Criminology. 15:2, p.118.

Tesfaye A. 1976. *Juvenile Delinquency: An Urban Phenomenon.* In: Marina Ottaway (Ed.). "Urbanization in Ethiopia: A Text with Integrate Reading". Unpublished. Addis Ababa University.

United Nations. 1957. *Urbanization in Africa South of the Sahara.* In: "Report on the World Social Situation". New York. pp.144-169.

LES DEVIANCES DE SUBSISTANCE

Elisabeth Michelet*

1. Introduction

Peuple de l'abîme, damnés de la terre, monde "d'en dessous", avec ses codes, ses rituels, ses agenouillés, gueux et misérables, truands, quart-monde et inégalités ... l'humanité, en tous temps et sous tous les cieux, halète, souffre, crie et agonise ... la pauvreté, un destin.[1]

En criminologie, une approche plurielle est nécessaire selon les aires géographiques qui produisent, entretiennent, renouvellent un terreau misérable. D'où l'intérêt d'une étude régionale qui photographie le paysage de réalités fort diverses selon les lieux.

En Afrique sub-saharienne, le terme "déviances de subsistance" paraît convenir à la qualification du processus de la pauvreté. Cette explication étiologique s'est imposée à nous dès 1980 (Michelet, 1980 et 1981).

Il est sans doute difficile de théoriser cette approche expérimentale d'une situation vécue au Sénégal. Cependant, l'analyse des déviances de subsistance peut servir de guide à la compréhension de la marginalisation rencontrée dans les pays en développement pour les régions sub-sahariennes.

Pour preuve de l'éclectisme de la situation des déviants selon les zones où elle se déploie, en France on n'utilise pas le terme "déviances de subsistance" mais "nouveaux pauvres" ou "stiffs" (Porquet, 1987:276).

Pour critique que soit la situation en Afrique, malgré la dégénérescence de millions d'êtres, elle n'est pas la pire en humanité. Ainsi, à Bogota en Colombie, on abattrait les enfants errants. La rumeur publique attribue ces assassinats à un mystérieux groupe, le M.A.G., "Muerte a los gamines" qui organise de véritables battues meurtrières contre les "enfants des égouts", la tête d'un gamin pouvant valoir jusqu'à 50.000 pesos. On enregistre près de 200 victimes en deux ans, tuées par balles pour la plupart, corps sans nom que personne ne réclame, étiquetés à la morgue "non identifiés" (Montali, 1990).

Nous réserverons donc l'expression "déviances de subsistance" aux pays en développement dont une partie de plus en plus importante de la population se trouve en position de survie, sans que les pouvoirs publics ne

---

* Maître de Conférences à la Faculté des Sciences Juridiques et Economiques de l'Université Cheick Anta Diop de Dakar, Senegal.

puissent la contrôler, contribuant à entretenir toute une atmosphère, une pression délinquantielle, si palpable dans la rue qu'elle crée une insécurité permanente.

Les déviances de subsistance ont donc engendré toute une stratification sociale d'indigents, qui, du point de vue criminologique, invitent à créer de nouveaux instruments d'analyse. Elles dépassent le cadre de la politique criminelle en raison des implications économiques, sociales, culturelles et de l'aide internationale, pour en faire l'un des drames de notre temps, car ce monde de la marginalité est de moins en moins celui d'une minorité.

La déviance se définit par rapport au conformisme: "tous ceux qui ne se soumettent pas aux canons des bonnes moeurs, de la bonne conduite, en somme tous les opposants aux vérités transmises par la tradition, et appuyées par les pouvoirs établis, sont considérés comme déviants" (Szabo, 1978:52).

Cette déviance est dite "de subsistance", car - et c'est là sa spécificité - elle est liée à la sous-alimentation.

La sous-alimentation est un facteur criminogène. Le but de la mendicité est la *conservation biologique*. L'être vivant est alors, selon l'expression de Stanciu, "obligé d'arracher sa nutrition" (Stanciu, 1956:153). Dans les cas limites, vol alimentaire par exemple, l'acte de s'emparer de la nourriture se produit avec la violence de la nécessité. C'est la loi biologique générale.

Le vagabondage, dans le cas qui nous occupe, revêt un aspect structural. Il n'est pas la conséquence d'évènements naturels imprévisibles et indépendants des structures sociales, telles une épidémie, une famine - encore que la désertification et la sécheresse soient à prendre en considération - mais résulte directement de la structure et des institutions d'une société donnée laquelle n'est pas sans base politique, juridique, religieuse ou économique. Il en est ainsi pour les chômeurs, les dépossédés, les émigrés.

Les déviances de subsistance sont liées à la faim, au chômage, à la misère. Survivre implique se mettre hors des lois. L'obéissance aux lois ne peut être suivie que par des personnes qui ne sont pas en situation infra-humaine et de dérive sociale.

En soi, ces déviances ne devraient pas intéresser la criminologie, et être condamnables, puisque, du point de vue juridique, on pourrait invoquer la contrainte ou l'état de nécessité. Au niveau primaire, il n'y a pas de faute. Cependant, le déviant s'accommode rapidement d'un certain relâchement moral, s'immunise contre les principes reçus de la famille, du village, de la tribu, de la tradition et même de l'honneur. "Etre malin", "se débrouiller", être inventif à n'importe quel prix, devient une qualité dans un environnement compréhensif: toutes les solutions sont bonnes si elles amènent un peu d'argent. Le nombre des nécessiteux déviants augmentant chaque jour, le danger social qu'ils représentent devient évident, car de la déviance de subsistance, on passe vite à la petite criminalité, et pour certains jeunes, à la grande criminalité, selon un cursus logique d'escalade dans les risques pris par le délinquant. A ce titre, les déviances de subsistance, en tant que ferment criminogène, doivent être étudiées sans complaisance.

Pour circonscrire le champ d'application des déviances de subsistance, on peut procéder de deux manières: au sens restreint, les déviances de subsistance concernent la mendicité liée au vagabondage, les larcins et petits vols alimentaires, certaines formes de prostitution, les activités commerciales irrégulières sur la voie publique, puisque sans aucune ressource l'être humain doit d'abord se nourrir pour subsister. En élargissant cette notion, on pourrait y inclure l'usage de la drogue comme dérivatif à la faim et au stress des malnutris. L'étendant encore à l'échelle familiale et villageoise, dans certaines régions, à la culture, à la production, à la commercialisation de stupéfiants, aux déprédations dans les forêts sur la flore et sur la faune, particulièrement dans les parcs protégés, au braconnage, à la contrebande. Beaucoup d'infractions seraient ainsi liées de près ou de loin au manque de moyens et à la pauvreté.

Nous pensons qu'il vaut mieux retenir la première formule, avec les infractions dont l'objet tient strictement à un impératif alimentaire, car l'homme est acculé à dévier d'une façon quasi incontournable. La culture des stupéfiants, la contrebande relèvent moins de l'urgence et de la nécessité que de la commodité, d'autres solutions pouvant être trouvées.

Au Sénégal, les individus concernés par cette déviance de subsistance sont de trois sortes. Il s'agit d'abord de personnes invalides qui ont reçu l'appellation de "délinquants majeurs" en 1975. Dans cette catégorie prennent place les aveugles, les handicapés physiques et les lépreux. Il s'agit ensuite de personnes valides, et sans travail réel, qui traînent à longueur de journées dans les rues, vivant d'expédients, et parmi celles-ci, bon nombre de mineurs. Il s'agit, enfin, d'une grande partie des prostituées dont la délinquance est, elle aussi, nutritionnelle.

Les plus déshérités parmi les pauvres, qui font partie de ce que l'on a appelé ailleurs "lumpen prolétariat", ont reçu au Sénégal le qualificatif critiquable autant que pitoyable "d'encombrements humains", parce qu'ils n'appartiennent pas à la ville dont ils viennent fausser l'apparence et l'harmonie, parce qu'ils gênent, ils encombrent. Dakar, comme toutes les capitales et grandes villes africaines, polarise toutes les données de ce fléau. L'émergence du terme date du début des années 1970. En 1971, est créé un comité national de lutte contre l'envahissement de Dakar par les mendiants, vagabonds et colporteurs, appelés "banas-banas"[2] qu'ils soient valides ou invalides, majeurs ou mineurs, aveugles ou lépreux, et qui se livrent à des activités répréhensibles sur la voie publique.

La question des encombrements humains ne se pose pas en termes de recensement démographique, car le Sénégal, avec sept millions d'habitants, n'est pas surpeuplé.[3] Elle se pose en termes écologiques de "pollution humaine", pour tous ceux qui essayent de tirer leurs moyens de subsistance d'activités non autorisées, troublant l'ordre public, et portant atteinte à la dignité nationale, surtout à cause de la réaction qu'ils suscitent auprès des touristes, soumis plus que d'autres au harcèlement des mendiants, colporteurs et quémandeurs, dont la tenacité n'a pas d'égale pour inspirer pitié et s'imposer à votre charité.

Les mass-média ont diffusé l'expression "encombrement humain" par la voie de la presse[4], celle de la littérature avec le livre d'Aminata Sow Fall (1979), dont le thème porte sur la grève des mendiants refusant de tendre leur calebasse[5], par le cinéma, avec certaines séquences du film "Xala", produit par le cinéaste sénégalais Ousmane Sembene, évoquant la pratique des rafles de mendiants, pour dégorger la capitale, à la veille de l'accueil d'hôtes de marque, et leur retour précipité par tous les moyens de locomotion une fois la fête terminée.

Peu à peu, le terme s'est officialisé, jusqu'à paraître dans les rapports de présentation, dans l'exposé des motifs des textes législatifs. Il est définitivement passé dans le langage courant.

Beaucoup d'efforts ont été déployés pour endiguer le phénomène, mais le mal à combattre reste entier. Il s'agit d'une sorte de recherche de Sisyphe, tant il est vrai que tout a été essayé sans résultat.

Il est difficile de parler d'une déviance de subsistance. Sur le plan étiologique, il existe des déviances de subsistance, que nous étudierons tour à tour, ainsi que les actions entreprises dans le cadre de la politique criminelle, tant au niveau des adultes que des mineurs.

2. Les déviances de subsistance des majeurs

On en recense trois: la mendicité, les activités irrégulières sur la voie publique, la prostitution.

2.1 La mendicité

Jusqu'à une époque récente, il n'y avait pas de mendiants valides majeurs. Tous étaient des cas sociaux, économiquement démunis, en raison d'un handicap.

194

Pour identifier ces derniers, il faut se poser deux questions:
- D'où viennent-ils?
- Qui sont-ils?

Ces déshérités proviennent essentiellement des campagnes, des taudis dominés par l'indigence, l'absence d'hygiène et de salubrité. La misère dans les campagnes, à cause du manque de travail et de la sécheresse, entraîne le mouvement de tous ces hommes vers les bidonvilles pauvres de la périphérie des centres urbains. La misère dans les bidonvilles entraîne, elle aussi, un déplacement de ces mêmes personnes vers le centre urbain. Par ce double mouvement, les encombrements humains finissent par prendre demeure dans les plus belles artères de la cité. Il en est ainsi pour la quasi totalité des handicapés physiques, aveugles, lépreux d'origine rurale.

Qui sont-ils? Des individus marqués par les stigmates de leur maladie ou de leur infirmité; encore plus démunis que les autres dans la recherche d'un emploi, malgré leur désir de travailler et d'être traités comme leurs semblables. L'attitude des citadins à leur égard est peu avenante, parfois nettement hostile. Exclus de la production économique, ils ne peuvent compter, pour survivre, que sur ceux qui disposent de revenus plus substantiels. A la tête de familles, d'enfants en bas âge, la mendicité en ville constitue pour eux la principale source de leurs maigres revenus.

C'est pourquoi ces marginaux se regroupent par cinq, dix, pour former une sorte de société. Le plus souvent, ils se marient entre eux, et leurs enfants vont rejoindre les "encombrements humains". Le regroupement des handicapés se fait à partir d'une similitude de l'infirmité. On note des groupements d'handicapés visuels, d'autres, d'invalides paralysés. Ils se cotisent pour faire face à une cérémonie familiale ou organiser une tontine.

Depuis quelques années, ces mendiants invalides se disputent les places rentables (devant les mosquées, églises, postes, pâtisseries, pharmacies, carrefours) avec des mères de famille et leur progéniture qui s'installent, dès l'aurore, sur un bout de trottoir dont elles deviennent pratiquement indélogeables jusqu'au crépuscule, avant de regagner leur banlieue éloignée. Si le lieu est bien choisi, elles peuvent gagner suffisamment pour assurer leur nourriture et leur habillement.

On note aussi la présence de vieillards. Avec la perte du sens de la solidarité familiale, des vieillards sont abandonnés et livrés à eux-mêmes, ce qui était impensable dans la tradition africaine.

On a pu voir également des groupes de femmes d'âges divers appartenant au même village, "partir en campagne", selon leur expression, pour passer plusieurs mois dans la capitale, en vivant de mendicité. Elles se dispersent dans la journée pour vaquer à leur activité et se retouvent le soir sur le

195

trottoir d'une avenue résidentielle pour passer la nuit allongées sur des cartons.

Ces·pratiques sont encouragées par le devoir d'aumône, l'un des cinq préceptes du croyant en terre d'Islam. C'est un devoir de solidarité consistant à aider son frère. Mais il est faux de tolérer la mendicité parce qu'elle permet des actes charitables requis par le devoir religieux. L'aumône doit s'adresser à des personnes choisies par le croyant, musulman ou chrétien, mais non à celles qui, au mépris de leur dignité, vont au devant pour la réclamer.

Lẽ sens profond de l'aumône s'est dégradé et perverti. Faire l'aumône constitue souvent un rite magique conseillé par le marabout, pour se purifier, pour gagner une faveur ou avoir une influence. C'est un commerce avec le ciel, pour en retirer un avantage purement personnel.

Sous cet aspect, on comprend mieux que la mendicité n'est pas un acte honteux dont on doive se cacher. Elle bénéficie non seulement de la caution de la religion, mais aussi de celle des traditions coutumières et familiales respectables, toujours vivaces et ancrées dans la vie des populations.

Des dérogations importantes sont apportées par l'article 245 du code pénal à l'infraction de mendicité. En principe, interdite en temps ordinaire, il est permis de solliciter l'aumône le vendredi, le dimanche et les jours de fête religieuse, aux alentours des mosquées et des églises.

La loi 75-78 du 9 juillet 1975 et ses décrets d'application[6] ont donné aux magistrats saisis d'un délit de vagabondage, mendicité, vol simple, commis par un handicapé physique, la possibilité de ne pas prononcer les peines prévues par le code pénal, mais de prendre des mesures de placement dans un établissement de soins et de protection sociale dépendant du Ministère de la santé publique et des affaires sociales, à condition que les faits qui leur sont reprochés ne paraissent pas devoir être sanctionnés par une peine d'emprisonnement. Leur placement est ordonné pour un an et peut être prolongé par périodes successives d'une année. L'intéressé qui a fait l'objet d'une pareille mesure peut, à tout moment, demander à la juridiction qui l'a prise à son égard d'y mettre fin.

Pour les lépreux bacillifères appréhendés pour vagabondage et mendicité, la loi du 25 mars 1976 a prévu de les faire soigner dans des villages pour lépreux. A l'issue des soins, les lépreux blanchis doivent être réinsérés dans des villages de reclassement social.

Nous ne pouvons qu'approuver cette dépénalisation, compte tenu des mesures d'indulgence prises par le législateur en faveur de personnes victimes de leur état.

2.2   La prolifération des activités irrégulières sur la voie publique

En raison de conditions climatiques, parfois très défavorables, le paysan anxieux de sa situation précaire, veut chercher en ville, dans le salariat, la solution à ses conditions de survie. Sans aucune qualification professionnelle, il trouvera rarement un emploi et devra compter sur les ressources de son imagination pour s'organiser une occupation de survie sur la voie publique. Elle sera praticable en toute saison, à la différence de ce qui se passe pour les travaux agricoles, essentiellement saisonniers. Son origine sociale ne diffère pas beaucoup de celle de l'handicapé. Comme lui, il se contente de vivre au jour le jour et il dispose de ressources très limitées.

Devant la prolifération de ces activités irrégulières, qui ajoutent aux encombrements humains sur la voie publique, le législateur est intervenu pour en réglementer l'accès en les distinguant de la vente ambulante, elle-même réglementée, à cause de la concurrence illicite qu'elle fait aux commerçants. Les points stratégiques de ces activités sont les marchés, les avenues commerçantes et le port de Dakar.

Elles sont souvent le fait de mineurs. La loi du 29 novembre 1967 et le décret du 10 juin 1968 précisent que les activités de gardien, laveur de voitures, cireur, porteur, sont soumises à autorisation préalable et rigoureusement interdites aux mineurs de 15 ans.[7]

En tout état de cause, il est interdit de racoler les clients dans la rue, ce qui est le propre du métier de marchand ambulant, très florissant dans les pays en développement.

Est considéré comme marchand ambulant toute personne qui parcourt pour son compte ou pour celui d'autrui, même de façon occasionnelle, les agglomérations urbaines et rurales, en vue d'offrir et de mettre en vente sur la voie publique, des produits industriels locaux ou importés, des denrées alimentaires et des produits de l'artisanat. Afin d'éviter leur prolifération anarchique, le commerce ambulant est réglementé avec beaucoup de précision par le décret du 9 juillet 1966 interdisant le stationnement sur les trottoirs, ainsi que l'installation d'étals aux abords des marchés, des magasins et le racolage de la clientèle dans la rue.

Devant l'encombrement de Dakar, un décret du 6 janvier 1976 est venu purement et simplement y interdire la vente ambulante. C'est la vente à des points fixes, désignés par arrêté du Gouverneur, qui est seule réglementée.

De contravention, l'infraction est devenue délit, d'où la possibilité d'utiliser la procédure de flagrant délit. Ces textes ne sont pas appliqués, car il est impossible d'endiguer la montée des chômeurs et désoeuvrés qui sillonnent la ville à l'affût d'une occasion de gagner quelques pièces de monnaie. Les rafles épisodiques opérées au cours d'opérations "coup-depoing" par la police n'améliorent pas la situation de façon durable. A ces occasions, on constate que, parmi toutes les personnes en situation irrégulière, les marchands ambulants sont en tête.

Les sanctions ne servent à rien. Les impératifs nutritionnels qui sont à la base de toutes ces désobéissances aux réglementations en vigueur, rendent les textes caducs et inobservables dans les faits. En soi, s'il n'y avait un impératif d'ordre public qui sert d'alibi au législateur, il faudrait dépénaliser ces activités illicites, qui, à la différence des vols alimentaires, ne sont pas une étape vers des délits plus caractérisés. Ces infractions, qui sont d'ordre économique, devraient rester contraventionnelles. Elles font du tort à la concurrence, sans doute, mais elles ne sont ni violentes ni malhonnêtes, ne portant pas préjudice à la propriété d'autrui; elles ont plus un caractère astucieux.

Devant une déviance de subsistance, l'amende ou la prison ne peuvent avoir de portée et sont inappropriées. La police et la Justice le sentent si bien que les textes restent lettre morte.

2.3   La prostitution

Le contexte prostitutionnel dakarois met en évidence que ce fléau est directement lié au sous-développement. Il est en partie alimentaire, aussi nous le situons essentiellement comme une déviance de subsistance. Plus de 80% des femmes qui se prostituent sont motivées par la recherche de moyens de subsistance qu'elles ne peuvent trouver que dans la prostitution. C'est sous le prisme du sous-emploi, du chômage, de leurs conséquences sur les ressources familiales et sur la promotion individuelle liée à l'argent que l'on peut comprendre la nature de ce type de prostitution. Déviance de subsistance, la prostitution l'est dans son but: nourrir sa famille. Déviance de subsistance, elle l'est dans le moyen pour y parvenir: faire de la prostitution un métier.

2.3.1 La prostituée, soutien de famille

La prostituée a le plus souvent des charges familiales extrêmement lourdes. Elle peut se trouver soutien de famille, aussi bien dans ses liens avec ascendants et collatéraux que dans ses liens matrimoniaux et avec les enfants qui en sont issus.

Dans ses rapports avec sa famille d'origine, elle a la charge de parents âgés, infirmes ou sans travail, entourés de nombreux frères et soeurs. Pour survivre, les siens s'appuyeront, presque exclusivement sur l'argent qu'elle enverra à la famille restée au village. La plupart des prostituées sont d'origine rurale. Elles se sont rendues à Dakar dans l'espoir d'apporter une solution au drame que vivent leurs parents. Faute de trouver du travail, elles tombent dans la prostitution pour leur venir en aide. Certaines ont même une très haute idée du bonheur qu'elles doivent apporter à leur famille, qui est rarement au courant de leurs activités. Interrogees par une assistante sociale à l'Institut d'Hygiène Sociale, cette motivation revient souvent au cours de l'interview.[8] Si les parents apprennent la situation, ils se taisent et laissent faire, à regret. Pour la prostituée célibataire, ce travail est un palliatif. Elle pense le laisser dès qu'elle aura "trouvé un mari".

Dans le mariage, en ce qui concerne ses rapports avec son mari et ses enfants, il arrive qu'elle doive pallier la grande misère qui découle d'un décès, d'un accident, d'une séparation, d'un abandon. Divorcée, veuve, délaissée pour une co-épouse, mari au chômage, mère célibataire, autant de situations dramatiques qui peuvent entraîner une femme à se prostituer, bien qu'elle soit mère de famille.

Il arrive aussi que la femme se prostitue à des moments déterminés, notamment à la fin du mois, lorsque les ressources alimentaires sont épuisées, ou lorsque le mari ne donne pas une somme suffisante pour faire le marché ou se procurer les produits nécessaires à l'alimentation de base du foyer. Dans ces conditions, la prostituée estime qu'elle "aide son mari à entretenir la famille dans la dignité, car elle ne quémande pas, elle ne vole pas et l'on peut-être heureux".[9] A travers ces propos relevés auprès des prostituées, on voit à quel point la prostitution est une déviance de subsistance, comme substitut d'un emploi stable.

2.3.2 La prostitution, substitut au problème de l'emploi

La plupart des femmes sont venues à Dakar pour trouver un travail honnête. Le secteur urbain, saturé, n'offre pas d'emploi aux personnes sans diplômes. Elles ne peuvent que se placer comme employées de maison, lorsqu'elles ont la chance de trouver un patron. Beaucoup d'entres elles sont sous-payées. Pour un travail de forçat, on leur donnne un salaire de misère, très au-dessous du taux prévu par les lois sociales et exigé dans le cadre de leur emploi.

A titre d'exemple, leur salaire couvre à peine les frais occasionnés par la location de leur chambre. Peu armées pour la vie, d'un niveau intellectuel très bas, certaines vont se laisser entraîner vers la voie de la facilité. Pour celles qui n'ont rien trouvé, la prostitution est la seule issue. La famille "laissée au pays" ne saura rien. Elles s'y aventurent avec une certaine naïveté, une certaine innocence, concevant la prostitution comme un métier, pour celles qui l'exercent à titre principal, et en tirent des moyens d'existence que la loi n'interdit pas formellement. Elles s'y situent comme exerçant une profession, profession qui se développe dangeureusement avec le tourisme de masse. Les largesses des clients encouragent le commerce de la chair. Ce fléau prend des proportions inquiétantes, à cause de la propagande occidentale qui entoure le marché du tourisme.[10] Sous la dénomination d'hôtesses ou de serveuses sont engagées des femmes destinées à satisfaire la clientèle sur le plan sexuel. Les prostituées vivent la situation où elles se sont mises, comme un palliatif à leur détresse. Pourtant, certaines n'en sortiront plus. Derrière leur apparence, derrière leur innocence ou leur aggressivité se découvre le désespoir d'une vie gachée.[11]

2.3.3 Les actions entreprises

Les mesures prises par le Sénégal en matière de prostitution sont exclusivement définies par rapport à une politique de salubrité publique: ordre public et bonnes moeurs, ordre sanitaire et social. Ce qui est en cause, c'est la réputation de la capitale à travers les manifestations les plus choquantes de la prostitution, avec l'interdiction du racolage, de l'homosexualité, de l'outrage public à la pudeur, de la gestion d'établissements de prostitution. Ce qui importe surtout, c'est la protection du public contre les maladies sexuellement transmissibles, en luttant contre les effets épidémiologiques de la prostitution. L'émergence du Sida est trop récente pour que les pouvoirs publics aient pris des mesures appropriées, d'autant plus que le Sénégal est encore peu touché par cette maladie.

Les mesures d'assistance aux prostituées, et de reclassement, sont, pour l'heure, totalement inexistantes. Les mesures curatives ne le sont que dans le but de dépister les maladies vénériennes. Ce n'est pas la prostitution qui est pourchassée, mais les "M.T.S.". La réglementation, exclusivement tournée vers les mesures sanitaires, découle de plusieurs textes introduisant l'obligation du fichier sanitaire et social, des visites sanitaires et du carnet sanitaire.[12] Bien des prostituées ne sont pas recensées, ce qui rend cette réglementation assez illusoire. La misère économique engendre la misère sexuelle.

3. Les déviances de subsistance des mineurs

Ce que nous avons étudié à l'échelle des adultes se retrouve à celle de ceux que l'on appelle "les enfants de la rue".

3.1 Les enfants de la rue en quête de subsistance

3.1.1 Les talibés

Sous le pseudo prétexte d'inculquer une éducation religieuse à leurs enfants, certains parents les abandonnent à des marabouts, maîtres coraniques, qui les obligent à mendier pour gagner leur subsistance. Ces enfants sont exploités. Ils doivent verser chaque soir à leur maître une somme forfaitaire sous peine d'être châtiés. Exiger du jeune talibé une somme si modique soit-elle, qu'ils n'espèrent obtenir qu'en mendiant, c'est le pousser à voler.

Ces enfants sont souvent maltraités et sous-alimentés. En bandes, rachitiques et déguenillés, ils remontent les files de véhicules arrêtés aux feux de signalisation, pour présenter une boîte vide aux usagers bloqués sur la chaussée. Leur très bas niveau de vie explique leur misère vestimentaire. Ils n'ont pour toute garde-robe, de jour et de nuit, que ce qu'on leur voit sur la peau, des vêtements en lambeaux. Cela préjudicie à leur santé et met à l'épreuve leur amour-propre. Ces enfants, habitués à la vie errante, s'intègrent très difficilement, après l'école coranique, dans un cadre de vie plus organisé. Ayant souvent perdu le contact avec leur famille, ils ne veulent plus, ou ne peuvent plus rentrer chez eux, et deviennent des marginaux (Baro, 1978).

3.1.2 Les autres enfants errants

En dehors des talibés, des enfants exercent des "petits métiers" illicitement, à la sauvette et se livrent à du "petit brigandage" dans les rues, lorsqu'ils n'obtiennent pas satisfaction. Il s'agit d'enfants en difficulté scolaire, ou n'ayant jamais pu aller à l'école, s'en étant fait renvoyer, ou encore d'enfants titulaires du C.E.P.E. (Certificat d'études primaires élémentaires), qui ne trouvant pas d'emploi, ne peuvent s'intégrer dans la société active. Il s'agit aussi d'enfants totalement abandonnés à eux-mêmes, les parents n'étant pas à la maison. Ces jeunes s'improvisent gardiens de voitures, porteurs de paniers, laveurs de voitures, cireurs de souliers, guides dans les lieux touristiques. Devant les magasins, à l'entrée des cinémas, à l'abord des grands hôtels et des marchés, de jour comme de nuit, ils quadrillent certains quartiers de Dakar jugés "rentables". S'ils n'obtiennent pas satisfaction dans leur quête de quelque argent pour subvenir à leurs besoins immédiats, ils n'hésitent pas à se livrer à des actes de vandalisme sur les voitures. Le vol à la roulotte devient un sport.

Ces activités sont interdites par la loi aux mineurs de 15 ans. Les enfants sont raflés par la police épisodiquement et aussitôt relachés faute de solution à leur proposer.

3.1.3 La prostitution enfantine

Il s'agit surtout de la prostitution scolaire, qui, par certains côtés est déviance de subsistance, par d'autres autrement motivée. La prostitution des écoliers est due au fait que certains enfants, dépassant le cap du cycle primaire, se trouvent confrontés à des difficultés financières pour continuer leurs études. Des parents, économiquement faibles, ne peuvent pas payer le coût élevé de l'habillement et des fournitures scolaires dans les écoles privées. Ils laissent leurs enfants se débrouiller et tolèrent leurs agissements par leur silence complice.

Dans les archives de la brigade des moeurs, parmi les filles fichées pour prostitution et racolage, il y a un grand nombre d'élèves. Toutes les grandes écoles de Dakar comptent des élèves qui se prostituent. C'est généralement dans les bars ou les boîtes de nuit qu'elles rencontrent leurs clients éventuels.

Devant les nombreux problèmes de transport auxquels les élèves sont confrontés, l'auto-stop est un agent important de prostitution scolaire.

La prostitution masculine, inconnue au Sénégal jusqu'à ces dernières années est pratiquée de plus en plus fréquemment par des élèves du cycle secondaire, auprès des touristes femmes et hommes.

Dans une société qui reste attentive aux prescriptions de l'africanité, essentiellement spiritualiste, les débordements de l'érotisme sont interdits. Pourtant, en contradiction formelle avec cette éthique, on ne peut nier un laisser-faire des pouvoirs publics, débordés par les conditions socio-économiques et par la détérioration des moeurs amenée par le tourisme. Le tourisme est un agent de mimétisme et de perversion dans le domaine sexuel, d'où la montée de l'homosexualité, rigoureusement interdite par le code pénal, aussi bien pour les majeurs que pour les mineurs, et surtout de la prostitution masculine qui est un phénomène récent.

Au plan individuel, et en termes de pourboire, les touristes sont les meilleurs clients des prostituées. Le réseau touristique ne connaît pas de morte saison, en raison des conditions climatiques exceptionnelles dont jouit le pays.

Au plan général, et en termes de devises, l'apport aux caisses de l'Etat n'est pas négligeable. Sur le plan du développement économique, le secteur tertiaire, singulièrement le tourisme, est devenu un secteur des plus privilégiés. L'Etat investit dans la construction d'équipements touristiques et d'hôtels. D'où la concentration de déviants dans les zones touristiques. La prostitution est un fléau qui rapporte. Les déviances de subsistance ne doivent pas être traitées du seul point de vue individuel. Ce sont aussi des phénomènes de masse que l'on doit analyser dans le cadre de l'évolution des structures sociales.

3.1.4 Les adeptes du "Guenz"

Les jeunes qui n'ont pas les moyens de s'acheter les drogues classiques, notamment du Yamba, non local du cannabis ou chanvre indien, sont des adeptes de la colle forte, du diluant, du pétrole. Les petits talibés, les enfants de la rue, inhalent quelques minutes les émanations toxiques qui se dégagent de ces produits, qui ne figurent pas sur la liste des stupéfiants et dont l'emploi ne constitue pas juridiquement un délit. Mais ces jeunes ne sont pas à négliger par le criminologue, car, en détériorant leur santé, ils se mettent en état de dépendance, candidats à l'enchaînement de la toxicomanie vers les drogues dures. Nous n'entrerons pas dans l'analyse des motivations des jeunes drogués. Elles sont liées à la misère, source d'évasion pour les dépossédés, les malnutris, les enfants qui ont faim et qui s'ennuient.

3.2 *L'accoutumance à la transgression, évolution vers une plus grande criminalité*

L'étude de la montée des vols correctionnels au cours de ces dix dernières années, d'après une enquête menée en 1990 auprès d'un commissariat de police de Dakar, et l'évolution du vol selon la classe d'âge à laquelle appartiennent les délinquants concernés, font apparaître la place grandissante des jeunes dans la commission de cette infraction. La progression générale est de 300% entre 1980 et 1988. La tranche d'âge des 15-20 ans est allée de 15,9% en 1980, à 27,2% en 1985 et 36,8% en 1988[13], devançant la tranche des 21-26 ans qui était la plus dangereuse.

Après être passés par une situation de déviance de subsistance en agglomération urbaine, il est rare qu'ils retournent dans leur village. Il est fréquent qu'ils se risquent à accomplir des vols occasionnels en prenant le maximum de précautions. S'enhardissant dans cette pratique, ils finissent par faire du vol leur gagne-pain, opérant seuls, à plusieurs ou en bandes.

3.2.1 Du menu larcin au vol sélectif

Longtemps, les vols correctionnels ont été dominés par le menu larcin: linges, ustensiles de cuisine, effets vestimentaires, matériels de tout genre, sans grande valeur marchande. Ces objets étaient bradés au premier venu, dans des lieux douteux et à des heures suspectes. A ces menus larcins s'apparentent les vols commis par la technique du pickpocket, consistant à profiter des rassemblements, mouvements de foule, attentes et queues devant les stades, les cinémas, les magasins, pour faire la poche des personnes les moins vigilantes. Depuis quelques années, les délinquants semblent avoir opté pour une autre voie: le vol sélectif. Les voleurs ont jeté leur dévolu sur le secteur électronique; téléviseurs, chaînes à musique, magnétophones, magnétoscopes; également sur les bijoux en or, argent, ivoire, ainsi que sur les accessoires de voitures, les appareils électro-ménagers. Tous ces objets sont des biens facilement plaçables sur le marché. Ils ont une plus grande valeur financière. Cette tendance est favorisée par les receleurs qui préfèrent ces objets sur lesquels ils peuvent réaliser de plus gros bénéfices avec le moindre risque. Les bijoux sont revendus à des bijoutiers qui les fondent et créent de nouveaux modèles. Nul n'est indifférent au matériel électronique lorsqu'il est vendu à prix très bas.

La conséquence est qu'aujourd'hui nous assistons à l'émergence de véritables gangs, spécialisés dans le vol de matériel électronique et d'accessoires de voiture. Ce nouveau choix des voleurs rejaillit sur leur manière d'agir. Ces vols nécessitent une préparation minutieuse, une promptitude d'éxécution, un minimum de logistique, et une technicité qui relève plus du spécialiste en électricité et en serrurerie, que du bricoleur.

Les quartiers ciblés sont les quartiers résidentiels de moyen standing dont les habitants ont un niveau de vie qui leur permet d'équiper leur habitation, mais qui ne disposent pas forcément d'un garage, laissant leur véhicule sur la voie publique, avec tous les risques encourus. Ce sont des quartiers dans lesquels les habitants s'ignorent le plus souvent les uns les autres, chacun vivant sa propre vie et ne s'intéressant presque jamais à ce qui se passe chez son voisin. Il est facile au voleur d'étudier les habitudes des locataires et d'opérer dans la journée pendant que les enfants sont en classe, les parents au travail, la bonne seule à la maison.

Les quartiers de très haut standing sont moins visités à cause de la présence de gardiens, de veilleurs de nuit, de chiens de bonne race dressés pour la surveillance. Dans ces quartiers, tout déplacement à certaines heures est suspect et ne peut manquer d'attirer l'attention des gardiens.

Pour bien mettre en relief cette évolution qualitative, nous nous sommes appuyés sur les éléments fournis par l'un des commissariats de quartier de Dakar en 1990 qui reflète la tendance actuelle pour l'ensemble des six commissariats de la ville.[14]

Nous notons qu'en 1980, près de 83% des vols correctionnels sont relatifs aux menus larcins, effets vestimentaires, ustensile de cuisine et au pickpockets; soit 187 cas sur les 225 enregistrés. La deuxième catégorie, constituée par les objets électroniques, électro-ménagers, accessoires de voiture et bijoux, représente 17,5% des cas de vols correctionnels enregistrés, soit 38 cas.

Si nous nous intéressons, en revanche, à l'année 1988, l'évolution est manifeste. En effet, la première catégorie (effets vestimentaires ... etc), ne représente plus que 45,3% soit 179 cas enregistrés pour un total de 429. Par contre, la deuxième catégorie (électro-ménager, électronique, bijoux, accessoires autos) passe de 17,5% en 1980 à 54,7% en 1988, soit, en chiffres absolus, de 38 cas à 250 cas enregistrés.

Les vols de matériel électronique passent de 14 à 92 cas alors que les ustensiles de cusine volés ne représentent plus que 6,9% des cas enregistrés en 1988, contre 18% en 1980.

De la même façon les accessoires de voiture passent de 5 en 1980 à 69 en 1988, soit de 2,5% des objets déclarés à 16%. Les vols de bijoux passent de 3 cas en 1980 à 36 en 1988, soit, en nombre relatif de 1% à 8,3%.

3.2.2 L'émergence des bandes

Les déviances de subsistance chez les mineurs qui vagabondent favorisent les regroupements au sein des quartiers les plus pauvres. Après les troubles sociaux dus aux élections présidentielles de février 1988, et lors de la crise due au conflit Sénégalo-Mauritanien d'avril 1989, s'est précisé un phénomène nouveau par son ampleur: les bandes de voleurs.

Ce sont des voleurs qui n'agissent qu'en groupe, comme des loups, profitant du moindre évènement pouvant engendrer des manifestations ou des mouvements de foule. Ces bandes profitent de toutes les occasions pour créer des incidents qui masqueraient leurs forfaits: meetings politiques ou syndicaux, grèves, marches pacifiques.

Ces petits groupes vivent dans les quartiers à très forte densité de population, où ils peuvent se fondre et se dissimuler sans attirer l'attention.

Si certaines de ces bandes sont formées de délinquants aguérris, qui se sont rencontrés en prison ou dans des lieux douteux qu'ils fréquentent, beaucoup d'entre elles sont constituées par des jeunes oisifs et sans profession. Livrés à eux-mêmes, ces jeunes s'assemblent pour s'adonner à leurs passe-temps favoris: le cinéma et la drogue. Pour satisfaire ces besoins, le premier recours est le vol. Ils sont liés à des receleurs qui écoulent la marchandise.

Nouvelle donnée venant s'ajouter aux difficultés que rencontre la police dans sa lutte contre la délinquance, les bandes sont aussi informelles. Au moindre phénomène de rue - si fréquent avec la tension politique et sociale créée par les mouvements d'opposition - elles éclosent en quelques heures, pour faire razzia sur les boutiques, casser, détériorer, piller les marchandises et la caisse.

Après leur forfait, elles s'évanouissent dans la nature, attendant le prochain moment favorable pour renouveler leur exploit. Ces expéditions se disent parfois "punitives" et "d'assainissement social", lorsqu'une personne ne leur plaît pas: vente d'alcool, débauche et prostitution favorisée par un tenancier de bar.

Ce phénomène, fort inquiétant, nous fait penser que par un enchaînement de la déviance de subsistance, on est entraîné vers la violence gratuite, la violence comme fin et non plus comme moyen. Lorsque l'Etat et la police ne peuvent pas faire face à leurs obligations, les jeunes s'instaurent "redresseurs de torts", et sous prétexte de rétablir la moralité publique, commettent des exactions dont ils tirent profit.

4. Conclusion

Devant l'appauvrissement économique des pays en développement, les déviances de subsistance ne peuvent qu'augmenter et rendre la société toujours plus criminogène.

Les déviances de subsistance suscitent un abaissement généralisé de la moralité publique et se génèrent également en raison de cet abaissement de la moralité publique. Lors des pillages des boutiques des ressortissants mauritaniens en avril 1989, toutes les couches de la société ont été impliquées dans le recel et l'achat à vil prix des marchandises volées par les casseurs et les violents. Une prise de conscience, a posteriori, a été une découverte étonnée de ce qui fut un mouvement spontané, autant qu'une blessure au flan d'un peuple connu pour sa fierté et son attachement à ses valeurs traditionnelles. Cet épisode sera peut-être sans lendemain. Mais les déviances de subsistance se déploient au sein d'un tout et l'on ne peut les traiter à la légère, sous prétexte qu'elles seraient "peu" ou "moins" criminogènes que la violence ou la grande délinquance, et empreintes de circonstances atténuantes.

Au plan individuel, malgré les apparences contraires, subsiste encore le sens du "DIOM", c'est à dire de "l'honneur", la fine pointe de l'âme sénégalaise. Pour se débarrasser d'un colporteur harcelant ou d'un mendiant trop zélé, il n'est que de dire: "Amolo diom"? C'est à dire "qu'as-tu fait de ton honneur?", pour le voir décrocher. Cette expérience est révélatrice: Faim, survie, mises en balance avec l'honneur ...? Lorsque c'est l'honneur qui l'emporte, on ne se trouve pas devant un délinquant en rupture, mais devant un pauvre acculé à ce mode de subsistance. Le terrain le plus profond de l'honneur est accessible. Rappeler la dignité perdue est encore ressenti comme une humiliation.

Mais les attitudes sociales de rejet persistent. Pour qu'il y ait réconciliation entre déviant et société, il faut un effort mutuel qui paraît lointain, tant il est vrai qu'avec le déclin de la solidarité familiale africaine et le sentiment d'une insécurité grandissante, l'abaissement du seuil de tolérance à la déviance emporte de plus en plus le rejet de l'individu. Or, toute politique de réinsertion sociale dépend de la tolérance des populations, véritable "quête du Graal".[15] Les communautés villageoises ne sont pas disposées à supporter l'implantation d'un centre pour mineurs délinquants, d'un village psychiatrique ou d'un village de protection sociale pour handicapés physiques, ou même un village de lépreux.[16]

Est-ce à dire que la tolérance à l'égard des déviants signifie "l'approbation de valeurs sous-culturelles"? (Szabo, 1978:189). Il ne saurait en être question. Mais on doit s'acheminer vers une action plus sociale que pénale lorsqu'il s'agit de petits délinquants victimes d'un problème de subsistance, en résonnance à cette appréciation d'un enfant du tiers-monde: "En grandissant, j'ai appris à connaître la rue. Compris que pour manger, il faut voler. Se droguer pour oublier le froid, la faim, la peur. J'ai appris tout ce qu'un enfant ne devrait jamais apprendre. C'est comme ça. *Faut survivre!* "Ne me jugez pas" (Montali, 1990:120).

Notes

1 Sur l'histoire des pauvres:
 Jacq London, 1902; Kromer Tom, 1937; Vexliard A., 1956; Mollat M., 1978; Porquet J.L., 1987, particulièrement, sa bibliographie.
2 Arrêté 10-878 du 26 août 1971, J.O.R.S. n° 4 186 du 25 sept. 1971, 932.
3 C'est à 10 millions d'habitants que la cote d'alerte sera atteinte, avec le très fort taux de fécondité.
4 Journal "Le Soleil": 6 juin 1972; 16 mars 1974; 12 janv. 1976; 8 fév. 1977; 1er mars 1980.
5 "Ce matin encore les journeaux en ont parlé: ces mendiants, ces talibés, ces lépreux, ces diminués physiques, ces loques, constituent des encombrements humains. Il faut débarrasser la ville de ces hommes - ombres d'hommes plutôt - déchets humains, qui vous assaillent et vous agressent partout et n'importe quand" (Sow Fall, 1979: 5).
6 Loi 75-78 du 9 juillet 1975, J.O.R.S. 1975: 1007
 Décret 76-213 du 24 février 1976, J.O.R.S. 20 mars 1976: 422
 Décret 78-540 du 16 juin 1978, J.O.R.S. du 22 juillet 1978: 921-922
 Loi 76-03 du 25 mars 1976, J.O.R.S. du 10 avril 1976: 534
 Décret 78-541 du 16 juin 1978, J.O.R.S. du 22 juillet 1978: 922-923
7 Loi 47-50 du 29 novembre 1967, J.O.R.S. du 9 décembre 1967: 3 930
 Décret 68-664 du 10 juin 1968, J.O.R.S. du 22 juin 1968.

8 En témoignent ces propos d'une jeune prostituée interrogée au centre d'hygiène sociale: "Je suis née dans la misere, de parents eux-mêmes misérables. Je n'ai qu'un regret, d'avoir perdu trop tôt mes parents. Je les aurai rendus heureux".

9 Autre propos relevé auprès de l'une d'elles au centre d'hygiène sociale.

10 "Revue Famille et Développement". Il s'agit de la certitude de trouver toute l'année les quatre "S": Sea, Sun, Sand and Sex. 1977: 9; 1978: 13 et s.

11 D'autres types de prostitution, non liés à la déviance de subsistance, existent au Sénégal comme partout: prostitution de luxe, prostituées de services administratifs et de colloques internationaux, prostitution universitaire. Cette prostitution n'entre pas dans le cadre de notre étude.

12 Loi 66-21 du 1er février 1966, J.O.R.S. du 5 février 1966; Décret 69-616 du 21 mai 1969, J.O.R.S. du 5 juin 1969.

13

Années	1980		1985		1988	
Ages	Nombre de cas	%	Nombre de cas	%	Nombre de cas	%
15-20 ans	19	15,9	54	27,2	139	36,8
21-26 ans	47	39,4	63	31,8	88	23,3
27-33 ans	21	17,6	40	20,2	70	18,5
34-40 ans	12	10,0	23	11,6	27	7,1
41-46 ans	14	11,7	9	4,5	36	9,5
47-53 ans	6	5,0	6	3	15	3,9
54 et plus	0	0	3	1,5	2	0,5
Total	119	99,6 100%	198	98,8 100%	377	96,6 100%

14

Années et %	1980	%	1988	%
Effets vestimentaires	37	16,44	41	9,55
Ustensiles de cuisine	41	18,22	30	6,99
Electroménager	16	7,11	53	12,35
Accessoires autos	5	2,22	69	16,08
Menus larcins (divers)	62	27,55	60	13,98
Pickpockets	47	20,88	48	11,18
Electronique	14	6,22	92	21,44
Bijoux	3	1,33	36	8,39
Total	225	100%	429	100%

15 Sénégal d'Aujourd'hui Magasine (1979). N°, 16, "Un peu de convialité pour les exclus".

16 Qu'on en juge par ces titres évocateurs d'articles parus dans le quotidien national: "Plaidoirie pour les blanchis du centre" (Soleil, 23/5/79); "Leurs mères étaient indésirables: les enfants creusent le puits du salut" (Soleil, 25/5/79); "Le tort d'être enfant de malade" (Soleil, 26/5/79).

Références bibliographiques

Baro R. 1978. *La Protection Judiciaire de l'Enfant*. Le Droit au Service de la Justice. Publication de l'Amicale des Juristes Sénégalaises. pp.89-90.

London J. 1902. *Le Peuple de l'Abîme*. Paris. Seuil. Collection 10/18.

Kromer T. 1937. *Waiting for Nothing*. Traduit sous le titre: *Les Vagabonds de la Faim*. Paris. Calmann-Levy.

Michelet E. 1980. *Cours de Politique Criminelle*. Non publié. Dakar. Faculté des Sciences Juridiques.

---- . 1981. *Politique Criminelle et Prophylaxie Sociale au Sénégal*. Annales Africaines. pp.111-167.

Mollat M. 1978. *Les Pauvres au Moyen-Age*. Paris. Hachette.

Montali J.M. 1990. *La Ville dont les Rats sont des Enfants*. Figaro-magasine. 1er juin, p.120.

Porquet J.L. 1987. *La Débine*. Paris. Flammarion.

Sow Fall A. 1979. *La Grève des Mbattus*. Dakar. Nouvelles Editions Africaines.

Stanciu 1956. *Délinquants Nécessiteux et Prévention*. Revue Internationale de Défense Sociale.

Szabo D. 1978. *Criminologie et Politique Criminelle*. Paris. Vrin.

Vexliard A. 1956. *Introduction à la Sociologie du Vagabondage*. Paris. Rivière éd.

VIOLENCE AS A WEAPON OF THE DISPOSSESSED

Ben F. Smit*

1. Introduction

There are several theories on, and explanations for, the concept of *violence* and its concomitants *disorder, terrorism* and *intimidation*. In the context of this article violence in South Africa is explained in terms of being a competition between possessor and dispossessed for a commodity.

Generally, it goes without saying that man *per se*, his history and his environment tend to be violent, and one may even say that violence comes naturally to man. This natural tendency to violence does not distinguish him from "other species of the animal kingdom". However, the very nature of human violence differs quite drastically. " ... Man is a killer distinct from the others. Hardly ever among the 'lower' animals of a given species does a 'fratricide' (literally killing of a brother) occur. There may be combat over mates and territories, but the fighting ends in submission, not annihilation" (Hartogs and Artzt, 1970:8).

History abounds with examples of man's bloody violence in competition for scarce commodities. Excluding wide-ranging wars, one could cite Cain and Abel (for God's mercy); revolutions (for freedom, equality and brotherhood), the infamous Molly Maguires of the United States (for economic equality), blood-drenched colonialisation and decolonialisation (for Africa's geographical space and collective freedom), the gas chambers of Auschwitz (for homogeneity and racial superiority), Northern Ireland (for religious tolerance), Kuwait (for basic materials and energy) and South Africa (for opportunities in the political, educational, economic and social fields).

Violence is also part of the human environment to such an extent as to be regarded as natural. It is an indication of a pressure building up against the chain of social relationships (Van Heerden, 1986:9). " ... many individuals in crisis signal a society in crisis ... Violent acts may be looked upon as society's early warning system, revealing deep-rooted ... conflicts which are gathering strength beneath the surface of social relations" (Kalinowski, 1980:57).

---

* Head, Department of Criminology, University of South Africa, Pretoria, South Africa.

2. Theories and explanations

These theories and explanations are, in the main, focused on possible causes, of which there are many. In an attempt to organize this medley of possible causes, this brief discussion will be classified into four main categories. Initially *cultural conditioning* (i.e. violence as acquired behaviour); *psychological factors* (i.e. violence as pathological behaviour); and *utilitarianism* (i.e. violence as goal-directed behaviour) will be discussed. The three categories will provide some blameworthiness: they would probably serve as indicators of whether violence is caused by a sick or confused environment or a sick or confused individual or whether it can be considered a rational approach to interaction. However, in this article, the premise would be on violence as a competition for scarce commodities in society. The approach is multi-disciplinary with the emphasis on certain structural-functional elements.

2.1 *Cultural conditioning*

This approach sees violence as acquired behaviour on the assumption that violence is part of the culture whose members or groups adhere to its values and customs. Thus, violence is not simply the outcome of individual idiosyncracy, but is consolidated by the environment. True, the capacity for violence resides in the individual, but social values determine the choice of behaviour. A society with a tradition of violence, which transmits to its youth, an attitude oriented towards violence, is bound to erupt into violence at some time or another. Kieselhorst (1974:16-23) lists the following cultural factors that give rise to the conditioning of violence:

a) Interpersonal relationship: violence is subtly presented as part of human interaction. In numerous ways violence creates the attitude that it is a sign of distinction, prestige, or power - the behaviour of people with superior status (parents, teachers, government, etc.) towards their inferiors. Its effects are supposedly salutary, but taken to extremes, it has the opposite effects. This could be taken even further to a form of cultural symbolism: the Zulus' insistence to carry cultural weapons and members of the white supremists' organization AWB (Afrikaner Weerstandsbeweging translated as the Afrikaner Resistance Movement) openly flaunting their fire-arms at meetings.

A child who grows up in such a society would be conditioned not to respond with violence to violent discipline (i.e. corporal punishment) on the part of a parent or teacher. Similarly, this society would condemn an aggressive response to moderate police violence. True, it creates a subtle relationship, but to the masses aspiring to prestige, self-identity, and a self-image, violence becomes a symbol of prestige and authority, the short cut to success. Toch (1969:183) maintains that this tendency among suppressed or subordinate people to form a favourable self-image in their relations with others, reveals two types of orientations that may lead to violence. In the first instance, other people are seen as a means to personal ends, and in the second, some are open to manipulation.

b) *Military mobilization*: with its attendant publicity stresses the latent presence of violence. In this context, compulsory military service for the whites in South Africa cannot be ignored. For quite some time, youths live with the idea of violence and the conviction that the survival of the nation and its possession of strategic materials depended on it. In the South African context, during the years 1975 to 1990 this had been made very clear to its citizens. South Africans of all walks of life had been made eminently aware of the Enemy: a multi-faceted and omnipresent Reality, called the Total Onslaught which could only be combated by the so-called Total Strategy. Briefly, the white part of society became militarized; the blacks radicalized. The security forces (especially the military) became inwardly directed, the population targetted and virtually all resources pooled in the National Security Management System. The last-mentioned had in fact become the system of government (Frankel, 1984; Grundy, 1983 and 1986).

This implanted new values which in civilian life were expressed towards potential enemies, or in an attempt to uphold one's own set of superior values/possessions.

c) *Mass media*: speeches, newspapers, radio and television may over-emphasize violence to the extent that it may be interpreted as essential for survival and, in fact, a normal feature of it. This conditions acceptance of, and identification with, violence. In this, the media has become the creator of syndroms (e.g. the "Beirut-syndrome" where violence forms part of the natural order of things; or the "Pretoria-Soweto-syndrome" where violence in itself is the absolute prerequisite for peaceful co-existence: *si vis pacem para bellum*).

d) *Collective theories:* the idea of violence (crime) as normal acquired behaviour is very much at issue in Sutherland's *Theory of Differential Association* (Sutherland and Cressey, 1955). Although this theory deals with crime generally, it nonetheless relates to violence as a special facet of crime. According to this theory, violence is inherent in all societies and constitutes an element of general socio-cultural processes. Violence is essentially an integrative (individually) and adaptive (collectively) form of behaviour.

Individually, its general nature is determined by particular associations, that is, the extent to which it is elevated by the group that represents the individual's main source of association. In these intimate, personal groups, behaviour (violence) is *acquired* in *interaction* through *communication* with people. In the wide spectrum of possible behaviour, the individual conforms to the behaviour that was most forcibly conveyed to him by such differential association (the Soweto-riots and aftermath).

Collectively, this theory not only emphasizes man's capacity to associate, but also to adapt to, survive in and thrive in a hostile environment: the prevailing ongoing and very lucrative arms smuggling in South Africa. This is an illustration of non-possessors creating an own economy (albeit a dark or alternative one). In this regard, the non-possessors may counter-moralize: the danger of the changes facing us is that as a group, we may continue to act only from the perspective of one economic quadrant without appreciating the totality of concealed economic transactions and their place in a society subject to constant and often violent change. Alternative and hidden economies are too large to ignore often too informal to detect, and too resilient to control. In this beleaguered status quo, smuggling often represents untapped potential for the dispossessed (adapted from Mars, 1982:227).

e) Merton's anomie theory (Merton, 1968): posits that crime (and by implication, violence) is the result of a state of tension and frustration developing in a culture (e.g. have's/have-not's; possessors/non-possessors). His approach is based on the assumptions, first, that there is a fairly generally organised system of values governing the behaviour of members of any social group, and secondly, that there are institutionalised means of controlling the attainment of cultural aims and accepted social objectives. When the approved means are inadequate for the attainment of prescribed goals, this gives rise to tension and frustrations - consequently to violence.

Srole approached anomie (a socio-cultural theory) from a psychological angle, calling it *anomia* (Szabo, 1966:187). This designates the mental condition of someone who believes that:

- the government is indifferent to his needs;
- little can be achieved in a society where everything is unpredictable;
- individual goals in life become blurred rather than actualised;
- life has little meaning and has nothing to offer; and
- there is no one to rely on when one needs moral and social support.

2.2   Psychological factors

Although these factors are normally utilized to explain individual behaviour, these could be relevant in analyzing group behaviour. It could serve as the common denominator of individuals in a group.

Most forms of violence are the result of the psychological effect of the environment. The following conditions can be listed:

a) *Deprivation-frustration* derives from the wretchedness of existing living conditions, that is certain groups - in particular the lower socio-economic classes (non-possessors) - feel that they are being deprived or even robbed of the advantages of prosperity and progress. Theorists maintain that violence is the natural outcome of the resulting alienation, frustration, and anomia. Deprived circumstances give rise to frustration and ultimately to violence because they constitute obstacles primarily to the pursuit of basic human need satisfaction, and secondly, to a group's aspirations. This could serve as a psychological vantage-point to understand the colonialization and decolonialization processes in Africa (cf. Frantz Fanon's *Wretched of the Earth*. Fanon, 1967 and 1970).

The most common approach is that frustration is the outcome of obstructed goal pursuit. Individual reactions vary from modifying either the goal or the means of realising it, to withdrawal and aggression: "A person frustrated by submission to a stronger group or person may also 'scapegoat' or 'displace' or 'project' his aggression toward a weaker party (or object) rather than to the one responsible for his frustration" (Canfield, 1973:31). Groups react by competition/violence. In such cases actual aggression is very often directed at the police, the visible representatives of the total regime, or at structures like schools, police stations and other public buildings which serve as substitutes for the real cause of frustration (cf. Table 1). Research into riotous situations indicates, however, that they occur also in times of affluence. In the past (1968) the worst riots on university and schools campuses occurred at those institutions where education and facilities were best. Hence deprivation-frustration is manifestly not the only explanation for violence.

b) *Relative deprivation* is a theory in which deprivation is less important, and the emphasis is on expectations with regard to the goal and the hopes associated with these. Goal pursuit is intensified when the satisfaction of realising the goal is anticipated (as in the case of South Africa since 2 February 1990); but if this does not materialise, frustration is aggravated. Frustration is really accepted only when hope has been abandoned. Rapid change and political or social instability arouse higher hopes than can be fulfilled, that is to say, the hopes are unrealistic. "Thus, the deprivation felt may be largely dependent on or relative to, the level of anticipations, expectations, and hopes. The higher the hopes, present or future, the greater the deprivation likely to be felt and the greater the potential for violent reactions to such frustrations of hopes" (Canfield, 1973:34). In the light of this, and even though things could be better in South Africa, group violence would still stay a long time.

c) *Relative deprivation as a perception of injustice* puts the accent on the expectation of political activists. In this regard, violence is a motivated action aimed at removing all forms of injustice, inequality, and discrimination, that is, basic obstacles to being treated and regarded as dignified fellow members of the group.

Basically, psychological or pathological theories fall into two categories. Violence is regarded on the one hand as irrational, inherent behaviour, and on the other, as something with a rational foundation in that it relates to aspirations and the frustrations incurred in the process of trying to realise them. The latter provides a useful explanation for violence deriving from frustration, but it does not explain all violent behaviour, or why frustration should trigger violence in some cases and not in others.

2.3 Utilitarianism

The utilitarian approach puts greater emphasis on the rationality of violence. According to this theory, a rationalised pattern of behaviour offers the sole means of reaching a goal (Kieselhorst, 1974:26-35). In terms of this approach, violence relates logically to some form of individual or group goal.

Individual goal-oriented violence is:
- a reaction to deprivation of need-satisfaction;
- assistance to others;
- a response to violence;
- forms of reprisal; and
- individual conflict.

Political or group goal-oriented violence, on the other hand, is:
- a means of obtaining freedom, equality and justice;
- a symbol of and commitment to the group;
- a form of group reprisal; and
- a means of protecting and extending power and privilege.

The perceived positive effects of violence enhance its utility value:

a) *Conspicuousness*. The advantage of violence over other forms of behavioural expression is its conspicuousness. Violence absorbs people's attention and forces the non-involved to reflect on problems and issues which would otherwise have been ignored. For its advocates, violence is captivating and dramatic action which has a mysterious appeal to the casual bystander.

The part played by the media in publicising violence must not be underestimated (the press in South Africa is now relatively free). Through wide and detailed news coverage, opinions are expressed, alleged grievances are made known, and action and counteraction are praised or criticised. Propagandists sometimes use reports on violence to stir up further violent action.

b) *Attracts attention*. Both the collective and individual components of this particular behavioural expression are important. It can be assumed that violent groups consist of individuals whose past appeals for, or claims to, attention have been largely ignored. For them, as individuals and as members of a specific group, violence ensures the necessary attention. Also, through violence, attention is drawn to scarce commodities in South Africa such as political representation, social equality, economic affluence and opportunities for education.

c) *Goals are attained*. Violence is an efficient means of attaining short-term and immediate goals. Black militants often claim that bloody riots and acts of arson have elicited a greater and more real and positive reaction from the White establishment than has ever been accomplished by the total effect, over many years, of non-violent and fruitless efforts such as peace marches and demonstrations. Violence forces politicians to handle problems personally and urgently. Also commissions of inquiry are appointed and legislation is passed with far-reaching effects on civil rights (Kieselhorst, 1974:36)."The policy concerning the medium of instruction was one of the main reasons for the first eruption (Soweto 1976) and the first thing to be rectified by the authorities .... So successful was the demolition of the existing system (of education) that White and Black speakers publicly advocated the abolition of Bantu education ..." (Commission of Inquiry, 1980:537-538).

d) *Provides emotional release*. On the individual human level, the agitator is given the opportunity of ridding himself of accumulated anxiety and suppressed emotions. The frustrated individual uses the practice of violence as a psychological discharge process which enables him to return to a state of emotional balance.

e) *Non-violence is meaningless.* Sorel states that violence emphasises the social inequality and the potential for conflict between classes. Unlike non-violence, violence prevents class assimilation, which extinguishes the flame of revolutionary zeal (Kieselhorst, 1974:36-37).

Through violence, groups which have become passive and resigned are activated. "The young people or a large group of them, feel that the riots have prepared and inspired them" (Commission of Inquiry, 1980:546). For the oppressed and colonised masses, violence is labour: labour which builds the national character with positive and creative qualities. "They (Sorel and Fanon) are suggesting that violence is very effective in arousing the masses, shaking them out of their resignation, and inspiring them to action that will bring about the fundamental social and political changes that are so badly needed. In short ... violence is a good way to get the revolution started" (Kieselhorst, 1974:37).

Not only groups, but also individuals are encouraged by violence (this also points to the irrevocable and magnetic nature of violence). "During the riots in the United States ... stress was laid on the value to a riot movement of someone who had lost his fear of violence and the reaction to it as a result of previous experience. It was said that those who went through the baptism of fire were taught by the 'spontaneous' violence to lead the nation in revolt" (Commission of Inquiry, 1980:547).

3. Defining points of departure

This essay is a criminological explanation of the violence in South Africa. This explanation is based on part of the principle of causality: cause -> means -> consequence. It is presumed that *cause* denotes the existence of scarce commodities in a given society whilst *means* are indicative of the competition (i.e. violence) to obtain those scarce commodities.

3.1 Competition

Van Heerden (1986:86) maintains that competition is the impersonal rivalry for desired but limited gains such as wealth, prestige, higher social status, work, promotion, better living conditions and more influence with regard to social and political questions. Unfortunately, this description does not address the essence of competition. It merely lists commodities which, under certain circumstances, may be regarded as scarce.

The following elements of the concept *competition* are of importance:
- competition is a form of human interaction;

- this interaction does not occur according to rules;
- the interaction is spontaneous (unexpected), instrumental, intense, destructive, unjustified and illegal. Hartogs and Artzt (1970) say that it is precisely the last two adjectives which distinguish *state violence* from *terrorists' violence*, for instance. State violence may be unjustified but is normally not illegal. Terrorists' violence, however, is always unjustified and illegal.

From the description above, two parallel concepts, namely, *aggression* and *conflict* may be deduced.

In reality, the nature of the interaction is perceived to be aggressive. Aggressiveness is a purposeful willingness to compete. "Aggression is broader than any single theory; it is the resultant of many factors, an inborn drive shaped by learning and development, released by circumstances within the person and his environment. In modified form, it has utility and value: one can hardly imagine a salesman, or a ball player, or a junior executive being praised for his lack of aggressiveness ... Violence may be defined as an extreme form of aggression making illegitimate use of force" (Hartogs and Artzt, 1970:14).

The other concept is *conflict,* which is seen as " ... being designed to resolve divergent dualisms and a way of achieving some kind of unity, even be it through the annihilation of the one of the conflicting parties" (Ahn, 1977:9). However, Deutsch, warns against the tendency to use the concepts competition and conflict interchangeably and as synonyms. This leads to confusion. "Although competition produces conflict, not all instances of conflict reflect competition. Competition implies an opposition in the goals of the interdependent parties such that the probability of goal attainment for the one decreases as the probability for the other increases. In conflict that is derived from competition, the incompatible actions reflect incompatible goals" (1973:10).

For the purposes of this study, competition is regarded as the aggressive and conflicting human interaction between parties where violence is the visible, but possibly unjustified and illegal component.

3.2 Scarce commodities

For various reasons, certain commodities in South African society are regarded as scarce (limited). In essence, these are scarce because people have been dispossessed (deprived) of them and there is a general refusal to share. One should, however, keep in mind that dispossession and its concomitants are largely dependent on individual and group perceptions. In this essay, political power (freedom) and expression, social equality and homogeneity, economic affluence and survival, equal opportunities for education, equality before the law and impartiality are, *inter alia*, regarded as limited.

4. Manifestations of competition

There are generally two approaches to competition. The reason for these two approaches is probably the result of a difference in opinion as to proportionateness or tolerability of competition. Is competition in a society abnormal or is it normal?

a) *The consensus (or equilibrium)* model regards conflict and violence as deviations and stability as the normal (or desired) state. "... violence is seen largely as the failure of the ruled in complying with formal authority" 25. (Ahn, 1977:8).

b) *The conflict* model is an alternative viewpoint of violence. "This model posits essentially that at every point of social change, disensus and conflict are normal phenomena" (Ahn, 1977:9).

The latter theory stresses the antagonism and conflict between groups of people as an explanation of violence (crime). White points out that some theorists adopt the view that conflict is to be explained in terms of the behaviour of groups and individuals (behavioural theories), while others believe that conflict relates to social structure (structural hypothesis) (Masotti and Bowen, 1968:158).

Behavioural theories emphasise attitudes and how they are formed. This includes the degree of tension and anomie, the processes responsible for tension and aggression, and the processes of socialisation. It also incorporates the classical *frustration-aggression model*, according to which conflict arises when a gap develops between individual expectations and the ability to satisfy them. Conflict and concomitant aggression may arise, for example, in times of economic recession (as in South Africa), or when a group or an individual is unable to earn the same income as the rest of society.

The *structural hypothesis*, on the other hand, cites objective social conditions as the main causes of conflict, stressing economic circumstances, social stratifications and mobility or geographical and demographic (national, ethnic and racial connection) factors. Smelser (Masotti and Bowen, 1968:158), believes that conflict, especially as manifested in riots, is best examined in terms of structural effectiveness and structural tension. Structural effectiveness refers to religious, ethnic, racial and class differences that may lead to conflict, the potential being higher when economic, political and racial membership coincide. It may also relate to the channels used to air grievances. Smelser states that "it is important to inquire into the possibility of expressing protest by means other than hostility. Are these other means permanently unavailable (i.e. politically dispossessed)? If so, aggrieved people are likely to be driven into hostile outbursts" (Masotti and Bowen, 1968:159). See also the view of Le Grande (1967:393), that depriving people of the right to demonstrate peacefully or air grievances, leads to aggressive and violent civil disobedience.

Structural tension concerns the overall social situation when structural effectiveness is present. Many tensions in South Africa have been institutionalised and relate to the effectiveness of the structure; for instance, inherent structural differences of colour which are exacerbated by the influx into urban areas and concomitant housing and unemployment problems. In these circumstances open hostility is directed at unjust legislation, police brutality, job discrimination and housing. These factors overlap with the broad structure and may be regarded as belief that conflict relates to social structure (structural hypothesis) (Masotti and Bowen, 1968:158).

Behavioural theories emphasise attitudes and how they are formed. This includes the degree of tension and anomie, the processes responsible for tension and aggression, and processes of socialisation. It also incorporates the classical *frustration-aggression model*, according to which conflict arises when a gap develops between individual expectations and the ability to satisfy them.

4.1 Reasons for competition

Three main reasons can be put forward for the competition in South Africa:

a) It goes without saying that individuals and societies are not absolutely homogeneous. South Africa has many role-players: whites (approximately three million), coloured (approximately two and a half million), Indians (approximately one and a half million), Zulus (approximately seven million), Xhosas (approximately seven million), Sotho-speaking people (approximately six million) and other indigenous people (approximately three million).

b) The existence of demographic, social and political processes, spatial mobility (segregation and penetration of people) (Van Heerden, 1986:84), urbanisation (and squatting), population growth, and so on. Specific examples are the attacks of Inkhata-supporting, mainly Zulu-speaking inhabitants of mine hostels on squatters. The former grouping regards those squatters as potential opponents in the competition for a very scarce commodity: the availability of labour.

c) The human response and adaptation to the processes. Merton's (1968) mechanisms of adaptation could be cited as examples: conformism, innovation, ritualism, withdrawal and rebellion. The latter in particular could be a typical violent adaptation: it rejects the structure and means by which these structures are maintained.

4.2 Patterns of competition

In this article violence occurs in three patterns, namely violence (as generality) and disorder and terrorism, (specifically).

However, one should distinguish between *disorder* (in the form of civil disobedience) and *terrorism* as patterns of competition. Similar characteristics are:
- both are rationalised by the urgent and just nature of a particular cause; and
- in both violations, participants usurp the authority to decide when the law must be respected and when it may be violated.

Thus to summarise: "Civil disorders are manifestations of exuberance, discontent or disapproval of a substantial segment of a community ... . Terrorism is an act of extraordinary violence, the work of a comparatively small number of malcontents or dissidents who, their rhetoric notwithstanding, threaten the security of the entire community" (United States, National Advisory Committee on Criminal Justice Standards and Goals, 1976:1).

Kalinowski sees the distinguishing features between disorder and terrorism as follows: "The ... terrorist tries to achieve his objectives by the effect his unlawful actions have on strangers. The civil disobedient seeks his political end by violating the law but at a risk only to himself. Civil disobedience, because of its non-violent character, may cause inconvenience, but the violators do not intend to instill fear and inflict no pain. The civil disobedient does not run away, he protests in public, identifies himself and exposes himself to punishment" (1980:23).

Generally, South Africa can be regarded as an extremely violent society: a high murder and grievous assault rate (14,000 and 124,000 for the 1990-1991 period respectively) and violent deaths on the road (approximately 10,000 per annum) are indicative of this statement. South Africa has a population of thirty million people: Comparing the 1989-1990 figures of some crimes, one sees a marked increase: murder (+28.6%), robbery (+19.0%), arson (+57.2%) and malicious damage to property (+10.8%).

In this society, unrest-related incidents and acts of terrorism are fairly common features.

Terrorism has become a major threat for the security of South Africa in the 1980s, due to its unpredictability and the tendency to choose 'soft targets' (i.e. innocent people).

Table 3 reflects the number of terrorist attacks in South Africa for the period 1980-1989.

In comparison to other acts of violence, the number of terrorist attacks seems relatively low. As far as the community is concerned, however, the loss of life (sixteen killed in 1989), the effect on survivors and bystanders, and the damage to property makes this figure incalculably high (cf. the Chinese proverb: "Kill one, frighten ten thousand"). The propaganda value of excessive news coverage provides immense advantages to the attackers, terrorists or terrorist organizations. A few of the incidents caused a sensation as a result of the loss of human lives and damage to property, for example, Church Street, Pretoria; Magistrate's Court, Johannesburg; a supermarket in Amanzimtoti and a bar in Durban. On the other hand, it seems that, due to earlier excessive news coverage, most terrorist attacks no longer attract so much attention.

5. Scarce commodities in South African society

The nature of the scarcity is dependent upon the model accepted. The *consensus* model accepts the fact that scarce goods exist. Through consensus, it should be decided how these should be used. The *conflict* model regards scarcity as the result of structural violence. The system is solely responsible for societal, political, cultural and economical limits. One example is the following: "Underdevelopment is a chronic state of violence ... The first form of violence is expressed in inhumanly high rate of birth and death rates, degrading poverty, ignorance and non-participation in significant decisions" (Ahn, 1977:12).

5.1 Prerequisities for scarcity

The question here is why certain commodities in a society are limited (the obvious that the possessors refuse to share should not be forgotten).
- Unconditionally important: primary goods such as air, water and food.

- Strategically important: secondary goods such as minerals, energy and information.
- Goods becoming scarcer due to the inherent transitoriness, irreplaceability and demographic processes.
- The fact that certain goods are available to members of society to a lesser extent: *personal goods* such as wealth, status and power; and *system-related commodities* connected to politics, social structures the economy and education.

5.2 Structuring scarcity

In the last instance, it relates to what commodities are scarce in this society. It is difficult to identify such commodities. On the one hand, commodities overlap one another or often stand in a difficult-to-comprehend causal relationship to one another.

5.2.1 Political structures

According to Mallin, violence in this structure has two objectives: "*1)* As a means for ... regimes to maintain themselves in power, and *2)*, as a method whereby revolutionary groups achieve psychological effects which they expect will further their cause" (Kalinowski, 1980:28).

Violence in its various forms and as an option for competition functions basically for four reasons in this structure:
- To destroy the existing system. The Klu Klux Klan was founded in the United States to help the former slaveholding Confederate Democratic political establishment to regain power from the Black Republican Coalition which controlled the South (Kalinowsky, 1980:4). The process of de-coloniaization can also be cited as examples (Fanon, 1967 and 1970).
- To speed up political processes. This concerns the phenomenon of people and groups who are too slowly institutionalized politically (cf. the "Huntington-theory" in Ahn, 1977:67).
- To propagate a certain ideology. Literally, millions of people have died for slogans such as freedom, equality, fraternity and peace. This senseless idealism is possibly the oldest and most familiar motivation for violence.
- To create a political constitutency of power base. The most visible form of a political power base nowadays, is probably the so-called mass mobilisation of the African National Congress (ANC). "To some, mass mobilisation or mass action, is a legitimate form of

passive resistance, rooted in the Gandhi tradition of *satyagrapha*. To others, it is a clear and present danger, which threatens to unravel the very fabric of society, destabilising political and economic institutions and presaging increasing anomie and anarchy" (Jeffery, 1991:3). Mass mobilisation has two immediate aims: to compel the state to abidicate its power and to ensure that the negotiation process does not become bogged down. Mass mobilisation can be regarded as a type of the so-called Chinese option, where persuasion and intimidation by sheer numbers play especially important roles.

5.2.2 Social structures

In these structures, the competition revolves around equality and the impossible dream of homogeneity. This society is characterised by classes and group domination: sometimes subtle divisions and distinctions amongst people. The minority groups especially are responsible for attempting to break down the barriers. This process of breaking down is an important element of social mobility.

Social mobility is regarded as a process where "major clusters of old social, economic and psychological commitments are eroded or broken and people become available for new patterns of socialisation and behaviour" (Ahn, 1977:67-68). An increased demand is created to meet the expecations of the masses. This is known as the gap-theory. This theory is more social than political and was implemented to explain the black unrest in the United States in terms of prevailing discrimination and segregation, black migration and white exodus and the existence of black ghettos (Will and Vatter, 1970:191).

Does the factor of race *per se* play a part at all? Padmore, (creator of the African-unity idea and intellectual father of the Pan-African Congress) and Fanon concur definitely. Fanon, when writing on violence, (in contrast to de-colonisation and the "getting rid of the European") states: "At the level of individuals, violence is a cleansing force. It frees the native from his inferiority complex and from his despair and inaction; it makes him fearless and restores his self-respect" (Kalinowski, 1980:46-47). Greyling (1985:64), however, maintains that there is no correlation between race and terrorism.

South African society is seemingly characterised by a search for cultural (not racial but perhaps ethnic) alliances. This search has certain ethno-political directives: Xhosas -> African National Congress (in spite of this organisation's declared heteorgeneity); Zulus -> Inkhata; and Sotho-speaking people -> Pan-African Congress (?).

Other so-called minority groups who agitated in the past and will probably play a competitive role in the future are the Feminists in all their variations, the Gay-rights movements and certain ecology-oriented organisations.

5.2.3 Economic structures

The economic sphere is competitive by nature. As a matter of fact, the theory of relative deprivation (Van Heerden et Al., 1989:chapter 2), is mainly an economical explanation of violence. An increase in economic growth in developing countries (like South Africa) could be de-stabilising.

Flanigan and Fogelman (Ahn, 1977:46) found that the most violent countries tend to be those at the lowest levels of development. However, on the other hand, the accumulation of wealth and industrialisation have socially dividing effects. (In South Africa 87% of the population possess only 13% of the land). Important economic components are the possession of strategic materials, job opportunities (compare the feud between the inhabitants of the hostels and the squatters) and also poverty (affluence is regarded as a scarce commodity). Greyling (1985:62) asserts that poverty *per se* is not a stimulus for violence. Poverty which can be combined with development affords hope for a better tomorrow. Add limited education to these and a new social entity is created: the ambitious poor; the poor rebel; in other words the masses of the revolution which have nothing to lose but much to gain.

5.2.4 Teaching/educative structures

For various reasons, teaching and education are scarce commodities in our society. This statement does not necessarily refer to favouring, but to opportunities for education. The proven reason for the Soweto unrest (1976), was an education-related matter (Van Heerden et Al., 1989:20). The ironic consequence, however, was that no solution was found, and education has become even more scarce (people refer to the lost generation of black school children).

5.2.5 Legal structures

Two elements are of importance here:
- the accessibility, comprehensibility and applicability of the law;
- equality before and impartiality of the law.

226

These elements are important causes for the creation of the so-called People's Courts.

5.2.6 Other structures

Other more subjectively inclined scarce goods are the following:

a) *Order.* The police force as an institution competes to create a stable and non-violent society and to maintain the status quo. The quality of the competition determines the image of the police (Klockars, 1983:35). Due to charges levelled at the police for, *inter alia*, being over-zealous (an understatement, see Hansson and van Zyl Smit, 1990; Scharf, 1989) and the burden of governmental image (Holden, 1986) this image has been tarnished;

b) *Prestige and glamour.* " ... terrorism is seen by the disinherited and disenchanted as a means of aquiring prestige and glamour" (Kalinowski, 1980:1).

6. Conclusion

Gurr (Kalinowski, 1980:56) declares that violence has been resorted to by individuals of every social background and while acting on a variety of motives. "... there is fallacy in the assumption that all wants must be satisfied to minimize discontent. Man's resorting to violence (terror) *is in part unreasoning, but it does not occur without some reason"*.

South Africa bleeds daily. The people themselves are looking at possible remedies. Dhlomo in his address to the Conference on Violence and Political Intimidation (1991), suggested the following healing processes:

a) A Code of Conduct drafted and endorsed by all political parties and spelling out the rules of the democratic game according to which parties would pursue their political objectives. This Code of Conduct should be accompanied by a vigorous grassroots campaign of education for democracy aimed at assisting communities to inculcate the democratic values of tolerance and freedom of association;

b) Legislative and other measures to effectively combat political intimidation;

c) A concerted effort to combat criminal violence as distinct from political violence;

d) Endorsement of the idea of a Standing Commission on Violence whose structure, terms of reference and powers would have to be thoroughly debated by all significant political and community players;

e) A permanent police presence in unrest areas;

f) A strategy to rationalise and co-ordinate policing functions in the country, with a view to the establishment of a single law enforcement agency;

g) A properly co-ordinated and effective programme of social reconstruction to rehabilitate the victims of violence;

h) Effective use of the media to combat violence and promote peace and political tolerance;

i) An effective and meaningful partnership between Government and extra-parliamentary leaders in managing the process of socio-political transition.

Tables

Table 1: Analysis of targets for attacks of terrorism (1980-1989) expressed in percentage.

Target group	1980	1981	1982	1983	1984	1985	1986	1987	1988	1989	1990
Police	26.3	22.0	12.8	7.1	31.1	28.7	34.2	41.3	30.2	31.7	31.1
Defense force		5.1	2.6	3.6		6.6	3.0	7.2	5.0	3.0	4.5
Administration of justice			5.1	8.9	4.5	2.9	0.9	0.9	2.8	2.0	2.2
Government	10.5	16.9	15.4	14.3	13.3	21.3	12.6	10.2	20.6	16.6	15.8
Economy	47.4	50.9	61.5	51.8	37.8	22.1	13.4	10.2	14.2	23.6	21.6
Civilians	15.8	5.1	2.6	14.3	13.3	18.4	35.5	28.9	26.7	21.6	24.2
Others							0.4	1.3	0.5	1.5	0.6
Total	100.0	100.0	100.0	100.0	100.0	100.0	100.0	100.0	100.0	100.0	100.0

Table 2: Geographical breakdown of fatalities due to unrest-related incidents between 1 September 1984 and 30 April 1991.

Year	Cape	Natal	OPS	Transvaal	Unknown	Total
1984	--	--	--	--	--	149
1985	455	117	17	285	5	879
1986	398	101	12	776	11	1.298
1987	65	451	17	124	4	661
1988	79	912	8	150	--	1.149
1989	70	1.279	--	54	--	1.403
1990	247	1.811	92	1.547	2	3.699
1991	--	--	--	--	--	1.000
Total	1.314	4.671	146	2.936	22	10.238

Table 3: Number of terrorist attacks in South Africa for the period 1980-1989.

Month	1980	1981	1982	1983	1984	1985	1986	1987	1988	1989	Total
January	3	1	1	3	1	2	20	20	5	15	71
February		1	1	3	3	7	22	11	10	13	71
March		1	1	6	2	9	21	12	19	11	82
April	2	2	2	2	3	4	13	23	15	19	85
May	1	10	10	4	6	8	26	29	17	18	129
June	7	10	9	1	4	31	26	22	22	25	157
July		8	3	5	6	12	25	28	31	25	143
August		6		6	8	11	17	14	19	19	100
September	2	2	1	6	6	9	15	15	46	18	120
October	2	6	1	6	1	8	17	23	54	6	124
November	2	6	5	7	1	16	16	23	22	10	108
December		6	5	7	4	19	13	15	21	20	110
Total	19	59	39	56	45	136	231	235	281	199	1.300

References

Ahn C.S. 1977. *Development, Equality and Political Violence: Cross National Analysis of the Correlates and Causes of Domestic Political Violence*. Unpublished. Hawaii. University of Hawaii. D. Phil-thesis.

Canfield R.B. 1973. *Black Ghetto Riots and Campus Disorders*. San Francisco. R. & E. Research.

Commission of Inquiry. 1980. *Riots at Soweto and Elsewhere*. Vol.1. Pretoria. Government Printer.

Deutsch M. 1973. *The Resolution of Conflict*. New Haven. Yale University Press.

Dhlomo O. 1991. *Solutions to Violence*. Unpublished. Address to the Conference on Violence and Political Intimidation (24 and 25 May 1991). Pretoria. CSIR.

Fanon F. 1967. *A Dying Colonialism*. New York. Grove.

---- . 1970. *Towards the African Revolution*. London. Chavalier, Cox and Wyman.

Frankel P.H. 1984. *Pretoria's Praetorians: Civil-military Relations in South Africa*. Cambridge. Cambridge University Press.

Greyling R.J. 1985. *Terrorisme: Die Feite*. Pretoria. Van Schaik.

Grundy K.W. 1983. *The Rise of the South African Security Establishment: An essay on the Changing Locus of State Power*. Johannesburg. The South African Institute of International Affairs.

---- . 1986. *The Militarization of South African Politics*. London. Tarris.

Hansson D., Van Zyl Smit D. (Eds.). 1990. *Towards Justice?: Crime and State Control in South Africa*. Cape Town. Oxford University Press.

Hartogs R., Artzt E. 1970. *Violence: Causes and Solutions*. New York. Dell Publishing House.

Holden R.N. 1986. *Modern Police Management*. Englewood Cliffs. Prentice-Hall.

Jeffery A.J. 1991. *Mass Mobilisation. Spotlight. March, No. 1*. Johannesburg. South African Institute of Race Relations.

Kalinowski S.A. 1980. *Leftist Terrorist Motivation*. Los Angeles. California State College. M.Sc. Thesis.

Kieselhorst D.C. 1974. *A Theoretical Perspective of Violence Against Police*. Oklahoma. Bureau of Government Research, University of Oklahoma.

Klockars C.B. 1983. *Thinking About Police: Contemporary Readings*. New York. McGraw-Hill.

Le Grande J. 1967. *Non-Violent Civil Disobedience and Police Enforcement Policy*. Journal of Criminal Law, Criminology and Police Science. 58: 3.

Mars G. 1982. *Cheats at Work*. London. George Allen and Unwin.

Masotti L.H., Bowen D.R. 1968. *Riots and Rebellion*. Beverly Hills. Sage Publications.

Merton R.K. 1968. *Social Theory and Social Structure*. New York. Free Press.

Momboisse R.N. 1967. *Riots, Revolts and Insurrections*. Springfield. Thomas.

Newman G. 1979. *Understanding Violence*. New York. Lippincott.

Scharf W. (Ed). 1989. *Policing and the Law*. Cape Town. Juta.

Sutherland E.H., Cressey D.R. 1955. *Principles of Criminology*. New York. Lippincott.

Szabo D. 1966. *The Socio-cultural Approach to the Aetiology of Delinquent Behaviour*. International Social Science Journal. 18:2, pp.176-193.

Toch H. 1969. *Violent Men: An Inquiry into the Psychology of Violence*. Chicago. Aldine.

United States National Advisory Committee on Criminal Justice Standards and Goals. 1976. *Disorders and Terrorism*. Washington D.C. Government Printing Office.

Van der Westhuizen J. (Ed.). 1982. *Crimes of Violence in South Africa.* Pretoria. University of South Africa.

Van Heerden T.J. 1986. *Introduction to Police Science.* Pretoria. University of South Africa.

---- , **Smit. B.F., Coetzee M.R.** 1989. *Police Science.* Pretoria. University of South Africa (only Study Guide for POL2O1-M).

Will R.E., Vatter H.G. (Eds.). 1970. *Poverty in Affluence.* New York. Harcourt, Brace and World.

2.3 Ses actions entreprises

4. Les moyens de subsistance des mineurs

TEACHING AND RESEARCH NETWORK IN AFRICA IN THE FIELD OF CRIMINOLOGY

Adewale Rotimi* and Olufunmilayo Oloruntimehin**

1. Introduction

Concern about crime is probably as old as history, but attempts to understand the causes and etiology of it, from a scientific point of view, date back to only a couple of centuries.

In Africa, attempts to study crime in a scientific manner are relatively recent, dating back to only to two or three decades. This new interest in the study of crime has been stimulated by an unprecedented increase in the crime rate in many developing African countries. Many of these countries have been exposed to crime due to rapid urbanization and industrialization. The social changes and the speed at which they have and are taking place in newly-independent African states, have been made at a 'quicksilver' pace previously unknown in the history of the world (Clifford, 1974). All of these changes, as rapid as they are, have had a great influence on criminal behaviour.

Another observation was made by Mushanga (1976:5) who argues that the impact of abrupt social change with the emphasis on development, without adequate provision for non-delinquent social values, has led to a disproportionate rise in the crime rates, especially those involving property. Mushanga further focuses on other factors including urbanization, the disrespect for traditional values, the introduction of the financial economy, conspicuous consumption and other factors, which have contributed to the rising crime rate in Africa.

Commenting on the impact of the rapid rate of urbanization, Clinard and Abbott (1973:7) asserted that the percentage of African cities with a population of 20,000 or more, increased from 7 percent to 13 percent and the urban population grew from 13.8 to 36.4 million within a short period of time. The cities are the centres of trade and culture where job opportunities are concentrated. Clinard and Abbott agree with the observations of

---

* Criminologist and Senior Lecturer at Obafemi Awolowo University, Ile-Ife, Nigeria.
** Professor of Sociology, Criminology and Sociology of Law at Obafemi Awolowo University, Ile-Ife, Nigeria.

Mushanga, that is, that property crimes constitute the bulk of the crimes committed.

In many African countries, concern has been expressed by governments who have resorted to imposing harsher punishments as a way of curbing the crime rate. A common observation reveals, for example, that deterrence seems to be the most popular penal policy. Unfortunately, the use of harsher punishments has not resulted in a drastic reduction in the crime rate, and this situation has compelled many governments and researchers to examine more critically, the causes of crimes with the intention of preventing them. This probably explains why criminology is taught as a subject in many institutions of higher learning in Africa.

Despite the knowledge that criminology is new in Africa, there has been a general lack of organization among those scholars who are involved in the teaching and research on this subject, and this paper will initially focus on some problems that have been encountered. After which, it will focus on the necessity of maintaining a network among African scholars.

When commenting on the teaching and research of criminology in Africa, one has to exercise caution about making some generalizations. This is because Africa has many regional characteristics. For example, the northern part of the continent has been greatly influenced by Islamic or Koranic jurisprudence, whereas Africa South of the Sahara, on the other hand, has been influenced by Roman and Cartesian jurisprudence.

Even within the non-Islamic regions, the influence of the English, French, Portuguese and German systems are to be discerned. South Africa, until very recently, operated a rather 'closed system' because of its racist policies which isolated her from the rest of Africa. These regional diversities would have made the subject matter of criminology a more interesting and stimulating one had there been an effective network among the various African states.

In relationship to other disciplines, criminology world wide is in its infancy. As Clifford (1974) has observed, criminology is related to other social sciences; sociology, economics, political science and psychology, and these social sciences are relatively new areas of speciality in many African countries. Opolot (1983:611) observes that Makerere University in Uganda was among the first universities in Africa to teach criminology at the post-graduate level. Mushanga (1976:4) also notes, that the study of criminology has tended to remain in the faculties of law and occasionally, medicine, in Europe. Whereas, in the United States, criminology is to be. located in the departments of sociology and anthropology. Recently, however, there have been more or less autonomous departments or institutes of criminology both in the United States and the United Kingdom.

The first course in criminology to be offered in Nigeria was that by the Faculty of Law at the University of Lagos (Kayode, 1983). Currently, many Sociology Departments in Nigerian Universities now offer courses in Criminology (Oloruntimehin, 1990).

Apart from the Universities offering courses in Criminology, a major and bold attempt was made in the early 1970s to forge a network between African criminologists. This was to be done by the establishment of the Institute of Criminology at Abidjan, in the Ivory Coast, and was sponsored by the Canadian International Development Agency (CIDA) in collaboration with the International Centre for Criminology of the University of Montreal, Canada. According to Brillon (1985), each year from 1972 to 1975 the Institute in Abidjan organized meetings with representatives from Senegal, Nigeria, Niger, Upper Volta, the Cameroon, Zaire, Ghana, Togo, Gabon, Mali and Dahomey. Scholars from the countries mentioned above gathered to exchange information and ideas.

At the meetings in Abidjan, the subjects discussed centred on the "needs and perspectives in the matter of crime prevention and the treatment of delinquents in West Africa" (Brillon, 1985). Other subjects dealt with the kinds of crime committed in West Africa, as well as crime prevention and planning. According to Brillon, in 1973, a seminar was held in Lagos, Nigeria on the subject of 'Criminal Law and the Law Courts'. Unfortunately, the tempo of the Institute slowed down after 1975, and countries in Africa failed to give the Institute the necessary financial support. The organization went into decline and, as a result, the first major opportunity to maintain an effective network between African criminologists who were involved in teaching and research slipped away.

The contract between the Canadian International Development Agency, the International Centre for Criminology of the University of Montreal and the Government of the Ivory Coast expired. So the International Centre for Criminology would not continue to second staff to the Institute in Abidjan and there was no local professional staff available to continue. The Ivory Coast was, in fact, only the host country.

In 1986 the United Nations African Institute for the Prevention of Crime and the Treatment of Offenders (UNAFRI) was established in Kampala, Uganda. The Inauguration Ceremony was attended by representatives from twenty-three Member States of the African region, the Organization of African Unity and the United Nations.

The principal objectives of UNAFRI are to provide assistance in the formulation of programmes for the prevention of crime and the treatment of offenders in the context of overall national development planning, undertaking joint action, promoting technical co-operation, exchanging information, data, publications and experience in the field of crime prevention and control.

Although there is a surge of interest in the subject matter of criminology, those who are engaged in the teaching and research in it face some problems characteristic of a new discipline. These problems include paucity of data for research, dependence on foreign theories which have not been tested on the African soil, definition of terms which may be foreign to students, lack of practical programmes to complement students' theoretical knowledge, the lack of books, journals, funds and a host of others.

2. General Indication of the organization of criminal studies in universities in Africa

As far as the organization, planning and objectives of the teaching of criminology in African universities is concerned, relevant information can be found in Asuni (1990) from which we have taken the following excerpt:

"The role and relevance of University education in Africa, especially in Africa South of the Sahara is being questioned not in terms of the need for University education, but in terms of the type of education that the Universities offer. It is sometimes pointed out that the Universities educate graduates away from their roots and traditions making the graduates alien to their culture and background. Quite often, University education, instead of making the mind more inquisitive, makes the diploma or certificate the end of learning. The way University education is perceived in a country where the level of literacy is very high, is bound to be different from the way it is perceived where the level of literacy is very low, like in Africa South of the Sahara. It is like a one-eyed man being king in the country of the blind.

The attitude to scholastic learning will be different between a student who has come generations of scholarly background and the one who is first generation, which a large proportion of African students are.

It is against this background that this presentation should be taken.

Furthermore it is necessary to call attention to the problem of generalising about Africa. The independent countries of Africa have inherited the educational traditions of their past Colonial overlords, and these traditions are being modified in different

236

degrees to suit their present situations and to reflect their national educational objectives, and their economic capacities.

Some generalisation is however valid in view of similarity in national aspiration, economic circumstance, rate of development etc. The following statements should, therefore, be taken as generalisation deriving from some specific national situations.

Necessity of Criminology: For those who already know something of criminology, and those who are involved in the control of crime and treatment of offenders especially at a higher level, the need for a broader and deeper knowledge is obvious. It can be argued and easily proven that policies based on sound knowledge of criminology are likely to be more effective than those based on anecdotes and untested assumptions. The practitioner who has a broader knowledge of criminology than what is only needed in the performance of his duties is likely to be more effective than the one who does not have broad knowledge.

The cost of crime in terms of the machinery set up to prevent and control crime, in terms of the material and non-material losses due to crime is enormous enough to call attention to the importance of criminology at least with the objective of reducing the cost, the gain from which can be diverted to other constructive and development programmes.

The administration of Criminal Justice interferes with the much-valued area of the fundamental human rights of the convicted citizens. It also interferes with the liberty, property and even life of the offending citizens. Some of the measures taken against the convicted citizens also impinge on the non-offending citizens - like spouse, and dependents of the criminal.

Institutions where Criminology is taught: From a theoretical and philosophical point of view, the study of criminology adds more to our knowledge of men. So far, there is no institution in Africa South of the Sahara which is concerned with the teaching of criminology exclusively. There are, however, several institutions in which it is taught as part of a bigger programme. The Department of Sociology or Social Sciences in a number of Universities teach the subject of deviance which is mainly criminology at both Undergraduate and Postgraduate levels. In University Law Departments, criminology is taught at the Undergraduate and Postgraduate levels.

In addition to these University programmes, there are also in some countries Prison Staff Colleges and Police Colleges in which criminology is taught. These colleges often use University dons in relevant subjects in teaching where they are readily available and accessible.

Without a diploma or degree in criminology, one therefore needs to see the Course content of the Sociology or Law Department to know how much criminology is taught. It is to be expected that criminology taught in the Sociology Department will have a different emphasis from that taught in a Law Department. This difference may be reduced and minimised if there is inter-departmental co-operation and participation.

General structure of teaching, hours of lectures, percentage of theoretical and practical classes

All these will depend on the availability of staff to teach the subject. In some University Departments of Law, there are three hours per week devoted to Criminology in the final year of a three year programme. There are lectures and tutorials given during this 3 hour period, in addition to this there may be visit to law courts, police installations and Penal Institutions. The students may also participate in research activities in the department.

At the Post graduate level in law, depending on the interest of the student, the programme may be more focussed on criminology. The student will be expected to present a dissertation based on some research project, under the guidance and supervision of an appropriate don. The minimum period required is usually stipulated and it may not be less than one year of full time engagement in the programme.

In the departments of Sociology, deviance or criminology may not be taught at all if there is no qualified staff to teach it and if there is no inter-departmental relationship and collaboration with the department of law. Where it is taught, it is usual to have at least 2 hour lectures and 1 hour tutorial per week in the final year of a 3 year undergraduate programme. The students are expected to present a dissertation on a modest research project.

At the one year post graduate level at least 2 hours per week may be required for lectures and tutorial. A dissertation based on a research project may take more than one year to complete under the guidance and supervision of a don. It may be only during the process of collecting data for research that the students come into direct contact with criminological institutions like the police, law courts and corrections.

Conditions of accessibility for professors and students

In some Universities there are academic advisers who are designated for students for their guidance. On the other hand, professors can utilize their students in their research projects as part of the education of the students. The level of interaction between professors and students will depend on the personality of the professors, the number of students in each class, and the physical facilities available.

Diplomas and Certificates

What is awarded at the successful completion of a University programme is a degree in the relevant department like Bachelor of Law or Bachelor of Science, and the post graduate can be a masters and doctorate. This applies to Anglophone countries which are similar to the British, Canadian or American tradition.
The Prison Staff Colleges and Police Colleges award their own certificates the value of which may be limited to the enhancement of the career of the candidate within the system. The certificates do not have the same general significance as a University Degree or diploma where this is awarded by a university.

Financing of Education and Investigation

The trend in Africa is towards tuition-free undergraduate education. Which means that it is the government which carries the brunt of the financing of University education and research. It is sad to note that in general the funding is most inadequate. The classes are over crowded and the departments are under staffed.
To curb the empire building tendency of some departments, some Universities have embarked on a Rationalisation Exercise,

to combine courses in order to avoid the duplication of similar programmes, etc.

There is usually some departmental vote for research but in these days of economic crunch, a central research committee with limited funds tends to be the vogue. In short, there is little or no money for research.

Text Books

Practically all the text books of Criminology and related subjects used in Africa South of the Sahara are foreign from Europe and North America. Moreover most of these text books are beyond the economic reach of the students. Even the University libraries these days cannot afford to stock up-to-date text books.

This is unfortunate because what is learnt from most of these text books are culture bound and a number of students do not appreciate this. The theories propounded in most of these text books have social, cultural and economic specificity which is not usually stated as they are written usually by the authors for their own students in their own country.

Publications

What regular local academic or professional journals are available in the field of Criminology in Africa South of the Sahara? There is practically nothing. The result is that academics in Africa tend to publish their papers in European or North American journals. In doing this, they have to strive to conform with the expectation of the foreign academic community ideas for their papers to be accepted for publication. Journals with a transcultural perspective will of course accept such papers more readily than others"(1990:311-314).

3. Problems of paucity of data

The connection between teaching and research is too obvious to merit much elaboration here. It is through research based on accurate and up-to-date data that current information can be passed on to students. Unfortunately, however, in many African states, research activities are hampered by the lack of reliable information. In many cases where data are available, they may be difficult to interpret (Clifford, 1965). In the case of Kenya, for example, as observed by Mushanga (1976), the annual police reports for murder and attempted murder are calculated together; also, figures for rape and attempted rape are sometimes unified. In Nigeria, political crime statistics do not generally reflect the sex of the offenders, and information, such as the occupation of the offender, is not usually provided.

Indeed, in many African countries there is a lack of the comprehensive registration of births, marriages and deaths (Clifford, 1965). This situation makes it difficult for researchers to draw correlations between some demographic variables and crime. Clifford also notes that the recording of unemployment, migration, income levels, the size of families and mental illness leaves much to be desired. In many cases, social taboos prevent parents from disclosing the number of children they have and women are forbidden from talking to strangers. In some countries, it is almost impossible for researchers to obtain crime data from the police. Bureaucratic formalities and the uncompromising attitude of the police, court and prison officials, conspire to erect barriers and prevent researchers from obtaining data.

In some cases, it is easier to obtain crime data from Interpol than from the police departments in the researcher's own country. Africa has yet to develop a precise and accurate instrument for measuring the intelligence and personality of a person (Clifford, 1965). It is thus, difficult to accurately distinguish between 'normal' and 'abnormal' behaviour. The lack of precise, accurate and reliable instruments for measuring intelligence has prevented researchers from drawing any correlation between intelligence and deviant behaviour. In America for example, many studies have established the relationship between a poor academic performance and deviant behaviour.

In Africa, Clifford (1965:12) observed that the criminologist encounters considerable difficulty in the process of investigating crime, especially when related to such variables as urban growth, poverty, the lack of education or the opportunities necessary for advancement. Because of the lack of adequate data to support research activities, African criminologists tend to rely on those theories developed either in Europe and America to explain criminal behaviour in their own environments. This has led to the popularity of the cross-cultural application of criminological theories.

4. Criminological theories and research and their cross-cultural application in Africa

In teaching criminology or the other social sciences the importance of theory cannot be over-emphasized. It is the theory that guides research and it is also theory that throws light on the understanding of criminal behaviour. As mentioned before, criminology, as a field of discipline, is in its infancy in Africa. As observed by Kayode (1978), what passes for criminology in the continent of Africa is either American or European in origin.

Common observations reveal that, at present, most criminological theories which are available to the African scholar tend to be limited in scope when they are applied to the local situation, because such theories were constructed in foreign countries (Vigderhous, 1978) through cross-cultural research.

Cross-cultural research began to gain popularity in criminology in the 1950s and the 1960s (Bennett, 1980). There are some advantages in cross-cultural research. Bennett observes, for example, that the method affords the researcher an opportunity to assess the power of a theory by either determining its scope, or generalizability. He further maintains that such theories could also expand our knowledge concerning the conditions under which certain theories operate.

Clifford (1965) points out that the hypotheses explored in the more developed countries could be tested in the less developed regions. He further maintains that Africa will gradually acquire similar methods for the collection and application of data on crime. It is also true that certain situations and conditions are likely to stimulate deviant behaviour, irrespective of a particular location in the world.

Clinard and Abbott (1973) observe, that extensive worldwide evidence demonstrates that criminal behaviour involves the learning of norms in the same manner as non-criminal behaviour is learnt. The authors also maintain that criminal norms are acquired primarily by group association and participation in deviant sub-cultures, such as those existing in slums, in youth groups and in certain occupations.

Ongom and Nwabingu (1978) note that urbanization, slums, indiscriminate association and opportunities are all significant in explaining criminal behaviour in both developed and developing countries. Muga (1975) observes that the theory of Bugess's' concentric zone is applicable, to some extent, in the study of the Kisumu municipality, although he cautions that the district with better residences and that of commuters was not applicable.

There are other situations where the cross-cultural application of theories would have limited relevance. Kayode (1978), in examining an earlier study by Bamisaiye, cautions that her study did not confirm the distribution of delinquency in the zonal patterns as earlier reported by Shaw and McKay. Bamisaiye's study, in contrast to Shaw and McKay's findings, demonstrated that the largest concentration of delinquency was to be found in an area with better housing and better amenities.

Those studies which tend to link social class to delinquency will be hard to apply to many African countries where the class pattern does not fit the Marxian model. In Africa, it has not been precisely defined what is meant by the term upper, middle or lower class. Therefore, any theory that links a sub-culture of delinquency to a lower class culture or to a reaction against middle class cannons or behaviour, will run into difficulties.

Another major problem the researcher may encounter in the application of cross-cultural theory, is that which is involved in comparing many forms of criminal behaviour which are culturally specific. Vigderhous (1978) points out that different cultures reflect a wide matrix of norms and values. Therefore, it is difficult to explain some deviant behaviours that have been observed in Africa with those theories already developed in Europe or the United States. The researcher and teacher in Africa finds himself or herself, in the dilemma of either applying those theories already developed abroad, or to await those yet to be developed, based on the African experience.

Closely based on the dilemma of relying on the cross-cultural application of criminological theories is the problem of explaining some terms to students who have no practical experience of observing these terms in their local environment. This situation may lead to problems in the teaching of criminology to African students.

4.1 Structural and environmental problems in the teaching of criminology in Africa

Teaching a new subject such as criminology to African students could be very exciting. Unfortunately, there are occasions when explaining some terms with which students are not familiar. It can be very frustrating. For example, in explaining various alternatives to incarceration, such terms as probation, parole, work release programmes and half-way houses, the teacher usually finds difficulty in giving local examples, leaving most explanations to the students' imagination.

The terms mentioned above are usually encountered in standard texts books in criminology which have been written in the United States or Europe. In Nigeria, for example, the prison establishment have probation and parole only on paper. In Uganda, Mushanga (1976) observes that probation is not usually put into effect, with only 1.1% of convicted offenders actually put on probation.

The lack of familiarity with some terms used in criminology is complicated by the lack of opportunities for practical experience by students.

These students would probably have benefited from an internship programme with some unit of the criminal justice system, such as the police force, the law courts or the prison service. The exposure of students to the practical operations of the day-to-day running of the institutions mentioned above, would, without doubt, have increased their understanding of the criminal justice system.

Closely related to the lack of practical experience by students is the scarcity of books and journals on criminology and on the criminal justice system. With many African countries groaning under harsh and crushing economic conditions, it is hardly surprising to discover that many university libraries are without books, journals or monographs in criminology. In many African countries, it is almost impossible for individual scholars to subscribe to journals due to the very stringent foreign exchange rate regulations and exorbitant subscription rates. In Nigeria, for example, it is common to observe that the cost of subscribing to a journal is as high as an individual lecturer's salary for a month.

4.2 *Future directions in teaching and research of criminology in Africa*

Despite some initial problems which are typical when a field of discipline is being slowly introduced, the future of teaching and research in criminology in Africa appears very bright. There are, for example, many areas of criminology which are begging to be explored. These areas include female criminality, drug trafficking, the effects of imposing alien laws on the native populations, the effects of a military dictatorship on the rule of law, the impact (or lack of it) of new religious movements on the crime rate; an examination of such bureaucracies as the police force, the courts and the prison service, and so on. The area of prison sub-cultures in Africa, as compared to those already identified and studied abroad, still remains unexplored. Since theories and methodologies developed in Europe and the United States may not have much validity and reliability in Africa, African scholars need to be inward looking.

To fully understand criminal behaviour in Africa, emphasis must be placed on ethno-criminological research. As Brillon (1985) observed, in many African states the customs of the past still survive and continue to affect the present. Rizkalla (1974) points out that in Africa South of the Sahara "the present dualism between an ancestral social structure and a new way of life not yet entirely assimilated, has an effect on all community institutions, whether family, religious or economic". Rizkalla concludes that this duality which is expressed in the culture conflict has some effect on the criminal justice system. He further maintains that a gap exists between contemporary justice and the mentality of the agricultural majority of the population, which is still faithful to an agricultural culture.

Brillon (1983) observes that the colonial system introduced a social control system which was totally un-related to the cultural reality of the African peoples' modes of thought and ethnic personality. He further points out, for example, that while European laws emphasize the protection of individuals and their rights, the tribal concept of justice tends to emphasize the good of the community. He goes on to suggest an ethnographic approach to the study of criminology in which the cultural peculiarities of the research subject are carefully considered. He therefore concludes that research questions in criminology must address the following: what is the importance of surviving tribal laws, why do tribal laws continue to exist and what factors explain the co-existence of two dependent judicial systems in most of Africa? To be effective in Africa, teaching and research must address the questions raised above. As Lombardo (1986) pointed out, private justice, private social control and mediation all beg to be more thoroughly explored.

4.3   The importance of maintaining teaching and research network

A common observation reveals that there is an apparent lack of a communication network among scholars who are engaged in the research and teaching of criminology in Africa. An initial effort was made to correct this anomaly through the establishment of the Institute of Criminology in Abidjan and of UNAFRI in Kampala. There is even a lack of effective communication between criminology scholars living within the same country. For example, criminology is taught either in the law faculty or in the social science faculty, without these faculties being involved jointly in research or teaching. Oloruntimehin (1990) notes, for example, in the case of Nigeria, the lack of collaboration between the two above-mentioned faculties in the teaching of the sociology of law.

Seminars and workshops are organized by UNAFRI in the area of crime prevention and the treatment of offenders, attracting scholars and practitioners from various parts of Africa. The information and data gathered by participants at the seminars, are useful for research and teaching in the higher institutions of learning of the countries of the participants.

It is hoped that this Institute will develop into a repository for information and data on the various aspects of crime and the treatment of offenders, not only in relation to Africa, but the world as a whole. Thus, it will be able to fulfill the aspirations of the founders, its operating personnel as well as the African scholars who are interested in the field of crime and the treatment of offenders.

The advantages of forging a communication link between criminologists in Africa seem too obvious to merit extensive discussion. However, a few examples deserve special attention. For example, many African countries share similar historical negative experiences with regard to colonial rule, and the consequences of colonial rule on the administration of the criminal justice system. Also, many African countries have experienced the devastating effects of urbanization. Hopefully, a research network will reveal similarities and contrasts in the effects of urbanization on the crime situation in many countries in Africa, and will reveal how different countries are coping with social change.

Even though it is evident that many African countries share common experiences with regard to colonialism and urbanization, differences do occur. For example, differences exist between the Muslim North and the Christian South. One may ask what are the differences in the impact of the administration of the Muslim/Hammurabic Code of Law in the Muslim States and that of the Cartesian and the Roman Law in the predominantly Christian States. Does the degree and severity of urbanization vary from one region to another? Are there any major differences and social control mechanisms among the same tribes who have been divided by artificial colonial boundaries? Answers to these questions will throw more light on crime and social control in Africa, than theories imported from the United Kingdom and the United States. Answers to these questions will materialize if African criminologists work towards maintaining an effective network.

It is imperative that an effective network be upheld among African criminologists. This must be achieved through the organization of seminars and the establishment of professional organizations such as the American Criminological Society or the Academy of Criminal Justice Sciences in the United States. It is also necessary to establish a journal where researchers can share research experiences and 'compare notes'. For the above to be realized, it is necessary to convince many African governments of the importance of hard data in the planning and implementation of social defence policies. As cautioned by Mushanga (1976), commonsense views and ideas cannot work in the scientific age.

Until an effective network is forged and maintained among teachers and researchers in Africa, we may be forced to continue to explain criminality which abounds in our immediate environment, with theories which have only been tested in Europe and the United States. This will be devastating to African scholars, since it will continue to frustrate our efforts at controlling the menace of crime which always seems to outpace our current social development.

5. Conclusion

‚The menace of high crime rates is a social fact in many African countries, and this is due to the strong impact of urbanization, industrialization and to social change. Many countries have shown an interest in the introduction of teaching and research in criminology as a way of meeting the challenges of the high crime rates. Unfortunately, many scholars and researchers in criminology still depend on the theories which have been developed in Europe and the United States in trying to explain the crime phenomena in their immediate environment. Little attention has been paid to ethno-criminological research which has more relevance to the understanding of the African crime situation.

Since effective and adequate funding is necessary for the realization of the suggestions made above, various African governments must be encouraged to offer the necessary financial support. It is only through an effective network among scholars who are engaged in the teaching of and the research in criminology, that hard and reliable data can be obtained for effective social defence planning in Africa.

References

Asuni T. 1990. *University Education in Criminology in Africa.* Eguzkilore-Extra. 3, pp.311-317.

Bennett R. 1980. *Constructing Cross-cultural Theories in Criminology.* Criminology. 18:2, pp.252-268.

Brillon Y. 1983. *Judicial Acculturation in Black Africa and its Effects on the Administration of Criminal Justice.* International Summaries. United States Department of Justice, National Institute of Justice.

---- . 1985. *Crime Justice and Culture in Africa.* International Centre for Comparative Criminology Montreal. University of Montreal.

Clifford W. 1965. *Problems of Criminological Research in Africa South of the Sahara.* International Review of Criminal Policy. 23, pp.11-17.

---- . 1974. *Introduction to African Criminology.* Nairobi. Oxford University Press.

---- . 1983. *Criminology in Developing Nations: African and Asian Examples.* In: Johnson E.H. (Ed.). "International Handbook of Contemporary Developments in Criminology, Europe, Africa, the Middle East and Asia". Westport (CT). Greenwood Press.

Clinard M., Abbott D.J. 1960. *A Cross-national Replication of the Relationship Between Urbanism and Criminal Behaviour.* American Sociological Review. 25:2, pp.253-257.

----, ---- .1973. *Crime in Developing Countries.* New York. John Wiley and Sons.

Kayode O. 1978. *Some Notes on Research into Crime and Punishment in Nigeria.* Australia and New Zealand Journal of Criminology. December, pp.241-254.

---- . 1983. *Nigeria.* In: Johnson E.H. (Ed.). "International Handbook of Contemporary Developments in Criminology, Europe, Africa, the Middle East and Asia". Westport (CT). Greenwood Press.

Lombardo L. 1986. *Nation Building and Social Control: Observations from The Ivory Coast and Tanzania.* International Journal of Comparative and Applied Criminal Justice. 10:2, Spring and Winter. .

Muga E. 1975. *Crime and Delinquency in Kenya.* Nairobi. East African Literature Bureau.

Mushanga T.M. 1976. *Crime and Deviance: An Introduction to Criminology.* Nairobi. East African Literature Bureau.

Mutngi O. 1977. *The Legal Aspects of Witchcraft in East Africa.* Nairobi. East African Literature Bureau.

Oloruntimehin O. 1990. *The Situation of the Sociology of Law in Nigeria.* In: Ferrari V. (Ed.). "Developing Sociology of Law: A World-wide Documentary Enquiry". Milano. Giuffrè, pp.593-604.

Ongom V. L., Nwabingu F.A.T. 1978. *Social Background to Juvenile Delinquency: A Study of Naguru Remand Home.* Kampala. East African Medical Journal. 55:2.

Opolot J.S.E. 1983. *Uganda.* In: Johnson E.H. (Ed.). "International Handbook of Contemporary Developments in Criminology, Europe, Africa, the Middle East and Asia". Westport (CT). Greenwood Press.

Rizkalla S. 1974. *Crime and Justice in the Developing Countries.* Acta Criminologica. January.

Szabo D. 1978. *Criminology and Crime Policy.* Lexington (MA). Lexington Books.

Vigderhous Y. 1978. *Methodological Problems Confronting Cross-cultural Research Using Official Data.* Human Relations. 31:3, pp.229-247.

ABSTRACTS

ADMINISTRATION TRADITIONNELLE, COLONIALE ET CONTEMPORAINE DE LA JUSTICE PÉNALE

Leonard P. Shaidi

Le présent article aborde la question de l'administration de la justice en Tanzanie au cours de la période pré-coloniale, durant le colonialisme ainsi que le système actuellement en vigueur.

L'auteur décrit les pouvoirs attribués aux chefs de tribus avant l'avènement du colonialisme et montre que leurs jugements étaient rendus de manière à satisfaire la victime tout en traitant le délinquant de manière équitable, et comment la compensation et les crimes plus graves étaient traités. L'auteur soutient que les lois en vigueur au cours du pré-colonialisme étaient beaucoup plus efficaces et plus justes et il présente les effets négatifs de l'introduction des systèmes juridiques allemands et anglo-saxons.

L'auteur décrit également la situation de l'administration de la justice après l'Indépendance du pays, les problèmes posés par l'utilisation du système juridique anglais et son adaptation à la réalité tanzanienne avec pour corollaire l'abandon du droit pénal coutumier.

Enfin, l'auteur signale que la Tanzanie, bon gré mal gré et bien qu'elle soit indépendante depuis de nombreuses années, applique toujours le code pénal du droit anglais.

LES VICTIMES D'ACTES CRIMINELS ET LEURS DROITS

Ntanda Nsereko

L'auteur définit ici le concept de victimes d'actes criminels. Il opère une distinction entre les victimes de crimes communs ou de la petite délinquance et les victimes d'abus de pouvoir. Ces deux catégories de victimes subissent un préjudice de par l'action du délinquant et sont en droit d'obtenir justice. Toutefois les victimes d'abus de pouvoir semblent être les plus frappées en raison du fait que les gouvernements et les représentants des gouvernements qui jouissent d'une certaine influence ou du pouvoir, ou toute autre personne liée au gouvernement, sont les transgresseurs. Ces derniers agissent de manière à cacher leur conduite criminelle et s'assurer que leurs victimes n'obtiennent pas justice

L'auteur examine la situation des victimes d'actes criminels dans le cadre, d'une part, de la loi et des traditions indigènes africaines et, d'autre part, du système africain contemporain de justice pénale. La loi et les traditions indigènes africaines privilégient la victime: elle doit pouvoir faire valoir ses droits. En revanche, le système africain contemporain de justice pénale vise avant tout à empêcher le délinquant de nuire: il s'agit de le détourner du mauvais chemin. Dans le cadre de la loi et les traditions indigènes africaines c'est la victime qui joue le rôle principal au cours de la procédure engagée contre le délinquant alors que dans le cadre du système africain actuel de justice pénale son rôle est marginal. La loi et les traditions indigènes africaines présentent la compensation comme le moyen de réparer le tort subi par la victime. Dans les systèmes africains contemporains de justice pénale, le rôle des tribunaux pénaux n'est pas de rendre justice aux victimes elles-mêmes, ces dernières pouvant l'obtenir auprès des tribunaux civils.

L'auteur attire l'attention des lecteurs sur la tendance, dans les pays industrialisés, dans certains pays d'afrique et aux Nations Unies, a donner la priorité à la victime et recommande chaudement aux pays africains d'en faire de même. De la sorte, ces pays permettront aux victimes d'actes criminels d'obtenir justice et renforceront la confiance du public à l'égard de leurs propres systèmes de justice pénale.

TIME LIMITS IN THE ADMINISTRATION
OF CRIMINAL JUSTICE IN MADAGASCAR

Andrée Ratovonony

Time limits (i.e. procedural laws which therefore have the aim of ensuring the rights of the defendant as well as guaranteeing the freedom of the individual) in the administration of criminal justice in Madagascar are far from perfectly respected. This is the case, despite the desire of the nation to establish a lawful state.

A series of texts (to improve the administration of justice and to renew the organization of jurisdiction) aimed at speeding up the criminal procedures following the promulgation of the Madagascar Code of Penal Procedures on 2 September, 1962, reveal an attempt to adapt the texts to the political, economic and social reality of the country.

But the claim to serve two tyrannical and exclusive masters (i.e., the state and man) at the same time appears to be an even more challenging enterprise in such a developing country such as Madagascar.

The origins of the sluggishness of criminal justice in Madagascar are not to be found in its procedures, but in the lack of operative personnel, means and above all financial resources, which affect the very functioning of the Administration of Justice in general, to the detriment of both the criminal subject (civil party, prisoner, convicts) and the State.

VINGT ANS DE VIOLENCE D'ETAT EN OUGANDA

Tibamanya mwene Mushanga

Le présent article traite de la violence qui a explosé en Ouganda puis submergé ce pays au cours des vingt années qui ont suivi la proclamation de son indépendance en 1962, laquelle mis fin à la domination du Royaume Uni.

Il décrit la situation dramatique vécue par l'Ouganda et sa population sous les règnes tyranniques de Idi Amin et Milton Obote, les tortures infligées et l'extermination de certains groupes ethniques au cours de cette période, l'émigration forcée de nombreux ougandais vers le Rwanda, les injustices et les atrocités commises quotidiennement.

Enfin, l'auteur forme le voeu que les politiques des gouvernements des pays de l'Afrique sub-saharienne évoluent vers le plein respect des droits de l'homme, l'élimination de la corruption et favorisent la formation d'un environnement socio-économique et politique moderne afin d'empêcher l'accession au pouvoir de dictateurs, une situation qui caractérise depuis trop longtemps la vie politique africaine.

LA CORRUPTION EN AFRIQUE:
UNE ÉTUDE DE CAS AU NIGER

Adedokun A. Adeyemi

Non seulement la corruption en Afrique est devenue un crime courant, mais également un catalyseur qui fournit matière à la perpétration d'autres crimes. Dans le présent article, la corruption est définie comme le fait d'offrir, de conférer, de donner ou d'accepter de conférer, de solliciter, d'accepter ou de donner son accord pour recevoir toute sorte de gratification, aussi bien pécunière que de toute autre nature en dehors des rémunérations légales, ou tout autre objet de valeur, sans tenir compte du fait - ou en sachant parfaitement - que cette action n'est pas juste.

Les données officielles sur la corruption au Nigeria sont considérées comme étant trop basses en raison de l'importance considérable du chiffre noir. Il est à noter que les cas de corruption enregistrés sont élevés chaque fois que le gouvernement témoigne de son intention de la contrôler et vice et versa.

Au Nigeria, les tendances de la corruption sont la conséquence des rapides changements socio-culturels, socio-économiques, socio-politiques et démographiques - ayant engendré une urbanisation accélérée - combinés à la montée de l'individualisme, au rapide développement technologique ainsi qu'à l'anomie et aux sentiments d'insécurité émotionnelle, sociale et économique qui en dérivent. Ces phénomènes ont eu pour corollaire de nombreuses suppressions d'emplois et l'appauvrissement des liens familiaux sans oublier les activités des ressortissants étrangers qui profitent de la situation interne afin d'assujetir l'économie nigérienne à celle de leur propre pays.

La corruption engendre l'inefficacité, qui elle-même conduit à l'absence ou au manque chronique de biens et de services. Cette situation stimule le désir, chez les citoyens défavorisés, d'obtenir coûte que coûte ces rares biens ou services. Avec pour résultat le fait que les coûts d'exploitation, et par conséquent le coût des biens a été multiplié par quatre, et dans certains cas extrêmes par dix.

Ceci a bien évidemment été accompagné d'une diminution du taux de développement qui s'est vu divisé par quatre, ne dépassant dès lors pas 25% sur le total des ressources dépensées pour le développement. Il s'agit là de l'une des terribles conséquences de la corruption sur le processus de développement. La corruption a également fait baisser les attentes morales de la société, d'où un certain cynisme qui est lui-même à l'origine de l'attitude mentale caractérisée par l'envie de 'devenir riche' et l'idée que 'la fin justifie les moyens'.

La corruption doit être combattue sur une grande échelle en se posant dans une perspective de prévention et d'intervention.

La prévention passe, entre autres, par le respect de la justice sociale, le bon fonctionnement de l'administration et la mise en place de systèmes économiques, technologiques et socio-culturels garantissant la stabilité socio-politique et le progrès socio-économique.

Par interventionisme on entend, sur le plan informel, la pleine utilisation et la mobilisation des liens synergiques de contrôle social; tandis que sur le plan formel, il s'agit de créer les conditions administratives qui permettront de venir à bout de ces engorgements et de l'inefficacité tout en mettant en place des structures chargées du monitorage des différentes composantes du système garantissant ainsi la continuité de l'efficacité et de la probité. D'un point de vue légal, il nous appartient de définir de manière adéquate la corruption, comme que nous l'avons indiqué précédemment. Ensuite, il faudra créer une Commission Indépendante pour la Lutte contre la Corruption, chargée des enquêtes dans ce domaine et qui disposera de son propre personnel ou fera appel à des enquêteurs externes autorisés. Les personnes contre lesquelles des preuves auront été receuillies devront être déférées devant les tribunaux pénaux et, outre les sanctions pénales, devront être condamnées à la restitution, à la compensation et à la saisie/confiscation en réparation des torts causés.

Il a été prouvé que si la volonté politique de combattre la corruption existe dans une société celle-ci peut être contenue. C'est le cas de Hong-Kong. Le Nigeria peut, et souhaite déjà en faire de même.

CRIMINAL POLICY IN CAMEROON:
A TENTATIVE APPROACH TO A TRANSITION MODEL

Nathalie Grelet

The concept of criminal policy is of both juridical and criminological origin. It is thus an interesting instrument which can be used to decipher the reality of a changing society such as Cameroon.

Beyond the modernity/tradition dichotomy, the analysis through criminal policy tries to bring to light the concrete practices of law, both on the part of the State and civilized society.

Two major trends appear from the theoretical construction of models of criminal policy - those of the state and those of society - covering the relative responses to the criminal phenomenon. This axis crosses Cameroon society in a policy coming from "higher up" (State) and a policy coming from "below" (society), and permits us to identify the "in-between" area in which new dynamics emerge.

Concrete examples in the field of juvenile delinquency provide evidence of original practices; however, the State in its hegemonic research cannot guarantee its hold on reality, while the answers provided by society remain isolated, without any real structure.

Admitting the existence of a crumbled criminal policy doesn't dispense with the need to examine the relations and networks of action that provide evidence of the reappropriation of rights by the those taking part in the Cameroonian judicial system.

By approaching a country through its criminal policy one can witness the reality and try to understand its individual mechanisms and connections.

Criminal policy is not only a juridical instrument in the literal sense. It is a reflection of the ideological instruments of a given society in its logic of civil repression at a given moment.

Criminal policy corresponds to the "collection of processes by which the social group coordinates its response to the crime phenomenon". In defining process, we should not limit ourselves to the repressive system, but extend it to reparation, conciliation and mediation; furthermore we should not limit it to reaction, but also include prevention.

Our objective is to try to identify the connection between the criminal policy conducted by a state and its reception by society. Our examples will deal essentially with juvenile delinquency.

LE TRAFIC DE STUPÉFIANTS ET L'ABUS DES DROGUES EN AFRIQUE

Tolani Asuni

Tandis que la consommation de cannabis, principale drogue utilisée en Afrique, plafonne à un haut niveau, celle de nouvelles drogues comme l'héroïne et la cocaïne est en augmentation constante. Le cannabis est cultivé librement dans la plupart des pays d'Afrique, ce qui n'est pas le cas de l'héroïne et de la cocaïne. Au départ, l'Afrique n'était qu'un lieu de transit et, comme on devait s'y attendre, l'abus de ces nouvelles substances parmi les populations indigènes ne cesse de croître. L'héroïne provient du Croissant et du Triangle d'Or et la cocaïne de l'Amérique Latine et toutes deux sont destinées à l'Europe et à l'Amérique du Nord, leurs principales consommatrices. Le Cannabis est exporté de l'Afrique vers l'Europe et vers l'Amérique du Nord.

Si les psychoses et les syndromes de perte de toute motivation provoqués par le cannabis conduisent ses utilisateurs à recourir à un traitement, c'est la destruction de la famille et le comportement anti-social et criminel des utilisateurs d'héroïne et de cocaïne qui attirent l'attention sur les besoins de ces derniers.

Le traitement prévoit la désintoxication et la réhabilitation, considérées comme un ensemble et non pas comme des éléments distincts. Compte tenu des risques de fuite motivés par les douloureux symptômes des états de manque, en particulier pour l'héroïne, les toxicomanes sont hospitalisés au sein d'unités psychiatriques, dans des hôpitaux publics ou dans des hôpitaux psychiatriques. Outre la réduction du risque de fuite, la psychiatrie offre également l'avantage d'une approche multidisciplinaire indispensable pour le traitement.

En raison du fait que la détention de ces drogues constitue un délit, le système de justice pénale prononce souvent des mesures de traitement pour les toxicomanes, les posant comme alternative à un procès pénal. Si le trafiquant est poursuivi en justice et fait l'objet de sanctions, en revanche le détenteur de petites quantités est orienté vers un traitement.

L'Afrique devrait trouver sa propre voie pour résoudre le problème de l'abus des drogues et non pas imiter les pays développés qui n'ont pas encore réussi à faire face à ce problème.

On pourrait tirer profit de l'importance des noyaux familiaux pour résister aux pressions extérieures et ériger une barrière de protection contre l'abus des drogues. L'attitude négative de la famille et de la communauté face à l'abus des drogues devrait être maintenue sans pour autant préjuger de l'éducation préventive, du traitement et de la réinsertion.

LES HOMICIDES RITUELS EN SIERRA LEONE

Muctaru Kabba

Le présent article décrit le phénomène des homicides rituels commis en Sierra Leone. Aux fins de l'analyse, il a été procédé à une classification présentant trois catégories: homicides communautaires, de groupes et individuels. Si l'homicide rituel de groupe a constitué la catégorie prédominante au cours de la période coloniale, en revanche l'homicide rituel individuel a acquis une importance considérable au cours de la période post-coloniale.

Cet article examine également les principes légaux, processus et méthodes traditionnels et occidentaux et montre que l'efficacité et la supériorité des pratiques traditionnelles en matière d'homicides rituels de groupe est imputable au fait que leurs procédures et méthodes étaient moins contraignantes.

La prédominance actuelle de l'homicide rituel individuel est liée à l'accroissement, au cours de la période post-coloniale, des possibilités d'acquérir santé, pouvoir, statut social. L'intensité des combats engagés pour acquérir ces valeurs engendre des incertitudes qui, associées à la croyance cristallisée en la capacité des experts des sciences occultes de manipuler les forces surnaturelles et permettre ainsi la réalisation des désirs individuels, ont facilité la continuation de telles pratiques, et ce, malgré les nombreuses sanctions rigoureuses imposées aux criminels.

L'auteur conclut en indiquant qu'étant donné que les lois, procédures et méthodes ne produisent pas d'effets dans une situation de vide socio-culturel, la lutte contre les homicides rituels sera probablement beaucoup plus efficace si les procédures occidentales et traditionnelles sont intégrées l'une à l'autre d'une manière constructive.

LA THÉORIE DE L'ÉTIQUETAGE: CONTRIBUTION À L'ÉTUDE DE L'OPPRESSION, DU CONFLIT ET DE LA VIOLENCE EN AFRIQUE DU SUD

Apollo Rwomire

Bien qu'indispensables dans les domaines de l'interaction sociale et de la communication, les étiquettes s'avèrent souvent dysfonctionnelles lorsqu'elles s'emploient dans un but de stigmatiser ou de défavoriser certains secteurs bien marqués de la population. Cette étude, fondée sur les perspectives du marxisme et de l'interactionnisme symbolique, et appuyée par des preuves d'ordre historique, explore les sources, la dynamique et les conséquences sociales de l'étiquetage négatif en Afrique du Sud.

Selon la théorie de l'étiquetage, tout individu officiellement désigné comme déviant (ou criminel) et traité comme tel, aura par la suite tendance à afficher les caractéristiques qu'on lui aura imputées. Loin d'être de simples catégories du comportement, la déviance et la conduite criminelle résultent du traitement que reçoit le contrevenant au sein des structures sociales. En conséquence du signe de l'infériorité et de la marginalité que les éléments plus influents de la société attribuent à certains individus, ceux-ci peuvent finir par formuler à leur propre sujet une conception négative, voire criminelle, en s'associant plus étroitement à des personnes ou à des groupes qui par leur nature renforcent cette nouvelle identité.

Appliquant la théorie de l'étiquetage à la situation en Afrique du Sud, l'auteur cherche à élucider certaines complexités et contradictions qui caractérisent cette société. Un abîme insondable sépare d'un côté les Blancs minoritaires, jouissant de tous les privilèges économiques et sociaux, et de l'autre la majorité noire, défavorisée et tyrannisée.

La discrimination officielle, ainsi que des préjugés raciaux plus généralisés, éléments de base des structures sociales sud-africaines, assurent que la puissance et la richesse resteront les domaines privilégiés de la minorité blanche. L'auteur prétend qu'il existe une corrélation entre le maintien par les Blancs d'un système qui les favorise, et la création et l'apposition d'étiquettes négatives qui servent d''instruments discriminatoires contre les Noirs.

Pour résoudre les problèmes des conflits sociaux et du comportement criminel qui en est une conséquence importante, l'auteur préconise l'annulation et la redéfinition des étiquettes négatives actuellement en vigueur en Afrique du Sud.

SOCIO-CULTURAL CHANGES AND THE MARGINALIZATION OF CHILDREN AND YOUNG PEOPLE IN AFRICA SOUTH OF THE SAHARA

Manga Bekombo

The term "street children" is a product of the evolution of criminological terminology which has tended to restrict the use of the terms "delinquency", "deviance" or "social maladjustment" when referring to those children and young adolescents who are considered to be marginalized, particularly in non-western societies with a low level of economic development. This evolution is due mainly to the contribution of sociological research on problems of socio-cultural changes linked to the phenomena of culturalization and social reorganization - phenomena which are particularly evident in the urban centres of African countries south of the Sahara.

The children concerned are divided into two main age groups of between 8 and 14, and 15 and 19 years of age. A small proportion come from native families, whereas the majority are from migrant families who have been attracted to the town from the rural areas. Most of these families live in suburban areas generally inhabited by groups of the same ethnic origin. Given their modest social and economic status, these families are in fact excluded from those social groups which reproduce the symbols of modernity. Although the young people strongly aspire to acquire these symbols they are frustrated by their social condition from actually doing so. On a more general basis, the transmission of values, norms and rules are blocked by a lack of traditional rules on the one hand and, on the other, by the inability of both young people and even their parents to control the effects of the processes of modernization, thus breaking the parallelism between historical and biological intervals which divide generations.

For these children, school was or has become inaccessible.
In contrast, the street represents a vast and welcoming, non-sectorized and unappropriated space of life which, besides absorbing all social strata and permitting all kinds of action, also provides the aspiration for all kinds of changes and plans. In this way, the street performs one of its basic functions, which it also performs, although in a slightly different form, in industrialized countries during periods of crises.

From a sociological point of view "street children" cannot be considered deviant (in societies where norms are not yet socially integrated or conceptually coherent) or delinquent (in social contexts where reference to the rules of behaviour is not based on a single ideological system). We are dealing with a global social phenomenon, since these children form their own social category and constitute an anomic society which reveals, although in a magnified way, its multiple internal conflicts.

MIGRATIONS RURALES VERS LES CENTRES URBAINS: CRIMINALITÉ ET DÉLINQUANCE

Andargatchew Tesfaye

Cet article étudie les conséquences des migrations rurales accélérées vers les centres urbains en Afrique. L'exode des populations rurales, commencé au cours de la période coloniale, a enregistré une accélération au cours de ce siècle en raison des divers attraits présentés par les zones urbaines, en fort contraste avec les zones rurales laissées à l'abandon. Les populations se sont déplacées à la recherche d'un emploi, de services éducatifs et sanitaires mais aussi pour bénéficier des divers autres avantages offerts par les cités. Très peu de personnes ont eu le courage de rentrer dans leurs villages après le choc initial de la vie urbaine.

Ceux qui choisissent de rester ont des difficultés à s'adapter et ils sont également incapables de subvenir à leurs besoins quotidiens. Ils finissent généralement par vivre dans les bas quartiers et subsistent pauvrement.

Ils ne bénéficient plus du soutien et du contrôle familial auxquels ils étaient habitués chez eux. Les dures épreuves qu'ils doivent affronter et le mode de vie impersonnel des zones urbaines les amènent petit à petit à perdre tout sentiment de honte, le sens de la dignité et la maîtrise de soi, et consciemment ou inconsciemment ils commencent à dévier des routes établies. Leurs différents modes de survie les conduisent parfois à sombrer plus profondément dans la déviance. On leur colle alors l'étiquette de voyous, mendiants, prostitués, délinquants et criminels. Ils n'ont guère d'autre choix que celui d'adopter ces comportements comme mode de vie et devenir des déviants à part entière - ennemis d'une société qui les a créés.

SUBSISTENCE DEVIANCE

Elisabeth Michelet

Subsistence deviance is the result of a process of marginalisation linked to the biological survival of the individual. Undernourishment is a criminogenic factor which explains the phenomena of vagrancy, begging, prostitution, irregular street activities, among other forms of pauperism, in developing countries.

The high number of people who resort to deviance for necessity poses a threat to society, since it can lead to petty crime and, sometimes, by learning and by example, to hard crime.

Hunger-related delinquency, comprised in part by the handicapped, blind, leprous, unemployed and deprived, takes place on the street and forms the so-called "human clutter", in the ecological sense of human pollution of the urban environment which finds itself harassed by the undernourished.

This article analyses these forms of deviance with reference to both adults and adolescents, as well as the attempts by Senegalese legislation to solve the problem.

It shows that, although subsistence deviance is insignificant at the individual level, it is largely responsible for the general increase in crime in African society which, for a long time, has been perceived as living in a state of sub-criminality compared to the industrialized countries. This is particularly evident in relation to the young people, who are more affected than others by socio-economic difficulties.

LA VIOLENCE COMPRISE EN TANT QU'ARME DES PERSONNES DÉFAVORISÉES

Ben F. Smit

Il existe différentes théories et explications sur le concept de violence et les phénomènes qui l'accompagnent tels les désordres, le terrorisme et les intimidations. Cet article donne une explication à la violence en Afrique du Sud en la présentant comme une lutte entre les détenteurs et les non-détenteurs de privilèges.

D'une manière générale, on peut relever que le genre humain, son histoire et son environnement sont marqués par la violence et l'on pourrait même dire que celle-ci fait partie de la nature humaine. Cette tendance naturelle à la violence de l'homme ne le distingue pas des "autres espèces du règne animal". Toutefois, l'essence de la violence humaine est sensiblement différente. " ... L'homme n'est pas un tueur comme les autres. On assiste rarement chez les animaux, même chez les "moins évolués" d'une espèce donnée, à des luttes fratricides. Des combats ont lieu pour une femelle ou pour le contôle d'un territoire, mais ils visent à la soumission et non pas à la destruction de l'adversaire".

La violence fait donc partie de l'environnement humain et ce, à un tel degré, qu'elle est considérée comme un phénomène naturel. Ceci est indicatif d'un accroissement de la pression contre la chaîne des relations sociales. " ... la présence de nombreuses personnes en situation critique témoigne d'une société en crise ... Les actes de violence peuvent être considérés comme un premier signal d'alarme, révélateurs de profonds ... conflits qui se renforcent au-dessous de la surface des relations sociales".

LA CRIMINOLOGIE EN AFRIQUE: ENSEIGNEMENT ET RECHERCHE

Adewale Rotimi and Olufunmilayo Oloruntimehin

Les auteurs du présent article évoquent les problèmes rencontrés en Afrique dans le domaine de l'enseignement et de la recherche criminologiques et la nécessité de créer et développer un réseau entre les criminologues africains. Ils expriment leur inquiétude quant à la récente montée de la criminalité, facteur qui a été aggravé par les rapides changements sociaux apportés par l'urbanisation et l'industrialisation du continent africain.

La criminologie, domaine ou discipline nouvellement inscrit au programme d'études de la plupart des principales institutions africaines, est considérée comme un moyen permettant de mieux comprendre et résoudre le problème de la criminalité. L'article souligne d'ailleurs l'importance de la réalisation d'activités de recherche en Afrique, sur la base de données fiables.

Et cela, afin de réduire la dépendance actuelle des théories développées en Europe et en Amérique pour expliquer le phénomène de la criminalité en Afrique. Les auteurs relèvent que le manque de données est préjudiciable à la réalisation d'activités de recherche significatives. Outre le manque de données, existent également des problèmes environnementaux et structurels qui militent contre l'enseignement et la recherche criminologique en Afrique. Ces problèmes incluent, par exemple, le manque de familiarité avec certains termes et pratiques criminologiques, le manque de livres et de revues, le manque de fonds pour la recherche, etc. Les auteurs affirment qu'en dépit des difficultés initiales rencontrées dans ce domaine, le futur s'annonce prometteur pour la criminologie en Afrique.

Toutefois, ce futur sera encore meilleur si les étudiants arrrivent à maintenir des rapports étroits entre eux au travers de séminaires, conférences, la création d'associations de criminologues au niveau national ou international, la publication de revues criminologiques, et éventuellement avec la création d'un Institut de criminologie pour les seuls pays africains.

LIST OF UNSDRI/UNICRI PUBLICATIONS AND STAFF PAPERS

Publ. No. 1   **Tendencias y necesidades de la investigación criminológica en America Latina.** (1969) 60p. F. Ferracuti, R. Bergalli.

Publ. No. 2   **Manpower and training in the field of social defence.** (1970) 152p. (1) F. Ferracuti, M. C. Giannini

S.P. No. 1   **Co-ordination of interdisciplinary research in criminology.** (1971) 44p. F. Ferracuti

Publ. No. 3   **Social defence in Uganda: A survey of research.** (1971) 129p.

Publ. No. 4   **Public et justice: Une étude pilote en Tunisie.** (1971) 186p. A. Bouhdiba

S.P. No. 2.   **The evaluation and improvement of manpower training programmes in social defence.** (1972) 33p. R. W. Burnham (1)

S.P. No. 3.   **Perceptions of deviance: Suggestions for cross-cultural research.** (1972) 84p. G. Newman

S.P. No. 4.   **Perception clinique et psychologique de la déviance.** F. Ferracuti and G. Newman
Sexual deviance: A sociological analysis. G. Newman
Aspetti sociali dei comportamenti devianti sessuali. F. Ferracuti and R. Lazzari (1973) 75p.

S.P. No. 5.   **Psychoactive drug control: Issues and recommendations.** (1973) 98p. J.J. Moore, C.R.B. Joyce and J. Woodcock (1)

Publ. No. 5   **Migration: Report of the research conference on migration, ethnic minority status and social adaptation, Rome, 13-16 June 1972.** 196p.

Publ. No. 6   **A programme for drug use research: Report of the proceedings of a Workshop at Frascati, Italy, 11-15 December 1972.** 40p.

S.P. No. 6   **Un programma di ricerca sulla droga. Rapporto del seminario di Frascati, Italy, 11-15 dicembre 1972.** 93p.

Publ. No. 7   **A world directory of criminological institutes.** (1974) 152p. B. Kasme (ed.)

Publ. No. 8   **Recent contributions to Soviet criminology.** (1974) 126p.

Publ. No. 9   **Economic crisis and crime: Interim report and materials.** (1974) 115p.

Publ. No. 10   **Criminological research and decision-making: Studies on the influence of criminological research on criminal policy in The Netherlands and Finland.** (1974) 220p.

Publ. No. 11   **Evaluation research in criminal justice: Material and proceedings of a research conference convened in the context of the Fifth United Nations Congress for the Prevention of Crime and the Treatment of Offenders.** (1976) 321p.

Publ. No. 12	Juvenile justice: An international survey, country reports, related materials and suggestions for future research. (1976) 251p.
Publ. No. 13	The protection of the artistic and archaeological heritage: A view from Italy and India. (1976) 259p
Publ. No. 14	Prison architecture: An international survey of representative closed institutions and analysis of current trends in prison design. (1974) 238p. (2)
Publ. No. 15	Economic crises and crime: Correlations between the state of the economy, deviance and the control of deviance. (1976) 243p.
Publ. No. 16	Investigating drug abuse: A multinational programme of pilot studies into a non-medical use of drugs. (1976) 192p. J.J. Moore
Publ No. 17	A world directory of criminological institutes. (2nd edition) (1978) 521p.
Publ. No. 18	Delay in the administration of criminal justice: India. (1978) 73p. S.K. Mukherjee and A. Gupta
Publ. No. 19	Research on drug policy. (1979) 93p. J.J. Moore and L. Bozzetti The effect of Islamic legislation on crime prevention in Saudi Arabia. (1981) 606p. (3)
Publ. No. 20	A world directory of criminological institutes. (3rd edition) (1982) 691p.
Publ. No. 21	Combatting drug abuse. (1984) 251p. F. Bruno
Publ. No. 22	Juvenile social maladjustment and human rights in the context of development. (1984) 504p.
Publ. No. 23	The phenomenology of kidnappings in Sardinia. (1984) 211p. I.F. Caramazza and U.Leone
Publ. No. 24	The rôle of the judge in contemporary society. (1984) 80p. (4)
Publ. No. 25	Crime and criminal policy: Papers in honour of Manuel López-Rey. (1985) 747p. P. David (ed.)
Publ. No. 26	First Joint International Conference on Research in Crime Prevention. Riyadh, 23-25 January 1984 235p. (5)
Publ. No. 27	Action-oriented research on youth crime: An international perspective. (1986) 275p. U. Zvekic (ed.).
Publ. No. 28	A world directory of criminological institutes. (4th edition). (1986) 582p. C. Masotti Santoro (ed.).
Publ. No. 29	Research and international co-operation in criminal justice: Survey on needs and priorities of developing countries. (1987) 264p. (6) U. Zvekic and A. Mattei.
Publ. No. 30	Drugs and punishment. (1988) 146p. (6) D. Cotic.
Publ. No. 31	Analysing (in)formal mechanisms of crime control: A cross-cultural perspective. (1988) 343p. (6) M. Findlay and U.Zvekic. Prison in Africa: Acts of the Seminar for Heads of Penitentiary Administrations of African Countries (1988) 286p.(7)

Publ. No. 32   **The death penalty: A bibliographical research.** (1988) 320p.(6)

Publ. No. 33   **La criminolog;a en America Latina.** (1990) 288p. (6) L. Aniyar de Castro (ed.).

Publ. No. 35   **A world directory of criminological institutes.** (1990) 661p. (6) C. Masotti Santoro (ed.).

Publ. No. 36   **Essays on crime and development.** (1990) 377p. (6) U. Zvekic (ed.)

Publ. No. 38   **Soviet criminology update.** (1990) 179p. (6) V. N. Kudriavtzav (ed.).

Publ. No. 39   **Diritti umani ed istruzione penale. Corso di formazione sulle tecniche di istruzione ed investigazione.** Castelgandolfo, Italy, 11-22 September 1989 245p.

Publ. No. 40   **Infancia y control penal en America Latina.** (1990) 417p. (9) E. Garcia Méndez and E. Carranza (eds.).

Publ. No. 41   **Toward scientifically based prevention.** (1990) 181p. (6) F. Bruno, M.E. Andreotti and M. Brunetti (eds.).

Publ. No. 42   **Ser niño en America Latina. De las necesidades a los derechos.** (1991) 434p. (10) E. Garcia Mendez and M. del Carmen Bianchi (eds.).

Publ. No. 43   **Compendio per la prevenzione. Vols. I/II/III.** (1991) F. Bruno (ed.).

Publ. No. 44   **Cocaine today: its effects on the individual and society.** (1991) 420p. (11) F. Bruno (ed.).

Publ. No. 45   **Justicia y desarrollo democratico en Italia y America Latina.** (1992) 343p. (6) G. Longo, U. Leone and M.Bonomo (eds.).

Publ. No. 46   **Development and crime. An exploratory study in Yugoslavia.** (1992) 350p. (12) U. Leone, D. Radovanovic and U. Zvekic.

PUBLICATIONS DEFERRED

Publ. No. 34   **Criminology in Latin America.** L. Aniyar de Castro (ed.). (8)

Publ. No. 37   **Prison labour.** (8)

NOTES

(1)   Also published in French and Spanish.

(2)   Available through The Architectural Press, 9 Queen Anne's Gate, London SWH 9BY, England.

(3)   At the request of the Government of The Kingdom of Saudi Arabia, UNSDRI published English, French and Spanish editions of this publication.

(4)   In collaboration with the International Association of Judges.

(5)   In collaboration with the Arab Security Studies and Training Center in Riyadh, The Kingdom of Saudi Arabia.

(6)   Available through United Nations Publications in Geneva (Palais des Nations, CH-1211 Geneva 10, Switzerland) or New York (United Nations Headquarters, Room A3315, New York, N.Y. 10017, U.S.A.).

(7)   In collaboration with the Ministry of Justice of Italy and the International Centre for Sociological, Penal and Penitentiary Studies, Messina, Italy.

(8)   Tentative title.

(9)   Joint UNICRI/ILANUD publication.

(10)   In collaboration with the UNICEF, ILANUD, IIN (Instituto Interamericano del Niño) and DNI (Defensa de los Niños International).

(11)   Also published in Italian.

(12)   Joint UNICRI/IKSI publication.